A SELF-IMAGE
OF PRIMARY SCHOOL TEACHERS

*A Cross Cultural Study
of Their Role and Status in
Twelve Cities*

A SELF-IMAGE OF PRIMARY SCHOOL TEACHERS

by Marion Edman

Wayne State University

WAYNE STATE UNIVERSITY PRESS   DETROIT, 1968

PREFACE

Yet all experience is an arch where thro
Gleams that untravell'd world, whose margin fades
Forever and forever. . . .
— *Tennyson*

THE RESEARCH HERE PRESENTED HAS BEEN AN INTERNATIONAL VENTURE. The idea for it came to me while I was a Fulbright Research Scholar in Korea in 1962. It began as an attempt to discover whether drastic changes in the political and social life of a nation, such as had occurred in Korea with the termination of the Japanese occupation, had brought about discernible changes in the thinking of elementary teachers about their own role and status. With the help of experts in teacher education in both the United States and Korea, I formulated a questionnaire for in-service teachers concerning their role and status as they conceived these. I tried out the questionnaire with several groups of Korean teachers for further refinement and clarification, and then with the cooperation of the Central Education Research Institute and the Ministry of Education in Korea, I administered it to a random controlled sample of 540 teachers in elementary schools. Two hundred of these teachers had less than five years' experience; 200 had from ten to fifteen years' experience; 140 had eighteen or more years' experience.

Two hundred eighty-two taught in elementary schools in Seoul; 258 taught in a rural province. Through the cooperation of the Fulbright Commission in Korea, the results of the study were published in 1962 by the Central Education Research Institute in Seoul under the title *Primary Teachers of Korea Look at Themselves.*

Following this pilot study, the cooperation of educational authorities was obtained in fifteen countries for the administration of the same questionnaire to a random sample of elementary teachers in an urban center of each country. While it might have been desirable to sample teachers in rural areas as well, it was agreed, because of problems of communication away from cities, that only teachers in metropolitan areas were to be included in the expanded study. A controlled random sample was taken in each city chosen of 100 teachers with less than five years' experience and of 100 teachers with more than ten years' experience. All teachers were asked to respond anonymously. How much the fact that the questionnaire was distributed and collected by school officials in positions of authority influenced the replies cannot, of course, be estimated. Every effort was made to exclude questions which teachers might avoid answering for personal reasons or which they would not answer truthfully because of possible official disapproval.

Cooperating officials supervised the translation of all questions carefully so that the meanings would not be changed in transposing from English to the language of the country. The exact numbering system of the questionnaire was likewise carefully maintained.

Completed questionnaires were all returned to the Central Education Research Institute in Seoul for tabulation and processing.

When final tabulations were completed, adequate samples had been obtained from teachers in:

Seoul, S. Korea	Yokohama, Japan
Manila, The Philippines	Saigon, Vietnam
Bangkok, Thailand	Lahore, Pakistan
Madras, India	Munich, Germany
Helsinki, Finland	London, England
Windsor, Ontario, Canada	Detroit, Michigan, U.S.A.

Unfortunately, the questionnaires from Oslo, Norway, were lost en route to Seoul; those from Athens, Greece, and Salerno, Italy, could not be used because some deviation from the English in translation had been made and these replies could not be tabulated with the others. I hope that the replies from Greek and Italian teachers can be used in a separate study.

To add dimension to the study, I included a small sample of students in training. Because the original questionnaire devised for teachers was not entirely applicable to students, some changes were made in it. The revised questionnaire was administered to a random sample of 100 students in three cities: Hong Kong, London and Detroit, all of the students sampled being currently enrolled in a teacher training college or the education college of a university.

In general, the response to the questionnaire was excellent. Very few teachers omitted replies to any questions, in spite of the fact that the questionnaire was long.

To the officials listed below go my sincere thanks for their willing cooperation in the administration of the questionnaire to the teachers in their cities:

Gordon Mann, Superintendent for Elementary Education, Windsor, Ontario, Canada.

Betty Adams, General Inspector of Education, London, England.

Olli Sampola, Director of Primary Education, Helsinki, Finland.

Anton Fingerle, City Superintendent of Schools, Munich, Germany.

N. D. Sundaravadivelu, Director of Public Instruction, Ministry of Education, Madras, India.

Isao Amagi, Director of the Research Bureau, Ministry of Education, Yokohama, Japan.

Hyun Ki Paik, Director, Central Education Research Institute, Seoul, Korea.

Ibrahim Shamin, Education Extension Service, Ministry of Education, Lahore, Pakistan.

Isabelo Manalo, Department of Public Instruction, Ministry of Education, and Epfanio Madali, Chief, Elementary Section, Department of Public Instruction, Ministry of Education, Manila, the Philippines.

Kaw Swasdi Panich, Educational Supervisor, Ministry of Education, Bangkok, Thailand.

Bui Chi, Faculty of Pedagogy, and Nguyen Van Buong, Directeur de l'Enseignement Primaire, Direction General de l'Enseignement, Saigon, Vietnam.

Robert S. Lankton, Director of Research and Development, Detroit Public Schools, Detroit, Michigan, U.S.A.

Clifford May, Deputy Superintendent, Board of Education, Oak Park, Michigan, U.S.A.

Theodor Photinopoulos, Chief, Department of Elementary Schools, Ministry of Education, and Konstantine Kolovos, Superintendent of Elementary Schools, Athens, Greece.

Francesco Vacca, Proveditore Adi Studi, Cosenza, Italy.

Kare Homstvedt, Secretary, Norges Laererlag, Oslo, Norway.

For samples of student teachers in training, I wish to thank the following:

Sam Young, Acting Principal, Northcote Training College, Hong Kong.

Betty Adams, General Inspector of Education, London, England.

I sincerely hope that their participation in this study has made these educational officials and teachers more aware of their common concerns and problems in educating the children of the world. No similar study of the primary school teachers' own assessment of their role and status in such a variety of countries has, so far as a search of the literature reveals, ever been made or reported.* I also hope that an increasing number of cross cultural and international studies will involve teachers and school officers and will help to build a feeling of unity within a profession which is world-wide in its responsibilities for helping children of all nations to take their proper places on an interdependent and shrinking planet.

Because of the nature of their contribution, most of those whose cooperation made this research possible must remain anonymous. They are the two thousand and more teachers and students who took time out of already overcrowded schedules to respond to a long questionnaire. Without their help this research could not have been accomplished. May their reward come in the knowledge that their cooperation has brought the members of their profession, certainly one of the most vital in the modern world, a little closer to one another in mutual understanding.

---

* A number of studies have been reported by such organizations as UNESCO, World Confederation of the Organizations of the Teaching Profession, various national organizations and a limited number of independent research workers, but these have almost universally relied on official data concerning education and teachers or on the appraisals of officials and observers other than teachers themselves. Several such studies will be summarized later.

My thanks are due also to the translators in the various cities who rendered into their own language the essential meaning of each of the questions, and to the research assistants at the Central Education Research Institute in Seoul, who hand tabulated the thousands of responses. Particularly, I must give credit to Dr. Hyun Ki Paik, Director of the Institute, who authorized and supervised the entire project, and to Miss In Soo Ri, Research Associate of the Institute, who compiled the many tables and who generally was responsible for carrying out the analysis of the data.

I also wish to express my thanks again to the Fulbright Commission and to the United States Information Service in Seoul for their encouragement and support of the pilot study made in South Korea, for without their help the present study could not have been undertaken.

I am indebted to the former dean of the College of Education of Wayne State University, Francis C. Rosecrance, and to the present dean, J. Wilmer Menge, for continued support and interest, and to my colleagues, particularly to the head of my department, E. Brooks Smith, who have been a source of strength in carrying this study to its end. A small research grant from the college provided for some of the expenses incurred in the study.

Finally, I must thank Alexander Brede, Chief Editor Emeritus of the Wayne State University Press, for invaluable suggestions in the preparation of the manuscript, and Zelda Rose, my secretary, who has given me continued and enthusiastic help in the many details involved in the research. To her, my debt of gratitude is considerable.

M.E.

CONTENTS

TABLES

The A tables give the summary data and percentages for the East and the West and for the younger and older teachers.
The B tables give the data for specific cities.
The C tables give the data for students in training. The items in some of these tables differ somewhat from the items in the other tables.

I
GENERAL PURPOSE
AND METHOD OF STUDY

Everyone has the right to education.
Universal Declaration of Human Rights, Art. 26, Sec. 1

THE MIDPOINT OF THE TWENTIETH CENTURY WAS MARKED BY A WAVE OF revolution that almost encircled the globe. This was in part political, in part economic, in part social, with extraordinary implications for the existing order in all realms of human affairs. Many institutions of long standing were either discarded or greatly modified. Perhaps for no institution were the changes more significant than for schools, for accompanying the revolution, and perhaps causally related to it, were three major phenomena: the explosion of population, the explosion of knowledge, and the explosion of expectations. While each of these had significant implications for education everywhere, they affected different nations of the world in varying degree and their institutions in different ways. In general, it was education that saw very great changes as a result of them. Education became a right, instead of being just a privilege.

This held for the so-called highly developed countries as well as for those just entering in upon the modern era of high industrialization. Illiteracy could no longer be tolerated in countries which for centuries had seen no need for the common people to have even the rudiments of formal schooling. And no longer was ability to command simple reading or ciphering, with scant knowledge of other matters, held to be adequate for the children of the masses in those countries which formerly were satisfied with this level of training, while they prided themselves on a much higher level of training for the elite minority.

In the industrialized countries, a new assessment of the total educational program had to be made. A common result was the reorganization of a long existing school system. Often new school forms were introduced, with new objectives and with corresponding new curriculums, and the enrollment of a new segment of society. Changes were deemed essential if the country wished to maintain a favorable place in a highly competitive international relationship and likewise wished to promote domestic tranquility and well-being.

The newer nations, emerging into political independence and all struggling with the transition from a simple agrarian society to a complex industrialized one, almost unanimously came to see that the development of a good educational system was a matter of highest priority. In most of these nations some system of formal education had been in existence for varying periods of time, either as a tradition from an ancient regime (as in Japan and Korea), as a legacy from colonialism (as in Vietnam and India), or as a gesture of humanitarianism by private or missionary effort (as in much of Africa). In every one of these new nations, whatever the tradition for education, only a small portion of the total population had been benefited. Recognizing that the wish of the people was almost universally for status and honor among nations, the governments of the new nations felt a strong need to give education high national and governmental priority in their desire for equality with the more affluent nations. In all nations, the need for more complete and more realistic schooling for all their children and youth, brought into sharp focus the need for a large and well-trained body of teachers, in order to bring to fruition the hopes of what might be accomplished through modern education to fit the needs of modern times. The current lack of such teachers was painfully apparent in all types of societies, but particularly acute in the developing nations where unique problems had to be faced.

With the increased demand for teachers in nations emerging from colonialism, came also the demand for highly trained native persons who could take over the government positions which had previously been held by representatives of foreign powers. There was likewise increasing demand for trained native personnel in various professions such as law, medicine, and business, where a great many nationals of foreign countries had previously held key positions. All of these demands had to compete with the demand for trained teachers, who could, at all levels, meet the nation's needs for education. In addition, often the demands on the resources of the new nations made agonizing decisions imperative where education was concerned. What part of an extremely limited total national budget should go for education? What part of the education budget should go for adult education? What part should go to the education of children and youth at what educational levels: primary, secondary and higher?

Whatever the stage of development of a nation, one of the major educational problems of all nations was how to recruit and train enough teachers of sufficiently high quality to guarantee the fulfillment of national aims and goals in education. In any program of education, the level of learning and the professional adequacy of the teaching staff are the factors, more than budget, or curriculum, or school buildings and equipment, which will determine the quality of education which can take place.

> The strength of an educational system must largely depend upon the quality of its teachers. However enlightened the aims, however up to date and generous the equipment, however efficient the administration, the value to the children is determined by the teachers. There is, therefore, no more important matter than that of receiving a sufficient supply of the right kind of people to the profession, and ensuring to them a status and esteem commensurate with the importance and responsibility of their work. With the rapid expansion in schooling, both in numbers and extent all over the world, these problems have acquired a new importance and urgency.[1]

It is, therefore, of paramount importance in trying to assess the educational proficiency of a nation to know something of the background, the training, and the personal and professional philosophy of the teachers who instruct its children. This holds true, whether one attempts to assess the educational program of new nations just beginning to organize schools for their children or of long established nations with well established school systems.

The rise of fervent nationalism in all countries following the post-war period gave rise to a kind of educational competition among

3

nations which placed particular emphasis on certain aspects of education, usually the areas of science and mathematics, particularly in developed nations. This was spurred, in part, by the early success of Russian scientists in exploring outer space and by the creation of atomic energy for use in armaments by several nations.

It was partially this spirit of competition that gave rise to the realization that the old systems of education which had met the domestic goals of a country in the pre-war era were no longer adequate. In the more developed countries, the challenge of the explosion of knowledge was perhaps uppermost in the minds of those responsible for education. This was also true to some degree in the less developed nations, although most of these were more directly affected by the population explosion and by the widening of their national goals and expectations.

Thus, there were insistent demands for improved quality as well as increased quantity in education. Demands for new types of skilled workers required new types of training. Established professions and vocations found that the widening bounds of knowledge challenged the old patterns of education. Moreover, the highly industrialized societies found that they had to educate their people for leisure, as well as for high productivity, because of their shortened work week and early retirement.

In the less affluent societies, the demand for teachers to meet the new challenges to education became a major consideration in developing the educational patterns which would be acceptable in the new age. More teachers were needed, in part because there were more children in schools, in part because the number of years of schooling was increased for many more children.

But the mere addition of numbers was not the only problem concerning the teaching profession. There would have to be new methods of pre-service and in-service training to guarantee that the goals sought would be realized.

In short, it can be said that in the era following World War II both developed and developing countries share a common concern with education: that it be made an instrument for building and for maintaining each nation's place in the family of nations and for building and for maintaining national goals of economic growth, social stability, and personal welfare. In both types of countries the adequate supply of well-trained and highly motivated teachers is a key factor in establishing the educational system which can realize these goals.

Many studies have been made of possible methods for recruiting, training and retaining good teachers. Each country has had to tailor its methods to the resources of the country and to the priorities it has decided to give to segments of the total educational endeavor. Since in all countries all other levels of schooling rest upon the primary level, the teacher of the primary school is the keystone of the entire educational structure, no matter what type of society he serves.

How he is recruited, what education he receives, what his conditions of work are, what salary he earns, how he is regarded in his society are matters of common concern, and to a degree all these have been studied in practically all major countries.[2] But one important area of study has been almost totally neglected: how does the primary teacher in various cultures view himself in relation to his work and to his society? Such questions as: Who is the teacher in a given country? What does he believe his status to be in the society for which he works? Does he believe his rewards are commensurate with the effort he must put forth in fulfilling his professional duties? Is he essentially happy and satisfied with his role?

Answers to such questions have remained largely in the realm of conjecture. The answers to these questions are extremely important in assessing the effectiveness of the teacher's work, for any teacher teaches *himself* as much or more than he teaches subject matter. It is difficult to see how teachers who feel themselves, in Harold Benjamin's phrase, "scared hired men," can bring their children to the level of personal and social competence demanded by their society and to equip them to take their places as adequately functioning adults in a modern world. On the other hand, teachers who feel secure in the importance of the role and status accorded them will undoubtedly be more capable of instilling in children the ideals of service and commitment to the goals and ideals set for them as adults who can fulfill their proper roles in the personal, social, political, and economic spheres of their national life. Thus it is extremely important, in assessing the effectiveness of the educational effort of a country, to know something of the self-image of the teachers in its schools.

Numerous studies have been made in various countries about how governmental officials or other observers *think* teachers feel about their role and status. These may be accurate on some points, inaccurate on others. So far as can be determined, no study has been made of the self-analysis of the role and status of primary school teachers on a cross-cultural scale. Whether such studies have merit or whether

5

teachers' answers to the questions suggested above have special merit must be determined by further study and analysis. It can be argued that many teachers will be either unwilling or unable to indicate their true feelings about themselves, their relationship to their profession and to the larger society in which they work. One can, indeed, point out many weaknesses in getting at the true state of affairs by the technique of a questionnaire distributed and collected by school authorities, even though strict anonymity has been observed. The chief compensating factor for these weaknesses is that any other approach has other difficulties which may vitiate results as much as or more than the method used in the current study.

One might raise a legitimate question concerning the efficacy of attempting to compare teacher attitudes toward role and status in several cultures. It has long been recognized, in comparative education, that direct comparison as a method of assessing value has little validity. Comparison does have value, however, in a descriptive sense and as a basis for trying to determine causal factors for a given phenomenon. In the present study no attempt has been made to compare teachers' responses on the basis of what seems an acceptable attitude or what seems an unacceptable one, as manifested by the combined answers of the teachers from a given culture. It is recognized that there is apt to be wide variance within a culture on any given point and general acceptance among the teachers of different cultures on other points.

Directions for sampling procedures and for translating and administering all questionnaires were sent to education officials in all the cities sampled.[3] These officials were interviewed personally to make sure that the purpose and the methods of the study were clear.[4] That it was sometimes not possible to carry out all instructions as planned became apparent as the replies were tabulated. Unfortunately the questionnaries from two European cities were not usable because of errors in translation, and the replies from one city, Oslo, Norway, were lost in transport. Thus the balance of European and Asian cities in the study is not as good as had been planned.

The sampling consisted of an initial 200 teachers from each city, half of whom were young teachers with less than five years of teaching experience, and the other half with ten or more years of experience. The reason for this choice of sample was that in most countries tremendous changes in education have taken place in the last two decades, and it seemed important to try to determine what effect, if any, these

6

changes have had on a teacher's self-image as measured by younger and older teachers. The sampling done in a pilot study of Korean teachers[5] has been included in the present study, except that the section dealing with teachers in rural areas has been omitted, since it was found impractical to include rural teachers in the cross-cultural study.

It may be argued, that a small sampling of teachers from a large metropolitan center can hardly be called an adequate sample of the entire teaching staff of a country, particularly in those areas of the world where there is sharp cleavage between the social conditions in the rural and urban life of the people of that country. Standards of social and economic life, including education, are apt to be higher in the city than in the less industrialized, remote areas. This fact is conceded in the present study, and the assumption underlying all generalizations made is that the sample of teachers from any country, taken from a large city, is usually a sample of the better trained and the more fortunately situated teachers of that country.

The pilot study made in South Korea confirms this assumption to a degree, and yet the differences between teachers placed in a large city such as Seoul and those in a rather remote rural province were not so marked as to warrant the conclusion that a sampling of teachers, either in rural areas or in metropolitan centers, would yield radically different results. Insofar as Korea can be taken as a prototype for a developing country, with rather marked differences between urban and rural society, one might conclude that the sample taken of teachers in countries somewhat similar to Korea would be a fair sample of teachers generally in that country.[6] In Western countries where the cleavage between rural and urban areas is less marked, differences between the teaching staff are also less marked. However, since all samples taken came from a large metropolitan area in each country, it can be assumed that it is possible to make comparisons from the responses made by the teachers in the cities. On this assumption, the responses have often been identified with the country, without I hope, distorting the accuracy of the conclusions.

The premise underlying the study is that the teacher's self-image of his role and status is an important factor in assessing the *actual* role of the teacher in discharging his professional duties and in fulfilling a role in his own culture.

Because of the nature of the data gathered, no sophisticated statistical treatment of it was attempted. Simple percentages show the comparative values of the raw data.

7

There are three sets of tables, all bearing the same titles, but differing in content. The A set covers the data for the East and the West as a whole, along with the differences in the responses of the younger and the older teachers and the percentages of the totals. The next set, the B tables, give the data for the five Western and the seven Eastern cities. The third set, the C tables, give the data of the responses of the students in training in three cities, London, Hong Kong, and Detroit. The questionnaire for the three sets was the same, except for the deletion of some questions for some places and some questions that were not relevant to students. There were also some changes in some questions to make them relevant to students.

II

THE CURRENT ROLE
AND STATUS OF TEACHERS

If we could first know where we are
and whither we are tending, we could
better judge what to do and how to do it.
Abraham Lincoln

THIS STUDY OF THE ROLE OF THE TEACHER HAS TWO MAIN OBJECTIVES.
The first is to determine what society thinks he *ought to do* in order to
fulfill his mission as the chief agent for carrying out the society's aims
for the schools it provides for its children. The second is to discover
exactly what he *does do* in the daily discharge of his duties, both in the
classroom and in the larger community, as evidenced by his behavior.
To determine the first is basically a philosophical and sociological
study; the second can only be learned, at least in part, by empirical
research.

On the first, much material has long been available in professional
literature. Manuals on teacher training as well as philosophical discussions of the place of education in the socialization of children have
long tried to spell out what sort of person is needed for the role of
teacher, how he should be trained for this role, and what his professional performance should be. To separate the teacher from his
teaching is indeed quite impossible. In every discussion of education,

9

the role of the teacher is implicit. The second objective has received increasing attention from research workers during the past several decades. Their research has taken several forms: evaluations by trained observers; by education officials of various ranks; by pupils; by members of community, including parents; and by teachers themselves.[1] While all methods of assessing the role of the teacher, both as ideally conceived and as practically carried out in the classroom, are valuable in judging the kind and quality of education being offered children by the teachers, one type of research is coming to have increasing significance. This is the study of self-assessment of what the teacher thinks he ought to do and what he actually is able to do under his everyday working conditions. While there are admittedly drawbacks to having the teacher draw a picture of himself as he sees himself, the study of this type of assessment promises insights into what is really happening in the classroom, for what the teacher *thinks* he is and does is probably a substantially true index of what he *in reality* is and does. To date, the great bulk of these studies has been limited to a single nation or society.[2]

A rather thorough research of the literature reveals that to date no main studies have been published on the self-analysis of the role of the teacher in several nations. One of particular interest, dealing with the English speaking nations of Australia, Canada, England, New Zealand and the United States is now in progress at the University of Missouri, under the direction of Bruce J. Biddle and a cooperating staff from the countries under study. When reported this research will, no doubt, receive world-wide attention.

In the following discussion, two main types of national studies have been drawn upon to describe the role present day society seems to want the teacher to fulfill: the role the teacher sees for himself as proper and possible; the role the teacher actually plays as evidenced by his behavior. Both of these are important in assessing the outcomes which can be expected from the educational endeavors in which nations are now engaged. The present study is concerned solely with the image which the teacher in a number of cities has of himself and of his place in forwarding the goals of his profession. That this image relates to the image that his society has of him and to his actual behavior seems reasonable to suppose.

"There can be little doubt but that teacher-held role conceptions are a major determinant of teacher behavior. Not only is this proposition suggested by role theory, but a major tenant [sic] of most teacher-education curricula is that through inculcating an appropriate conceptual framework, youthful teachers can be prepared to carry on the vital work of education."[3]

While the overriding objective of all educational effort for every nation has been, and continues to be, the socialization of its young, the transmission of its past culture has been and remains of extreme importance. An eminent British sociologist has characterized the traditional teacher as a "paid agent of cultural diffusion," who is hired to carry light into dark places.[4] The justification for this kind of missionary role is that an understanding of the culture of a nation by its young is indispensable to national survival. This means it is important for the teacher to understand his national culture and to be in command of the means for imparting it to the young under his care.

Recently teachers have been asked to assume far more than their roles as agents who have the responsibility of passing on the accumulated culture of the age. Because of accelerated cultural change in the world, it has become necessary for them to act as crusaders who will introduce those new ideas and measures which will bring about the changes deemed important and urgent in a society. How these two roles are to be reconciled and balanced is the delicate problem which faces teachers in practically all societies. In each society the problem is unique, since each one puts a different value on preserving the old at the expense of the new. In the light of the recent political, cultural, social, and scientific revolutions, which have virtually left no culture unchanged, it can safely be said that this dual role in the world today is particularly difficult for every teacher to reconcile, no matter where he serves.

In stable societies and in times of little or no change, the image of the teacher and his role were more or less fixed and he could rely heavily on tradition to guide him. Usually, he was not expected to be a crusader for change; rather he was a force in maintaining the status quo. While his position in many cultures may not have been an exalted one, he could consider himself a figure of authority, at least in his own classroom, with support from the community. Numerous studies have shown an erosion of that authority, so that he must now face new and hazardous responsibilities without feeling confident that he will have the necessary support for whatever he feels he must undertake. Because of the decline of his prestige and authority, some observers feel that the problem of determining his proper role has become almost insurmountable.

11

The problems facing teachers are formidable. We have seen how their traditional authority is undermined by social pressures over which neither they nor we can have much control, and how, if they are to achieve the indispensable ascending over their pupils, without which they cannot teach, they need to understand in a way that perhaps never before was necessary, the social dimensions of their work — the social determinants of the educability of their pupils, the hidden social tensions of the learning situation in contemporary schools.[5]

Another matter of considerable importance is the teacher's opportunity for involvement in the decisions and policy making for what goes on in his school. In some societies all matters of major importance pertaining to education are decided at high echelon levels (perhaps by a national ministry of education), and the individual teacher finds that his role is to interpret, as best he can, the specifics of such decisions as they are to be realized in the day-to-day discharge of his duties in the classroom. In other societies, responsibility is given to teachers, even in the lower echelons, to participate in the formulation of policies and to make decisions as to how policies are to be implemented in terms of classroom activities. In most countries, neither extreme is followed, so that the usual role of the teacher is to help decide, through democratic procedure, the general course that teaching practice and method ought to take in his particular school for his particular group of children. It is then his responsibility to cooperate with local and higher administrative officers in seeing that his performance conforms to what has been agreed upon.

Thus, in his professional role (only a part of his total role), a teacher is expected to be the possessor of knowledge which he can successfully impart to children; a student of the psychology of childhood; a disciplinarian responsible for conduct; an evaluator and counsellor of children's activities; a developer of curriculums; a public relations person dealing with parents; an eternal student in quest of new knowledge and new ideas for the pursuit of his profession. Furthermore, he must see clearly the major goals toward which education is to be directed in his society and to do his part to see that these goals are accomplished.

Because of the teacher's peculiar position in a society, his total role has always included much more than the performance of his professional activities. To a far greater degree than for the members of most other professions, the public is concerned with him as a person, as a citizen, as a representative of the culture. In some situations, some of the roles expected of him actually contradict one another, for the teacher is expected to be at one and the same time a leader and a follower, a conservative and an innovator, a member of the community but yet not really of it, a conserver of the culture and yet a dissipator of it, a paragon and yet an approachable human being.

Factors Determining the Status of Teachers

It is clear that status for a particular group or profession is a relative matter within each society. It can be assessed only in the total context of the respect, regard and privilege that a given group is accorded within the total pattern of hierarchies within a society. Status is a psychological as well as an economic and sociological reality. It can shift and change for any specific group because of shift and change within the value patterns and the sociological and economic evolution of a society.

Furthermore, teachers' roles usually vary with their sex, age, length of service, and level of cultural derivation, even though they may work under somewhat identical professional situations. The size of the community where they serve is also usually a variant of considerable importance. Generally, teachers in rural or small communities are much more at the mercy of the general public than are teachers in communities so large that they are culturally less visible to the general public.

A society's total role expectation of the teacher and his own concept of his proper role, even though they must be basically in harmony, vary from time to time. This fact may cause conflict within the individual teacher and may hamper him in fulfilling his most important role: that of being a professional person entrusted with the optimal development and guidance of the young. For that reason, he ought to be judged competent to create for himself the proper role to achieve this end. If he is to function at his best, in many societies he will have to free himself from his present ambiguous position. His anomalous role in relation to other workers has been described as follows:

> In the complicated structure of our modern civilization, the teacher holds an equivocal position. By one set of value judgments, he ranks no higher than the bus driver, the sanitary inspector, or the plumber. The teacher might reflect bitterly that he is not assessed even as high as the bus driver, since the latter's demand for pay increases, supported by strike action is usually effective, whereas his own are not. On the other hand, we expect a much higher

13

standard from the teacher in the matter of his public and private life, his moral and religious views, and in his general bearing before the public eye.[6]

For most societies in modern times, instability of position is certainly generally true of the teaching profession. In attempting to ascertain the position of teachers within any society, one must first ask whether the group can truly be said to have attained the status of a recognized profession, for a profession has, in itself, a certain status. If teaching is not recognized as a profession, then teachers must rank outside of what is generally considered a favored class. If it is recognized as a profession, then its status must be assessed with regard to its comparative position within the professional classification as well as with regard to the general place of the profession itself.

To judge whether teaching is a profession or not within a given society is difficult because the definition of a profession may vary from country to country. Usually a profession is defined as an occupation demanding specialized skills and knowledge; requiring an extended time for their acquisition; the practitioners of which carefully select and limit the numbers of members admitted to its ranks and maintain high standards of performance through methods of self-discipline. Because of its organization and the services to society a profession is uniquely prepared to render, it usually wields certain power, not only over those who render the services it gives but also over those who receive them. It does so by governing the conditions under which its members may be admitted and discharged and also by regulating the price exacted from the public for the services it gives. Judged by these standards, it is a matter of debate whether the total teaching staff in any country can, at the present time, be called a true professional group. Since there is doubt that teachers constitute a profession, it follows that usually they do not enjoy the high prestige given to medicine and law, which traditionally enjoy this designation, almost universally. However, university teaching generally does enjoy high prestige, as will be noted later, even though it may not qualify as a profession in quite the same sense as medicine and law.

Within any profession, a hierarchical system is usually maintained. This may be established through length of the training period, length of service, or the specialized skill and talent of the individual. This hierarchy is particularly evident in the teaching field. Status for the individual teacher may depend upon any of a number of variables, such as the social class of the pupils he teaches, the age of his pupils (nursery-school teachers often are at the foot of the ladder in prestige among teachers, while professors in graduate schools are often at the top), the subject he teaches (Latin is thought more reputable than physical education), the length and kind of training required for his qualification as a teacher.

Since this present study concerns only teachers in primary schools, the question to be raised is whether these teachers can be considered part of a profession and what position they occupy in various countries. One might consider a number of criteria.

The first criterion is that of salary, including various fringe benefits such as pensions, insurance, sick leave, family allowances and others. If a service is valued by a society, that society ordinarily rewards the workers adequately, so as to attract talented and intellectually and morally qualified young persons in competition with the demands of other services.

The second is that of mobility and promotion. This means both vertical and horizontal freedom to move about. If there are few incentives within a profession for improving one's position by rising to greater influence and greater recognition, many young people will look elsewhere in deciding where to expend their life activities. If any profession has a high turnover of personnel, one can assume that there is danger of that profession losing its status within the society. A unique factor in the teaching profession is that it traditionally attracts a large number of young women. For these the turnover is usually high because of the responsibilities of marriage and child rearing.

The third is that of appointment and dismissal. Protection through life tenure is extremely important, particularly in those professions where the pressure of public opinion is apt to be so strong as to interfere with the discharge of professional duties. Professions that pry into the religious and political views of applicants often repel the most competent youth. Young people of real ability ordinarily want freedom from restrictions on their beliefs.

Fourth and crucial is the selection and recruitment of well-qualified young people. Standards must be set which involve intellectual, physical, moral and spiritual qualities. Only those young people possessing these qualities in high degree should be admitted to the favored ranks of a profession in any society, because the society expects more of them in service and therefore expects to reward them accordingly. The standards for admission or exclusion should in general be set by the profession itself.

15

The fifth refers to the conditions of work which must be favorable. There must be freedom to carry on the usual life of a citizen, including the privilege of political action. There must be individual freedom for study and experiment and sufficient leisure to provide opportunity for this and for recreation. The relationship with superiors should be such that opportunities for creative work are possible.

The final criterion is the existence of a strong professional organization with the responsibility of safeguarding standards and of protecting the rights of the profession from encroachments by government, other professions or the general public for the maintenance of status. This organization must also demonstrate the will and the ability to exert disciplinary measures upon itself as an entity and upon individual members.

On the basis of these criteria, it is difficult to classify teaching as a true profession either in developed or developing countries. Particularly, the status of the primary school teacher must, in most societies, be classed far below the level of a profession. The many studies undertaken in this whole area, particularly by UNESCO and by the World Confederation of the Organizations of the Teaching Profession, have lead to the consensus that the status of teachers everywhere is far too low for the services they are expected to render in the modern world.[7] Reliable authorities assert that until this situation is changed, the results which various societies expect from education, be they the highly industrialized ones or those evolving into industrialization, will not be forthcoming. At the annual meeting of its general assembly held in Istanbul in 1955, the World Confederation passed the following resolutions on the status of the teaching profession, which it believes must be implemented before teachers can take their rightful place of honor and esteem.

1. In the interest of children and the nation, it is essential that the social and economic status of the teaching profession should be raised. In order to accomplish this and to secure a solid basis of knowledge and teaching ability, high standards of professional training should be established. It is in particular desirable that the level required for entry to the normal school should be the same as that accepted by the university, and, taking into account the system of training teachers peculiar to each country, it is necessary that the basic general culture of the primary school teacher be equivalent to that required for admission to the university.

2. Central and local authorities, universities and training institutions should provide facilities to enable teachers to keep abreast of educational thought and practice.

3. Teachers' salaries should be commensurate with those of other professions with equivalent training and qualifications whose responsibilities are of comparable importance. In order to attract and retain teachers of the quality required, salary scales should not only be adequate at the minimum but should proceed more rapidly to a satisfactory maximum. Pensions for teachers and their dependents should be such as will enable them to maintain reasonable standards of living.

4. One of the most important tasks of the teaching profession is to form strong professional organizations.

5. Teachers should be entitled to reasonable leave of absence with pay to enable them to participate in the activities of their professional organizations.

6. It is essential that the teaching profession should have permanent and close relations with the public authorities.

7. Teacher representatives on central and local government bodies should be appointed by teachers themselves.

8. Teachers in schools of all types should have the right to stand as candidates for administrative and political positions. While carrying out their duties in these spheres, their pension rights should be maintained by their continuing to pay contributions.

9. No teacher should be required, against his will, to give religious instruction.

10. It is impossible to envisage an efficient educational system and a sound education unless the necessary requirements of such an education are fully recognized by the whole country, which must be prepared to provide them.

11. Teachers' organizations should make use of all modern means of communication (press, radio, etc.) in order to rouse public opinion to the importance of educational problems.[8]

In the *Draft Recommendation Concerning the Status of Teachers* prepared by the joint commission of the International Labor Organization and UNESCO, assisted by WCOTP, for its sessions in Geneva early in 1966, in preparation for inaugurating a new world study on this topic, this statement of basic policy was presented for review:

Planning designed to improve the social and economic conditions of teachers would be given direction and coherence if it were to arise out of a conscious aim to accord teaching a public esteem and social standing commensurate with the high importance of the teaching function for the society. The teaching profession is an occupation wherein its practitioners render an intimate personal service on the basis of possession of a body of knowledge particular to the calling and a set of specialized skills gained initially through rigorous education and training demanding high intellectual attributes, and refreshed and reinforced from time to time in service. It is further marked by dedication to the welfare of others, a willingness to accept responsibility for

17

work outcomes with an accompanying authority to exercise independent judgment in prescribing procedures deemed to be in the interest of those whom the profession is called upon to serve. The members of comparable professions such as medical doctors and lawyers usually determine and safeguard standards of professional competence and practice. The exercise of such professions confers an appropriate social standing and remuneration.

In the light of these considerations, if teaching is to be accorded a social status of this kind it follows logically that conditions appropriate to preparation for professional practice and conditions necessary for the exercise of professional responsibility will have to be established. It also follows that persons will not come forward in sufficient numbers to staff the schools in terms of high requirements unless social, economic and working conditions are made compatible with professional status.[9]

Reasons for the Low Status of Teachers

If then, as evidence seems so clearly to show, the status of the teacher is currently judged to be low, what might be the reason? Sociologists find some explanation for it in the role he plays in most societies. In comparing the teacher with the doctor or lawyer, for example, a British sociologist points out these factors:

> His role appears to be less urgent, less dramatic, even though in fact it is no less vital. Because it is less urgent and less dramatic it receives less social respect, and carries less salary. We confer gratitude and rewards on those who put things right when they go wrong rather than on those who quietly keep things right. The element of the supererogatory is much more evident in the dramatic situation of the doctor's client or the lawyer's client than in the teacher's client where supererogatory acts must be more sustained if they are to achieve their end.
>
> Because teaching is a stable, normal need of society it requires more agents than do the law and medicine, which is, of course, another factor influencing social prestige and the conferment of rewards. There is no objective reason to believe that the special skills of the lawyer and of the doctor are particularly scarce in society. The abilities employed are probably potentially more abundant than those of a teacher. But these professions maintain a monopoly of training and keep lawfully recognized practitioners deliberately scarce. Of course, society needs fewer doctors and lawyers than teachers. The expansion of education has meant that whether people have high abilities for teaching or not they have to be accepted because large numbers of teachers are needed. As a profession it has never been in a position to choose whom it will have. Teacher training colleges rarely fail people; and graduates, merely by being graduates, are thought to be equipped to teach. There is no explicit professional ethic, no professional control of members and no expulsions — because

there have never been conditions in which adequate selectivity has been possible. Thus society accepts as dramatic and even glamorous those professional roles which "put things right" and accepts the myth that these abilities are scarce because the need for them is limited. It tends to disparage diffuse roles which are constantly and universally in demand, because a standard of performance is difficult to establish. This is so because the task is defined in terms of the general ends desired rather than in terms of the precise activities involved.

Because a teacher is concerned with a whole person over a prolonged period of time — and not merely with his delictual acts or his disturbed health — so *he* tends to become involved as a whole person. Since his role is difficult to define in terms of its action-content so it is difficult to delimit the extent to which his purely personal virtues are involved in it. The fact that the teacher employs his whole person in his role gives rise to unparalleled satisfactions, but equally to intense frustrations. A total commitment necessarily imposes strains — it means "living the job." And this is increasingly uncommon and uncalled for in our type of society in which specificity, time-calculation and contractual obligations are the rule. The diffuse role means diffuse involvement. The teacher carries his work around with him — because he has to "re-create" his role continually, to re-interpret, re-enact, re-structure relationships and behaviour patterns. He is the model for the child at a formative period and we know, and most teachers know in their work situation, that a child can be seriously disturbed if he discovers shortcomings in his model. The teacher has to be virtually beyond reproach. It is only because demand is great and selection limited that society has to put up with the uncommitted teacher. Thus there is no way of delimiting the role either in terms of the person dealt with or in terms of the role-performer himself.

Because our society is a society in which specialization continually increases, prestige increasingly attaches to the specialist. But there are distinct limits to the extent of specialization in teaching because the role is diffuse. Again, because our society relies on increasing technologization, it is instrumental roles which win social approval — in which clearly defined operations are undertaken and means are manipulated to achieve proximate ends, which in turn become means to further ends. In some measure, increasingly higher rewards are given to those whose roles involve them in the use of elaborate equipment — both technical and organizational. But the teacher's role is not directly instrumental — it is concerned with ends, with values. It is, of its nature, personal and direct. The results achieved are not dramatic achievements issuing from complex manipulation of elaborate mechanical or human machinery. They are imperceptibly gradual — and even when they are recognized the teacher's part in their achievement may not be credited — the boy was a bright boy, anyway! Results are always more manifest in instrumental roles, and the process — the equipment, jargon, tools, formulae, mystique — is impressive; but teaching has little of all this. Thus, diffuse roles tend to lack

19

the prestige of specific, instrumental roles. The same process has diminished the social prestige of the religious functionary. The process does not occur, of course, where the teacher is regarded as a vital agent of consciously-sought social change in accordance with an entrenched ideology — as is the case in the Soviet Union.[10]

But neither the numbers needed nor the peculiarities of the roles teachers are called upon to play, will alone explain the low status of the teaching profession in most areas of the world. As anthropologists and sociologists point out, in numerous and diverse cultures, teachers have traditionally been held in low esteem, partly at least because of the manner in which education and teaching evolved from a basically non-literate world into one of literacy and learning.

Margaret Mead, in describing the role of the teacher in American culture, calls to mind the part he played in former times in two diverse cultures, both of which reverenced learning but did not honor the teacher: Chinese and eastern European Jewry.

> Among the Chinese — in the village — the teacher was traditionally a poor relation or a stranger, a man who had failed to obtain a high enough rank in his examinations to win a place in the civil service and who was held in low esteem by the village community. To him was delegated the distasteful task of disciplining little boys into learning the hundreds of characters which must be mastered if anyone of them was to escape from the life of the village into the wider scene.
>
> If we turn to eastern European Jewry . . . the teacher, who had to make a living from teaching, rather than from being a great scholar . . . made life a misery for the little boys, boys often so small that they had to be carried to school, where they sat in cold, undecorated rooms pouring over tattered, inexplicable schoolbooks written in a language different from that which was their daily speech, a language which their mothers seldom understood at all. The teacher's weapons were an unbelievable vocabulary of sarcasm and vituperation; only one day a year were the devoted small boys permitted to go out into the fields; for all the rest of the year they studied, learning by heart great masses of sacred materials which they did not yet understand.[11]

For reasons which can be explained, the shadow of the past has not been fully dissipated for teachers generally, and most certainly not for elementary teachers. In most countries which have tried to delineate their position in contemporary society, it is almost universally a position of low prestige.

That teachers themselves tend to hold their group in low esteem is documented by two recent studies of American teachers. One of these was made in the eastern part of the United States of the teachers in smaller communities, the other made in the western part, of teachers in a larger community as subjects.[12]

In these studies, teachers defined their role as vague and confused. They did not perceive themselves as taking any positive action toward curriculum change or cultural change. They felt they had little respect from the community or the administrative officers of the school. Likewise they believed they had little part in developing educational policy and were hampered from doing so by their administrators. They felt that merit and creativity were not properly rewarded and that they were not growing professionally.

The teacher at the primary level tends to rate himself particularly low. In a study made in Germany, the primary teacher put himself lower in the social scale than did the general public.[13] In the Netherlands, primary school teachers considered themselves even lower than did the teachers of Germany, probably because they are not required to achieve the equivalent of university entrance before beginning training, as is the case in Germany.[14]

Perhaps a good part of the teacher's dissatisfaction with himself comes from his efforts to teach values which his society only partially supports. He has been led to believe that a teacher should represent moral values, integrity of mind, honest criticism, tolerance, loyalty, sensibility, and appreciative imagination. These qualities he finds are not valued in the judgment of his achievements.[15]

Another factor is the unsatisfactory conditions of his work. These include classes far too large for effective teaching, lack of proper teaching materials and aids of various sorts, undue assignments of work outside the regular teaching duties, inadequate sick leave and insurance protection, insufficient pension provisions.

The WCOTP sent out a questionnaire to teachers of its member organizations preparatory to its 1963 general assembly at Rio De Janeiro on the theme "Conditions of Work for Quality Teachers." This asked for the reactions of its membership to certain propositions which would raise the status of teachers through raising the quality of their contribution to society. Forty-one organizations responded.[16]

Crucial in these considerations is the matter of salary and fringe benefits. The teacher has always been poorly paid in relation to other professions with comparable requirements for admission, for length and kind of training required and for services expected. The reasons have been many, but basically the old law of supply and demand has been operative, particularly in those countries where large numbers of young women have entered the profession, usually as a stop-gap between school and marriage. In the present world situation, an almost universal shortage of teachers has led to serious efforts to raise salaries to the level where recruits will be attracted in sufficient number to allow for the expansion so desperately required.

The Burnham Committee of England in its salary negotiations with Parliament has advanced these major points in requesting a revised salary schedule: the longer training period now required, starting salaries out of line with those of competing professions and industry, the increased material standard of living for all kinds of workers, early marriage making the need for early income imperative, and the recent large increases in the salaries in other lines of work.[17]

The matters of low salary and poor working conditions as deterrents to building the kind of status for teachers and the kind of role attractive to intelligent and competent young people are particularly crucial in developing countries, although crucial to a degree throughout the world. In a study made by the International Federation of Teachers in seven new nations, the list of adverse conditions facing teachers is almost overwhelming: inadequate salary, little provision for in-service education, poor housing, existence of dialect and other language problems, isolation of rural areas, opposition of parents to school attendance of children, unjust dismissals, inadequate budget for creating the needed number of teaching posts, loss of best teachers to other needed government services, weak teachers' organizations, double sessions, large classes, lack of teaching materials, poor supervision, inadequate buildings, importation of teachers from other cultures, influences of foreign curriculum support, retention of aged and incompetent staff. Such a list can leave no doubt that in such countries there must be easier, more pleasant, more rewarding ways of earning one's living and spending one's life than in teaching.[18]

It is small wonder then that improving the economic status of the teacher has top priority in supplying the world with qualified and dedicated teachers. It is perhaps for this very reason that the ILO has joined with UNESCO in studying ways to improve the present deplorable situation.

> The draft Recommendation ends with a section on teacher shortage. This problem . . . has to be given special attention because even if every recommendation were fully implemented immediately some years would have to pass before the full effect was realised. In the meantime children are waiting

22

to be educated. Their need is for teachers now. In particular there is an extreme urgency in developing countries where there is no fully established school system on which to build and where financial resources are lacking. In many countries, emergency measures are likely to be the rule rather than the exception despite the fact that everywhere it is likely to be accepted that the final goal should be the provision of a professionally qualified teacher for every classroom.

Realistically, it has to be admitted, that, in most countries of the world, for a number of years to come, there will have to be employed many persons who cannot be deemed to be teachers in the professional sense. It is important that some way be found of using their services on a basis which does not detract from the status of those teachers who are truly professional and which at the same time gives them an opportunity to become fully qualified in service. Some of the proposals made in the final section of the Recommendation suggests ways and means through which every country can meet the immediate problem of staffing its schools and at the same time promote the high professional standards of its teachers.[19]

Rights and Responsibilities of Teachers

Like every other professional group, teachers must safeguard certain rights they feel must be maintained if they are to function according to their best standards. Likewise they acknowledge that they must make certain commitments to the public as to what it can legitimately expect of them by way of services. In all countries certain rights are safeguarded by law, others by custom. In many countries, so-called codes of ethics spell out the responsibilities for performance and conduct which teachers as a professional group believe they must assume in the proper discharge of their duties. Often these codes also spell out the rights to which teachers believe they are entitled. Usually the codes have been drawn up by teachers' organizations and are morally rather than legally binding upon society and upon members of the organization who are subject to disciplinary measures for violations of the code. Some codes provide for group action against the public in order to preserve and safeguard rights. Some codes are brief and general; others lengthy and explicit. The code of the Israel Teachers Union succinctly sums up the whole responsibility of teachers thusly: "The teacher should be exemplary in his way of life, in his honesty and sincerity, in his equal and responsible treatment of pupils, in his friendly relations with other teachers, and in his punctuality and initiative."

The code of the National Education Association of the United States goes into much detail. It was adopted by the Association at its Representative Assembly in 1963. It begins with this:

> We, professional educators of the United States of America, affirm our belief in the worth and dignity of man. We recognize the supreme importance of the pursuit of truth, the encouragement of scholarship, and the promotion of democratic citizenship. We regard as essential to these goals the protection of freedom to learn and to teach and the guarantee of equal educational opportunity for all. We affirm and accept our responsibility to practice our profession according to the highest ethical standards.
>
> We acknowledge the magnitude of the profession we have chosen, and engage ourselves, individually and collectively, to judge our colleagues and to be judged by them in accordance with the applicable provisions of this code.

There are then enunciated four principles of commitment: to the student, to the community, to the profession and to professional employment practices.

Under commitment to the student are pledged fair and considerate treatment, respect for his point of view, discreet use of information about him, activity on his behalf for special needs and services, and the provision of optimal learning materials and conditions.

> We measure success by the progress of each student toward achievement of his maximum potential. We therefore work to stimulate the spirit of inquiry, the acquisition of knowledge and understanding, and the thoughtful formulation of worthy goals. We recognize the importance of cooperative relationships with other community institutions, especially the home.

In commitment to the community, the Association pledges itself to work cooperatively with all community agencies dedicated to education for all, including the right to evaluate the deficiencies of such efforts, to work within policies laid down by law and to assume responsibility for full political and citizenship responsibilities, without using the teacher's position to promote political candidates or partisan activities. The summation statement is as follows:

> We believe that patriotism in its highest form requires dedication to the principles of our democratic heritage. We share with all other citizens the responsibility for the development of sound public policy. As educators, we are particularly accountable for participating in the development of educational programs and policies and for interpreting them to the public.

The commitment to the profession assumes responsibility for the conduct of its members, which should not hamper the development of policies affecting education; to assist in recruitment and selection of those entering the profession; to come to the aid of those unjustly accused or mistreated in the exercise of their rights as teachers; to assess administrative procedures to determine their value to students; to have a voice in employment and dismissal policies; to grow intellectually through appropriate in-service education; to deal honestly with colleagues; and to present honestly credentials and qualifications for employment.

> We believe that the quality of the services of the education profession directly influences the future of the nation and its citizens. We therefore exert every effort to raise educational standards, to improve our service, to promote a climate in which the exercise of professional judgment is encouraged, and to achieve conditions which attract persons worthy of the trust to careers in education. Aware of the value of united effort, we contribute actively to the support, planning, and programs of our professional organizations.

Finally, the Association commits itself to certain employment practices.

> We regard the employment agreement as a solemn pledge to be executed both in spirit and in fact in a manner consistent with the highest ideals of professional service. Sound professional personnel relationships with governing boards are built upon personal integrity, dignity, and mutual respect.[20]

Concerning teacher's rights, two matters seem paramount: academic and professional freedom for the individual teacher and collective action through the organizations representing the profession. Academic and professional freedom is generally conceived to be broader than the teacher's right to include in the curriculum matters of scientific truth which may be somewhat at variance with governmental policy or general public opinion. It includes also certain ways of working with superiors, parents, co-workers and children. The ILO and UNESCO in its Draft Recommendations for the Geneva meeting in 1966, included these points (points 73–83) as matters of importance in guaranteeing to teachers their rights in the performance of their duties.[21]

The matter of collective action through teachers' organizations may be purely academic, such as the preparation of curriculum materials, or it may be largely political, as in exerting pressures on legislative bodies for such concerns as salary increases or the amelioriation of working conditions. In some countries two kinds of organization exist: one to push academic interests, the other to push teachers'

25

economic and social welfare. In the latter, teachers' organizations may be affiliated with general labor organizations. Whatever their basic objectives, most teachers hold that these organizations are fundamental to the maintenance and development of true professional status. They insist that they should be recognized by law as having a key role in recruiting and selecting suitable candidates for the profession, in developing standards and curricula for training programs, in maintaining in-service training programs, in building curricula and in promoting the use of new teaching aids and methods, in revising and improving general school policies. How far teachers' organizations may properly go, in terms of general public welfare, in striving to maintain rights for their own group is at present a moot question. Collective bargaining is not carried on in a number of countries but is recognized in others. Some countries have recognized the right of teachers to call a strike, and strikes have occurred. Other countries think this sort of action not in the public interest. In general, strikes by teachers' groups have been, until very recently, rather rare and used only in extreme cases.

Other rights, which in the past have been denied to teachers and which are still not generally conceded to them, are the full rights of citizenship, including that of holding public office, and the right to be free of any obligations or restrictions due to religious affiliation or commitment.

Another right which teachers believe should be theirs is to leave the profession at any time, without prejudice. In some countries, they are now prevented from doing this by contracts entered into during their training period which obligate them to serve in schools a certain number of years. Because such arrangements are not usual for other professional workers, teachers argue it should not be required of them, for it is a deterrent to bright young people entering the profession.

The entire trend in the matter of teachers' rights and responsibilities is toward a more active and militant position: a position in which they can demand more from the public they serve and in which they can assume the obligation to take a more earnest attitude toward their responsibilities in the discharge of their duties.

Training of Teachers

As has been pointed out, teaching is unique as a profession because of the large numbers which are needed to man the schools of any given country. Recent developments, such as the rapidly increasing birth rate, the demand that all children be educated, the need to keep children in school for longer periods of time have increased greatly the need for many more teachers in practically every country. At the same time, the attractiveness of teaching as a life work has, for a number of reasons, been declining. Hence, teaching has not been able to compete with other professions in inducing qualified young people to enter its ranks, or even to recruit a sufficient number of any sort to meet the increased need. The teacher shortage is now world-wide. Because of the current shortages, teachers can be classified into three general categories in nearly all countries: the untrained (who are asked to serve briefly to take care of extreme emergencies), the un-qualified (those partially trained to take care of continuing shortages), and the fully qualified (those certified to make teaching a life career). Obviously, the definition of the teacher in each of these categories will vary from country to country. There are differences in the require-ments laid down for entering each category, in length of the training period, in the kind of institution in which training is offered, in the kind and quality of the curriculum to be followed. There are also wide variations in the proportion of teachers in each of the three categories which make up the total teaching force in any given country.

The usual pattern for the training of the primary teacher has traditionally been the completion of primary education with two to six years of teacher education or the completion of some level of secondary education, followed by one or two years of work in a teachers' training college, i.e., a normal school, devoted exclusively to the objective of training primary teachers.

In general, education in a normal school has remained at the secondary level. In a world survey of the teachers engaged in training primary school teachers, the International Bureau of Education reports that, for more than two-thirds of the countries replying, the type of institution reported was the normal school.[22]

In only a few countries were teacher training institutions open only to students who have matriculated or who can certify that they have completed secondary schooling. These institutions are exemplified by the teachers' training college in English speaking countries and by the *pädagogische hochschule* in certain of the states of West Germany.

> ... there are advantages in making a primary teaching career available to many more candidates by means of shorter, and consequently less costly, training, thus facilitating the task of educational authorities who are faced

by an ever growing demand for teachers. . . . But along with these practical advantages, the benefits of the more liberal and complete training . . . should not be forgotten. The very fact that a candidate has already acquired a good general education when he embarks on specifically professional studies permits a course to be taken which is more or less wholly devoted to subjects of a professional nature and to practical training; further, since in the majority of cases it is essential to have matriculated before proceeding to a university degree, any field of a specialization at the university is open to a primary teacher should he wish to enter it at some later date.[23]

In only a very few countries do training institutions include curriculums for the training of both primary and secondary teachers.

The curriculum in the various types of teacher training institutions is of three main kinds: general education, professional subjects, and special (non-academic) subjects. Because of the variations in entrance requirements, no generalization can be made of the relative stress placed upon or the relative importance of each of the three kinds. Where secondary education has been an entrance requirement to teacher training, there may be less stress on such subjects as literature, history, or mathematics, and these subjects are taught, if at all, as professionalized subject matter in connection with the methods of teaching the subject. In many countries, subjects such as civics, educational sociology, economics, and indigenous cultural backgrounds which are fairly closely connected with the political, social and economic aims and goals of the country have been recently introduced into the general curriculum. In some countries courses in agriculture are given special emphasis.

One problem of long duration seems no nearer solution now than when it was first propounded in the training of teachers: that of the relative importance of so-called subject matter and professional courses. An English educator poses this problem thus:

> . . . what should a good teacher know? Those who advocate the need for professional studies base their claims on the obvious advantages which are to be gained if the teacher understands (or knows) his pupils, recognizes the social functions of the schools, is aware of the aims of education in his society, and knows how to teach. These essential qualifications can, the argument runs, be best acquired through professional courses and practice in the classroom. It would seem, therefore, that the social sciences should be a vital part of a teacher's course, and some form of apprenticeship essential if he is to be a good teacher. The advocates of the subject-matter approach, on the other hand, often assume that teaching is an art — possessed in various degrees

by all people, but clearly not in the final analysis something which can be acquired through training. The argument of the "born teacher" is frequently used to illustrate this point. At the same time the possession of a body of information — subject matter — is regarded as a prerequisite of good teaching. The teacher must "know" his subject. Just so — but what subject or subjects must he know if he is to be effective in the twentieth century? At this stage the relative claims of the arts subjects and the sciences are debated, but the question is the perennial one of what should constitute a satisfactory general education for intending teachers. The answers are by no means clear, but certainly the American conception of a general education based on data from three overlapping areas — the social sciences, the natural sciences, and the language arts — has much to recommend it. The problems of giving this theory practical form are great, yet they are crucial, if teacher education is to be improved.[24]

Professional subjects usually include such courses in educational theory and background as psychology, child study, history and philosophy of education, and courses in teaching methods, including observation of classroom procedure and student teaching.[25] Non-academic subjects generally include courses in physical education, music and art in various branches. Certification for teaching normally follows automatically the completion of the prescribed training course.

In April 1963 the WCOTP reported a survey of the "Conditions of Work for Quality Teaching" made prior to its annual assembly held in Rio de Janeiro. Replies to a questionnaire were received from thirty-four nations. In reply to the question, "What deficiencies are there in present teacher training arrangements in your countries," these answers received highest priority: teacher training period too short, program training seriously inadequate in various respects, entrance requirements too low, training schools overcrowded. In suggesting improvements for teacher education, the following items were named most frequently: longer periods of training, improvements in type of program offered, higher entrance requirements, more rigorous selection procedures, graduate status for all teachers.[26]

In a study made of eighty-six countries in 1962, the International Bureau of Education reported that 43 percent of these countries were interested in reforming primary curricula or syllabi or both. They also favored lengthening the period of training. Fifteen countries reported that they were in process of reorganizing their training schools. The trends reported most frequently were: new kinds of training, reorganization of old forms, lengthening of courses, changes in curriculams and syllabusis.[27]

Thus the matter of training teachers in most countries currently presents a dilemma. Because of the teacher shortage the standards for their preparation have been lowered. Because standards are low, the most desirable young people are not attracted to the profession. This results in further lowering of standards. A vicious circle now exists, hard to break.

In-Service Education

Because of the rapid changes going on in all societies the teacher must remain in a perpetual state of learning if he is to keep up to date both in general knowledge and in education. So rapid are the changes, that teachers are often called upon to work with children who have come into a world which the teachers themselves find it hard to comprehend.

> ... children of five have already incorporated into their everyday thinking ideas that most of the elders will never fully assimilate. ... Teachers who have never heard a radio until they were grown up have to cope with children who have never known a world without television. Teachers who struggled in their childhood with a buttonhook find it difficult to describe a buttonhook to a child bred up among zippers, to whom fastnesses are to be breached by zipping them open, rather than fumblingly feeling for mysterious buttons. From the most all-embracing world image to the smallest detail of daily life the world has changed at a rate which makes the five-year-old generation further apart than world generations or even scores of generations were in our recent past, than people separated by several centuries were in the remote past.[28]

For these reasons an increasing number of countries place obligations of one sort or another upon even fully qualified teachers to continue their teacher training over a considerable part, if not over all, of the entire span of their teaching career. This may be a compulsory requirement for the renewal of the teaching license or it may be voluntary through such inducements as increased salary, promotion to higher positions, or to preferred status. The continuation study may take place through sabbatical leaves; summer courses at teacher training colleges or universities; late evening and Saturday classes when teachers are in the proximity of training institutions; special study groups within a school system; institute and special study days; reading circles;

correspondence courses; independent research; reading of professional publications, both books and periodicals; help from supervisory officers. Materials and activities by professional organizations of various sorts help teachers keep abreast of the times. Noteworthy among these are local, state or provincial, and national committees and conventions at which leaders in the field present new research and conduct discussions of new developments generally. Teachers' associations have more and more assumed responsibility for being agents of growth for teachers, both as promoters of good influences and as deterrents to backward steps.[29]

For nations with large numbers of unqualified and semi-qualified teachers as a more or less chronic situation, the matter of in-service education becomes crucial if the education of its children is to proceed in line with the nation's desire for schools to play an important role in the fulfillment of its objectives. This pressing need led UNESCO and the International Bureau of Education at the 1962 International Conference on Public Education held in Geneva to pass Recommendation No. 55, "Organization of Further Training," to the ministries of education on the further training of primary teachers in service.

The more pertinent of these recommendations are as follows:

1. It is becoming ever more necessary to organize systematic further training for primary teachers in service, whether they be insufficiently trained teachers requiring to complete their general and pedagogical education or qualified staff wishing to keep abreast of new methods and techniques, to broaden their general culture or, in some cases, to acquire further qualifications.

6. In organizing further training for primary teachers in service the competent authorities should consider three broad categories of teachers: (a) unqualified teachers; (b) qualified teachers, who may thereby supplement their general knowledge and improve their teaching techniques; (c) qualified teachers desiring to acquire additional qualifications or to train for other duties within the education service.

7. The provision of adequate training for unqualified primary teachers is essential in all countries where the shortage of teaching staff obliges the education authorities to recruit persons without the qualifications normally required.

8. However complete the professional training of the primary school staff may be, the education authorities should see that teachers have an opportunity throughout their career to broaden and deepen their general culture, to bring their pedagogical knowledge up to date and to become acquainted with new teaching methods and techniques.

9. In the interest of education itself, the education authorities should take the necessary steps to enable primary teachers so desiring to study for a higher level diploma, to take specialized courses in pedagogy or to qualify for other duties within the education service.

11. From the increasing numerous means available for promoting the further training of primary teachers in service, it would be an advantage to select those which best correspond to: (a) the specific needs of each category of teachers involved; (b) the material or other resources available; and (c) the characteristics and needs of primary education in the country concerned.

12. The provision of adequate training for unqualified teachers should be both systematic and regular and the duration of such training should be related primarily to the participants' level; the establishment of specialized institutions for this purpose might perhaps be contemplated.

13. When the aim is to supplement or refresh the general or pedagogical knowledge of qualified teaching staff, it is also important to prepare a systematic further training program.

15. Further training programs for primary teachers in service should not be exclusively theoretical in character but should also include practical work, demonstrations, model lessons, etc.

16. It is highly desirable to supplement further training facilities based on a set program by the occasional organization of education days, lectures and colloquia, visits to educational and other establishments, etc.

17. The promotion of discussion groups and study groups, within a school or at local or regional level, is to be recommended, as these enable teachers to exchange views and to take a direct and active interest in solving problems they may come up against in the course of their work.

18. It is important to introduce and extend further training correspondence courses, which offer the main advantage of enabling even isolated teachers to study without having to interrupt the exercise of their duties.

19. Greater importance should be given to educational and cultural books, pamphlets and periodicals; they should be distributed as widely as possible so that teachers may either receive them individually or be able to consult them without difficulty.

20. In further training work it is highly desirable to take the maximum advantage of educational documentation centers and of libraries, especially pedagogical libraries; in this connection it would be useful to expand traveling library and booklending services.

21. Judicious use should be made of the numerous opportunities afforded by gramophone and tape recordings, films, radio broadcasting and television.

22. It is desirable to encourage primary teachers to travel in their own country and abroad, either in groups or individually, with a view to their further training.[30]

Whether or not countries can assume large-scale or more moderate programs for in-service education, certainly no country in these days can avoid insisting that teachers keep abreast of new developments. Each country must arrange plans for its teachers to avail themselves of such opportunities as are offered them for continued growth.

In most countries, the problems arising out of the large numbers of women who enter the teaching profession and who temporarily withdraw from active service in order to bear and rear their children present a special challenge in the matter of in-service and continuing education. When these women return to teaching after an absence of several years, it is extremely vital that they be given help in gearing themselves into the on-going stream of educational effort. This help often takes the form of refresher courses at teacher training colleges.

Countries vary widely in the amount of supervisory help given teachers. In some countries, the ratio of teachers to each supervisor is so large that the supervisor's chief work is administrative rather than supervisory, entailing the handling of a great deal of paper work. In this event, the supervisor is a kind of liaison officer between the central administrators and the local school, rather than a real leader in teacher growth and development.

In some countries, the principal or headmaster assumes only a partial teaching load, or no teaching responsibility at all, in order to be free to administer the school and to supervise the work of the teachers. The quality and kind of supervision which is provided through this arrangement varies widely with local conditions and with the training and ability of the principal.

Certainly to a degree never before demanded, there is need for in-service education of teachers at all levels of competence. This need adds to the costs of education in no small measure, but, if properly met, helps to guarantee the adequate performance of the teacher, without which other moneys for education are inadequate to achieve the ends hoped for.

III

THE POSITION OF TEACHERS
IN EASTERN AND WESTERN AREAS
OF THE WORLD

---

*Education in the modern age
should be in harmony with the spirit of the times.*
Rabindranath Tagore

THE MIDDLE OF THE TWENTIETH CENTURY BROUGHT TO PRACTICALLY
every nation in the world the conviction that universal, public education
is an absolute necessity for maintaining its own identity and for
guaranteeing to its citizens the kind of life which they demand as a
result of what has been called "the rising tide of expectations." Accompanying this rising tide has been the explosion of knowledge.

This does not mean that the need for education itself is a recent
phenomenon. Every society, no matter how primitive, has always been
forced to assure its survival and to affect some means of successfully
inducting its young into the main stream of its culture. This has often
been accomplished through initiation ceremonies, sometimes simple,
sometimes elaborate; through training in practical skills while working
with their parents or other adults; and through simple imitation of
folk ways and folk mores.

When specialization of roles occurred in the economy and in the
social structure, enough recruits were apprenticed to them to insure

adequate supply to meet the needs for their continuation. For induction into preferred positions of power, such as the priesthood, usually special qualifications as well as more specialized training and apprenticeships were required. Anthropologists generally agree that one of the distinguishing marks of education in a primitive society was the relatively great equality of opportunity in all types of training offered and the lack of favoritism or preference shown because of family status or wealth.

With the evolution of complex societies, education became differentiated, not only because different skills had to be learned, but also because different qualities had to be developed. The development of writing meant the need for a whole complex of rather highly specialized skills. This is clearly discernible in Hellenic societies, where some of the young were to be trained as workers and some as leaders. For the training of youth in these two groups, different kinds of teachers and different tasks were assigned. The methods used and the ends to be reached were different. The selection of students who were to be educated became of vital importance. The sons of the wealthy or the noble could take advantage of the education for teachers and so were in possession of the certain means of maintaining their initial advantage, for their education led to an even more powerful place in their society.

With the rise of the church in medieval times and its responsibility for a literate priesthood, more and more formal schooling in Western nations was entrusted to the clergy. Though some effort was made to extend the benefits of learning to the poor, in the main, formal education was largely the privilege of the children of the elite. As political units grew in strength and importance through expanding trade and the growth of urban centers, the responsibility of the church for education was lessened. When the Renaissance and the Reformation challenged many of the existing ideas of authority and of social systems, democratic ideas concerning the goals of education began to take root. But even though the responsibility for educating the young shifted as a result of these new developments, the organization of education in the West remained firmly grounded in the idea that there were properly two kinds of education: one for those whose status gave them a position in government and the professions, and the other for those whose status gave them a position in trade and manual labor. Recruits for each kind came principally from the class in the culture which the education was calculated to perpetuate in a relatively stable status quo pattern. Even while democratic ideas for a more liberal policy of education were germinating, practices remained more or less static.

Several centuries passed before the idea really took firm root that all the children of a society must be the concern of whatever agency had assumed responsibility for the education of any segment of it. As occupations became more and more specialized for carrying out the goals of modern nations, leaving the education of the young to parents or to completely unsupervised teachers was considered far too haphazard a means for insuring industrial and social development. The Reformation emphasized strongly the need for universal literacy. The Industrial Revolution, with its concurrent urbanization and increasing complexities of social and economic structures, ultimately made it necessary to broaden the goals of education and to make it available to increasing numbers of children. So, into the modern world, with its infinite complexity, was born the idea of public, universal, compulsory education which must be the responsibility of the state. But, even under this idea, the old pattern was often preserved: a two track system with one kind of schooling   usually inferior in quality and shorter in duration — for the masses and another kind — with far greater prestige and longer in duration — for the elite. Elitism in education was based far more on the wealth and social class of parents than on the intellectual powers of the students.

Several common tasks were imposed on schools of both types, however. Chief among these were the development and maintenance of a national consciousness, induction into specialized vocational roles, and the perpetuation of the main streams of the inherited culture. In the United States and Canada and, recently in the U.S.S.R., because of economic, social and political developments, the traditional two track system, at least in administration, has given way to a single track system. There are evidences, even in these nations, that educational opportunities and goals for children are still partially dependent on the parents' position in society.

In all nations certain political and social developments of the twentieth century pressed for the common schooling of all children at the elementary level, even though differentiated education still persisted at the secondary level. Thus, at the present time, in nearly all the countries of Europe, during the early years of schooling, with minor exceptions, the children from all social classes are taught in common schools where attendance is compulsory. However, these children are fully aware that they will be shunted, some sooner, some later, onto one of the two tracks of education on a more or less involuntary basis. In the United States and Canada this division takes place during or following secondary schooling.

With two tracks of education in vogue, with different prestige values attached, a cleavage among teachers was unavoidable. Those teaching in the schools for the elite held favored positions and were required to pursue rigorous training. Those who taught the masses were held in low esteem and were required to have less training. As has been pointed out, there is considerable evidence to show that the status of the latter was from the beginning extremely low.

Since the primary school teacher has assumed responsibility for the education of children from all social classes, it might be expected that his position would thereby be improved. It is generally believed that in some countries this has happened, but, relatively speaking, in most nations it has not. One of the purposes of the present study is to determine what the teachers representing Western countries themselves think of their present day status and in what direction they believe it is moving. It is in these countries that the two track system has the oldest tradition. The responses of these teachers will be studied in relation to the ideas which teachers representing the Orient have of their present position. For historical reasons, the evolution of their place in society has been somewhat different.

Most of the so-called new nations of the East have in reality very old cultures, whose historical beginnings greatly antedate the nations of the West. Of the countries included in this survey, this is particularly true of India, Pakistan, and Thailand, whose cultures are among the oldest known. Korea and Japan, although having very ancient cultures, in early times borrowed rather heavily from the older and more highly developed culture of China, as did to a lesser degree India, Pakistan and Thailand. Though all these nations were frequently involved in internal and external wars accompanied by the rise and fall of dynasties and were plagued by many domestic troubles during their long history, they developed a high level of culture in the arts, in literature, in religion, and in governmental structure. These developments carried them far along the path to building an educational system which would guarantee for the present and future generations the benefits of this culture. There was also considerable exchange of ideas among these ancient civilizations. Some of the new ideas were carried by conquering armies and certainly some were transmitted by visiting leaders and scholars. This exchange gave the advantages of higher learning to those who lagged behind the more progressive nations. Written languages and a body of literature were developed early and the need for a literate group to read and to write became evident long before they arose in the West. Thus grew up the figure of the scholar, one versed in the great literature, which ordinarily incorporated the myths, the history and the heroes of the nation. The rise of the great religions of Hinduism, Confucianism, Buddhism and lesser sects gave impetus to the study of the literature embodying the teachings of the leaders of these faiths. Particularly in India, education was largely concerned with learning the religious writings.

The early development of classes in these nations, particularly a privileged class which was the ruling class, led to the establishment of schools and centers of learning where the sons of high degree could be prepared for government service and for practicing the arts essential to the life of a cultured gentleman. These schools and centers were well established long before the Christian era. For example a well-defined system of civil service examinations had been set up in China very early, which placed great stress on thorough knowledge of a great body of classical literature. The status of teachers in these schools was fairly high, taking as evidence the statement attributed to Confucious that "the king, the teacher, and parents are the trinity."

As these Eastern nations evolved and the social and economic life became more complex, the need arose for a greater spread of educational opportunity. The small number of students selected from the nobility and the most powerful families was no longer adequate to cope with the changing goals of the nation. New types of schools had to be established for the training of students in practical specialties. These new schools did not result in what might be called "universal education" for any considerable numbers of children although religious groups in India did provide some education for rather large numbers.

With the advent of contact with the industrialized West, came a vital change. Except for Japan and Thailand, the change was brought about by Western colonizing powers, who introduced the ideas of the industrialized state, which entailed changes for the general pattern of the society: socially, psychologically, and economically. Certainly the results of the changes after the conquest of Asian nations by Western powers are not yet fully in sight.

New demands were made for education both from without and from within. While the highest posts in the colonial government which were established were held by the nationals of the ruling country, there was need for the training of large cadres of native civil servants to fill minor governmental posts. For this training, the system of education in vogue in the colonizing country for civil servants was usually adopted, sometimes with minor local adaptations. Thus the basic outline of the English system came to India, of the Dutch to Indonesia, of the French to Indo-China. To a great extent, teachers, language, curriculums, textbooks, methodology and administrative procedure were all imports. Because of the great effort involved in such a system, the emphasis in education was for the favored few at secondary and higher levels. For the most part, education for the masses remained outside the interest of the colonial powers. Along with this introduction of an entirely alien system of education, some attempt was made to encourage indigenous groups to vivify the traditional education at the lower levels, with some emphasis on indigenous cultures and older patterns of schooling. Usually this necessitated major shifts from the older pattern so that graduates at the lower levels could fit themselves for entry into the higher levels. The higher education would, in turn, prepare them for favored positions in the Westernized society, which were now open to the indigenous population.

Needless to say, no attempt was ever made in any country under colonial rule to make education universal and free. Such educational changes as did occur were plainly made to serve that rule for very specific and narrow goals. It was designed to serve the exploitation, rather than development, of the natural and human resources of the occupied country.

With the end of the colonial period and the emergence of newly independent nations have come new demands for education: that it be universal, free, and suited to the unique and peculiar needs of the new nation. The desire to throw off completely the influences of the foreign systems has been voiced by many leaders of the new nations. To do this, however, has not always been simple. Teachers have had to be recruited and trained, sometimes in extremely great numbers (witness South Korea where most of the teachers at higher and secondary levels and many in elementary schools were Japanese nationals during the occupation of the country from 1910–1945). New curriculums had to be devised, new textbooks written, suitable administrative procedures set up. Furthermore, parents who had previously been in the habit of thinking that their children had no place in school were now required by attendance laws to send them.

The goals toward which education should now be directed were difficult to clarify and define. Academic rather than practical training had been the chief emphasis of the colonial period. Such utilitarian subjects as agriculture, health, animal husbandry, which might have been of greatest benefit to a developing nation, were unknown and had little prestige. Such subjects as these were considered by many observers as more essential than the highly academic ones in helping the new nations achieve a place of honor among other nations and to win for its people the good life in matters of health and economic well being which the nations of the West had already won for themselves. It was difficult for the new nations to realize that the nations of the West had traveled a long and circuitous path in reaching the levels of education and well being they had achieved.

In spite of all problems, however, the enrollment in primary schools in the world increased 57 percent during the ten-year period of 1950–1959, even though there was an increase of only 17 percent in the corresponding school age population. While nearly all countries showed some increase, the greatest came from the developing countries, because in the Western world, through earlier compulsory attendance laws, the saturation point had practically been reached during the early decades of the twentieth century.[1]

Thus the developing countries have made a clear commitment to the establishment of universal primary education and are laying plans to achieve it as rapidly as funds and teacher supply will permit. At a number of international conferences, notably the one held in Karachi in 1958, plans were developed for achieving universal compulsory primary education at various dates for various areas.

Believing it to be possible for them through education to push their countries along the road to modernization only with strong directives from above, most of the leaders of the countries have set up highly centralized systems of education. Japan, which after its defeat in World War II set up a decentralized form of administration at the suggestion of the United States Occupation Forces, has gradually reverted to a centralized form of control. Considering the demanding and peculiar stresses and strains under which the governments of many new nations operate, it might well be asked whether centralization will not ultimately establish the kind of education which tends toward the exploitation of the individual in order to further the state, just as did the form of education introduced by the colonial powers. This possibility is posed by such leaders in the field of international education as Robert Ulich.[2]

The present study is concerned with two main groups of teachers in primary schools: those who work in the West under long and well established school systems and those who work in developing countries, where learning has an old and proud tradition, but where schools in the modern sense have only recently been established. The nations sampled in the East (with the exception of Japan) have had, in the process of developing their current systems of education, first to free themselves of a pattern of education grafted into their older, indigenous pattern by the colonial powers which they have recently shaken off. In addition they have had to build a new concept of education for all children, particularly at the primary school level. The European countries sampled (with the exception of Finland) have a long tradition of universal education for children of elementary school age. Teachers there are conscious now, as were their predecessors, that the children they teach will be directed into two streams upon leaving the primary school: one stream to receive the education which will qualify them for elite positions; the other to receive that which will qualify them for less desirable economic and social places. In the United States and Canada, primary teachers know their children will all be taught in a common secondary school, but that they will meet with varying success in mastering the curriculum provided. Dropouts from the secondary school will constitute a major problem, with consequent loss to the society.

While schooling for all children of primary school age is theoretically available in all countries, only in Japan and in the countries of the West has the goal of universal primary education been reached. Furthermore, while compulsory school attendance laws are almost universal, only in the West and in Japan are these successfully enforced. In some countries of the East, attrition in primary schools is heavy after the first two or three years of attendance. This is particularly true for girls. In the West, boys and girls in almost equal numbers continue in attendance through seven or eight grades and attrition is practically non-existent.

Teachers in primary schools in the West may or may not be faced with the problem of preparing their children for an external examination at the end of the primary school education, which will determine the children's future schooling. This examination may be the "eleven plus" examination of England or Finland. In Germany, measures are used which require evaluation by teachers and parents. In the East, South Korea and Japan both administer tests, not to determine the

41

levels of future education, but to ascertain the quality of higher schooling to which a child will be admitted. In the U.S.A. and Canada the teacher administers and evaluates his own examinations. Undoubtedly, the examination requirements influence greatly both the content of the curriculum and the teaching methods used to achieve the mastery of subject matter expected.

Teachers are thus bound by tradition, by practical economic and political considerations and by their society's expectations of what can be accomplished through education. These are not the same for the developed nations of the West as for the developing nations of the East. What differences these considerations make in the teachers' own estimates of their role and status is the topic of the present study.

The Responses to the Questionnaire

Reference to the questionnaire (Appendix A) administered to 890 teachers in large cities of five Western countries and to 1252 teachers in large cities of Eastern countries will show that teachers were asked two types of questions: questions of *fact* about themselves and their work and questions of opinion of what they *would like* concerning their role and status. Some items in the questionnaire establish a check on the validity of other items. Consistency of the replies, or lack of it, will be noted. Furthermore, note will be taken of differences between teachers with a relatively brief amount of experience in teaching, from one to five years, and those with longer experience, more than ten years. In the light of the great social, economic, and political changes which have come to all areas of the world in recent years, differences of opinion in these two groups, or lack of differences, can have significance for the educational development of the countries involved in this study.

Table 1A shows that a higher proportion of teachers in the East are males than in the West, 39 percent and 26 percent respectively. Eastern teachers are younger, 73 percent being under forty years of age, as against 59 percent in the West.

In both East and West, considerably more than half are married, with a slightly higher proportion in the East. Few are divorced or widowed. However, slightly more than half in the West and slightly under half in the East have no children. Families are larger in the East with 26 percent of the teachers having more than four children.

TABLE 1A[a]

Sex, Age, and Family Status

| | WEST | | | | | | EAST | | | | | | TOTAL | |
| | 1–5 years | | Over 10 years | | Total | | 1–5 years | | Over 10 years | | Total | | Number | |
	N = 431	Per-cent	N = 459	Per-cent	N = 890	Per-cent	N = 593	Per-cent	N = 659	Per-cent	N = 1252	Per-cent	N = 2142	Per-cent
Sex														
Male	126	29	106	23	232	26	182	31	310	47	492	39	724	34
Female	305	71	353	77	658	74	411	69	349	53	760	61	1418	67
Age														
20–29	307	71	6	1	313	35	479	81	48	7	527	42	840	39
30–39	93	22	119	26	212	24	83	14	302	46	385	31	597	28
40–49	26	6	134	29	160	18	20	3	164	25	184	15	344	16
50–59	3	1	162	35	165	19	5	1	117	18	122	10	287	13
60–69	—	—	32	7	32	4	—	—	14	2	14	1	46	2
Marital status														
Unmarried	202	47	147	31	344	39	381	64	68	10	449	36	793	34
Married	219	51	262	57	481	54	203	34	555	84	758	61	1239	58
Divorced or Widowed	9	2	55	12	64	7	3	1	31	5	34	3	98	5
Number of children														
None	278	65	201	44	479	54	433	73	106	16	539	43	1018	48
1–3	130	30	205	45	335	38	107	18	244	37	351	28	686	32
4–6	11	3	26	6	37	4	25	4	214	32	239	19	276	13
Over 6	5	1	12	3	17	2	5	1	83	13	88	7	105	5

a. N = number of samples. The percents ignore decimals, are the closest in round numbers, and, hence, in the totals may not appear as the average of the East and the West percents. Where the percents do not total 100, the discrepancy is due to questions left unanswered.

TABLE 2A[a]

Teaching Experience

	WEST						EAST						TOTAL	
	1–5 years		Over 10 years		Total		1–5 years		Over 10 years		Total		Number	
	N = 431	Per-cent	N = 459	Per-cent	N = 890	Per-cent	N = 593	Per-cent	N = 659	Per-cent	N = 1252	Per-cent	N = 2142	Per-cent
Total Number of Years														
Less than five	431	100	—	—	431	48	593	100	—	—	593	47	1024	48
More than ten	—	—	459	100	459	52	—	—	659	100	659	53	1118	52
Years in Present Position														
Less than one	132	31	29	6	161	18	115	19	70	11	185	15	346	16
1–2	155	36	38	8	193	22	221	37	95	14	316	25	509	24
3–6	137	32	95	21	232	26	241	41	231	35	472	38	704	33
7–10	5[b]	1	98	21	103	12	8[b]	1	89	14	97	8	200	9
11–20	—	—	145	32	145	16	—	—	139	21	139	11	284	13
Over 20	—	—	53	12	53	6	2[b]	—	31	5	33	3	86	4
Type of School														
Public	429	100	458	100	886	99.5	542	91	602	91	1144	91	2030	95
Private	2	—	1	—	3	.5	36	6	44	7	80	6	83	4

a. N = number of samples. The percents ignore decimals, are the closest in round numbers, and, hence, in the totals may not appear as the average of the East and the West percents. Where the percents do not total 100, the discrepancy is due to questions left unanswered.
b. These cases may have had previous teaching experience in some other type of school.

44

Although in both East and West teachers in both age groups were predominantly female, in the East the proportion of females is increasing considerably (69 percent of the younger teachers as opposed to 53 percent of the older ones), while in the West this trend is showing a reversal (71 percent of the younger ones versus 77 percent of the older ones). A higher proportion of young teachers were unmarried in the East than in the West (64 percent versus 47 percent), while a greater proportion of the older teachers in the East were married than in the West (84 percent versus 57 percent).

While the study aimed to sample an equal number of teachers with less than five years' experience and those with more than ten, Table 2A shows that slightly more than half fall into the latter category. This may be because of the practice in some places of assigning teachers to posts in large cities (where all the sampling was done) only after they have served an apprenticeship in a smaller, less desirable community. The question regarding time spent in present teaching position denotes some, but not marked, stability in remaining in one post over a number of years, particularly in the East. Of those teaching more than ten years in the West, only 162 out of the 459 reporting had spent fewer than seven years in their present position, while in the East 396 out of the 656 reporting had spent this length of time in their present positions. Practically all teachers responding taught in public schools.

Table 3A indicates that practically all the teachers responding considered themselves fully qualified as teachers. There are, however, wide variations in the total years of schooling reported by both groups. Whereas 60 percent in the West had spent fifteen or more years in preparing for teaching, only 24 percent in the East reported like preparation. Qualification through examination was achieved by almost one-half of the teachers in the East, by only one-fourth in the West. Certification through completion of a regular training course was reported by 82 percent of the West; by only 56 percent in the East. Some of the teachers reported that both the completion of the course and an examination were required.

For both East and West, all younger teachers served a longer period of training than had the older ones. For the East a third of the younger teachers reported fifteen or more years of schooling as opposed to less than a fifth of the older ones. But in the West two-thirds of the younger teachers reported fifteen or more years of preparation for teaching, whereas slightly over one-half from the older group said this was true.

TABLE 3A[a]

Training and Qualifications for Teaching

	WEST						EAST						TOTAL	
	1–5 years		Over 10 years		Total		1–5 years		Over 10 years		Total		Number	
	N = 431	Per-cent	N = 459	Per-cent	N = 890	Per-cent	N = 593	Per-cent	N = 659	Per-cent	N = 1252	Per-cent	N = 2142	Per-cent
Qualification														
Fully qualified	411	95	456	99	867	97	554	93	614	93	1168	93	2035	95
Not fully qualified	19	4	3	1	22	2	34	6	35	5	69	6	91	4
Total Years of Education														
Less than 10	2	—	5	1	7	1	34	6	58	9	92	7	99	5
10	3	1	3	1	6	1	24	4	116	18	140	11	146	7
11	3	1	16	3	19	2	39	7	118	18	157	13	176	8
12	18	4	35	8	54	6	118	20	82	12	200	16	254	12
13	32	7	69	15	101	11	72	12	54	8	126	10	227	11
14	79	18	77	17	156	18	108	18	99	15	207	17	363	17
15	71	16	70	15	141	16	65	11	52	8	117	9	258	12
Over 15	216	50	178	39	394	44	123	21	68	10	191	15	585	27
Methods of Qualifying														
Regular government examination	88	20	157	34	245	28	288	49	360	55	648	52	893	42
Special examination	42	10	53	12	95	11	22	4	74	11	96	8	191	9
Completion of training course	362	84	365	80	727	82	358	60	346	53	704	56	1431	67
Special arrangement	32	7	16	3	48	5	11	2	41	6	52	4	100	5
Clock hours spent in observing or Teaching Children														
None	24	6	14	3	38	4	35	6	84	13	119	10	157	7
10–50	25	6	53	12	78	9	152	26	138	21	290	23	368	17
51–100	44	10	78	17	122	14	81	14	94	14	175	14	297	14
101–200	99	23	143	31	242	27	111	19	96	15	207	17	449	21
Over 200	230	53	162	35	392	44	173	29	177	27	350	28	742	35

a. N = number of samples. The percents ignore decimals, are the closest in round numbers, and hence in the totals may not appear as the average

It is recognized that a great deal of error may be present in the replies concerning one special phase of teacher preparation; namely, that of the number of clock hours in observation of children and student teaching. Definitions vary widely as to what is meant by these terms, and teachers may be only vaguely aware of the actual time thus spent during their training period. From the replies received, it is clear that this kind of preparation for teaching is considered far more important in the West than in the East, with 27 percent of the teachers in the West reporting 100 hours or less spent in observation and teaching as opposed to 47 percent in the East. For the younger group in the East, there was a marked increase over the older group in the number of hours reported.

No other questions concerning the preparation for teaching were asked because of the difficulty of common understanding of what is meant by course names or terms involving teaching methodology.

Table 4A shows that a much higher proportion of teachers in the West (70 percent) chose teaching because they felt it was a rewarding way of life than was true in the East (54 percent). Slightly more than one-third in each region had parents or close relatives as teachers and about the same proportion were influenced by teachers that they admired. Very few indicated that teaching was accepted as a second choice of profession. More teachers in the West than in the East indicated that a high scholastic average in school had been a factor in influencing them into going into teaching. While no fast conclusion can be drawn, perhaps a higher proportion of those earning good scholastic marks had been drawn into professions other than teaching.

In response to the question as to how they felt about the choice of vocation they had made, about half in each region were quite positive they had made the correct decision. More in the West than in the East said they "probably" would choose teaching again. On the whole, teachers in the West seem decidedly more happy with their choice of vocation than do those in the East. Indeed, teachers in the East seem to be losing a feeling of idealism about teaching, for more of the older teachers chose it as a rewarding way of life than did younger ones (58 percent as opposed to 49 percent). The opposite was true for the West (76 percent of the younger ones as against 64 percent of the older ones). For all ages and in both East and West, the influence of parents and teachers seemed strong.

When asked what degree of change they felt had occurred in their ideas concerning the purposes of education, 42 percent in the East

TABLE 4A[a]

Factors in the Choice of Teaching as a Profession

| | West | | | | | | East | | | | | | Total | |
| | 1-5 years | | Over 10 years | | Total | | 1-5 years | | Over 10 years | | Total | | Number | |
	N = 431	Per cent	N = 459	Per cent	N = 890	Per cent	N = 593	Per cent	N = 659	Per cent	N = 1252	Per cent	N = 2142	Per cent
Influences Affecting Choice														
Parent or close relative was a teacher	131	30	176	38	307	34	215	36	254	39	469	37	776	36
Chose to follow the example of an admired teacher	109	25	155	34	264	30	178	30	244	37	422	34	686	32
Felt that teaching was a rewarding way of life	328	76	296	64	624	70	291	49	382	58	673	54	1297	61
Took teaching as a second choice	40	9	43	9	83	9	69	12	82	12	151	12	234	11
High scholastic average	69	16	149	32	218	24	92	16	117	18	209	17	427	20
No special reason	35	8	19	4	54	6	74	12	59	9	133	11	187	9
Present Attitude Toward Choice of Vocation														
Positively would choose teaching	206	48	222	48	428	48	299	50	312	47	611	49	1039	49
Probably would choose teaching	119	27	124	27	243	27	95	16	97	15	192	15	435	20
Uncertain: depends on opportunities	74	17	70	15	144	16	113	19	131	20	244	19	388	18
Possibly would choose another occupation	19	4	21	5	40	4	46	8	87	13	133	11	173	8
Positively would choose another occupation	11	3	19	4	30	3	36	6	29	4	65	5	95	4
Changes in Ideas Concerning Purposes of Education														
Changed very much	73	17	125	27	198	22	225	38	297	45	522	42	720	34
Changed a little	193	45	234	51	427	48	263	44	208	32	471	38	898	42
Hardly changed at all	132	31	95	21	227	26	85	14	59	9	144	12	371	17
Do not know	32	7	2	—	34	4	17	2	81	12	95	8	129	6

a. N = number of samples. The percents ignore decimals, are the closest in round numbers, and, hence, in the totals may not appear as the average

acknowledged great change, while only 22 percent in the West agreed that they had changed a great deal. In contrast, one-fourth of the teachers in the West said they had experienced no change, while only one-eighth in the East admitted no change.

Taking older and younger teachers separately, it was the older teachers in the West who signified they had changed in greater numbers than the younger teachers. For the teachers in the East, the difference between the two age groups was not so marked. This is a rather surprising phenomenon, since the changes taking place in education in this part of the world have undoubtedly been more marked and more dramatic than the changes in the West. It is possible that change is still so pronounced in this part of the world that even the younger teachers in the East constantly feel the need for revision of their ideas and so they keep pace with their older colleagues who may have been called upon to make even greater changes in their thinking since beginning their careers as teachers.

In the East the teachers' place of origin (Table 5A) is rather equally divided among rural area, small town or city, and the large city, but in the West nearly one-half spent their childhood in the large city and one-fourth in each of the other types of locale. More of the older teachers in the East said they had spent their childhood in rural small town areas than did the younger ones. In the West the two ages were about equal. In both East and West more of the younger teachers came from large cities. Both East and West declared themselves definitely in favor of the large city as the place they prefer to teach in. About 10 per cent in each region said they preferred the rural area and a little better than one-fourth (29 percent) declared their preference for the small city or town. Answers to this question definitely point up the problem of making teaching positions outside the large urban centers attractive so that teachers will willingly accept posts outside the larger cities where there are obvious cultural and personal advantages.

For the group as a whole, family religious training seems to have been of minor importance. For the West 78 percent said their parents considered such training of some importance as against only 44 percent in the East. Nearly one-third in the East said their parents paid little attention to religion.

In contrast to their upbringing, teachers in the East would impose much stricter moral standards on teachers than would teachers in the West. Forty-three percent said standards for teachers should be higher than for other professional workers, as opposed to 20 percent in the

TABLE 5Aᵃ

Environmental Background and Choice of Teaching Environment

| | WEST | | | | | | EAST | | | | | | TOTAL | |
| | 1–5 years | | Over 10 years | | Total | | 1–5 years | | Over 10 years | | Total | | Number | |
	N = 431	Per-cent	N = 459	Per-cent	N = 890	Per-cent	N = 593	Per-cent	N = 659	Per-cent	N = 1252	Per-cent	N = 2142	Per-cent
Environment of Childhood														
Rural area or small village	106	25	146	32	252	28	171	29	227	34	398	32	650	30
Small city or town	119	28	112	24	231	26	176	30	244	37	420	34	651	30
Large city	203	47	195	42	398	45	243	41	185	28	428	34	826	38
Choice of Environment for Teaching														
Rural area or small village	39	9	45	10	84	9	86	15	82	12	168	13	252	12
Small city or town	142	33	118	26	260	29	168	28	198	30	366	29	626	29
Large city	244	57	292	64	536	60	336	57	374	57	710	57	1246	58
Parents' Regard for Religious Training														
Paid little attention to religion	51	12	33	7	84	9	204	34	190	29	394	31	478	22
Observed special rituals and ceremonies	58	13	46	10	104	12	130	22	159	24	289	23	393	18
Gave some emphasis to understanding basic meaning of religion	149	35	140	31	289	32	105	18	108	16	213	17	502	23
Considered religion very important	170	39	236	51	406	46	143	24	189	29	332	27	738	34
Attitude Toward Morals for Teachers														
Standards should be higher than for other professional workers	79	18	99	22	178	20	243	41	300	46	543	43	721	34
Standards should be higher than for the general public	224	52	237	52	461	52	277	47	297	45	574	46	1035	48
Standards should be the same as for the general public	121	28	116	25	237	27	63	11	54	8	117	9	354	17

a. N = number of samples. The percents ignore decimals, are the closest in round numbers, and, hence, in the totals may not appear as the average of the East and the West percents. Where the percents do not total 100, the discrepancy is due to omitted "Don't know" and

West; 46 percent indicated standards should be higher than for the general public as opposed to 52 percent in the West. Table 5A seems to indicate there is little relationship between the kind of religious training received in childhood and a teacher's present attitude toward the moral standards which should prevail for members of the profession. This seems particularly pertinent to the responses made by teachers in the East.

That religious training was important in their homes was reported more frequently by the older than by the younger teachers, particularly in the West. The older ones were likewise more insistent that moral standards for teachers should be higher than for other professional persons. Though younger teachers in both areas were laxer in their requirements for standards, those in the West were definitely more liberal.

There were no questions about income except one on the method to supplement it and the amount needed and one on preferences for deferring income to insure later payment of certain fringe benefits. Answers to these questions are found in Tables 6A and 7A.

About one-half in both East and West did not earn any supplementary income, although there are more in this category in the West than in the East. For those who did supplement income, the chief method was through the paid work of the spouse. More teachers in the East earned money through private tutoring; teaching in other schools was more popular in the West. The data do not show whether those replying were women or men. The supplemental amounts earned varied widely, but in only a small proportion of cases (about 11 percent) did it equal a full year's salary or more.

Between the older and younger teachers in the West there were no great variations in method of supplementing income and in amount earned. In the East over one-half of the younger teachers and only one-third of the older teachers indicated that they did not supplement their teacher's salary. The number earning more than their regular yearly salary was about equal for both ages.

In Table 7A, it is clear that the overwhelming choice of teachers in the West was for a high salary, but with deductions for a pension after retirement. While only a total of 12 percent in the West desired lower salaries with provision for many types of fringe benefits, 55 percent of teachers in the East would prefer this kind of arrangement. The data do not show differences of opinion among men and women on this point. It may be that teachers in the West, benefiting from

TABLE 6Aª
Adequacy of Income

| | WEST | | | | | | EAST | | | | | | TOTAL | |
| | 1–5 years | | Over 10 years | | Total | | 1–5 years | | Over 10 years | | Total | | Number | |
	N = 431	Per-cent	N = 459	Per-cent	N = 890	Per-cent	N = 593	Per-cent	N = 659	Per-cent	N = 1252	Per-cent	N = 2142	Per-cent
Method of Supplementing Income														
Not at all	238	55	241	53	479	54	335	56	240	36	575	46	1054	49
Teaching in other schools	20	5	21	5	41	5	7	1	8	1	15	1	56	3
Tutoring pupils privately	24	6	19	4	43	5	69	12	85	13	154	12	197	9
Writing educational books or articles	4	1	17	4	21	2	13	2	23	3	36	3	57	3
Working jobs outside of education	50	12	40	9	90	10	29	5	50	8	79	6	169	8
By the paid work of spouse	104	24	117	25	221	25	84	14	190	29	274	22	495	23
Other ways	53	12	67	15	110	12	80	13	110	17	190	15	300	14
Annual Amount of Supplement to Income														
Less than one month of regular teaching salary	52	12	57	12	109	12	117	19	135	20	252	20	361	17
One to three months	62	14	74	16	136	15	81	14	141	21	222	18	358	17
Four to nine months	22	5	29	6	51	6	31	5	56	8	87	7	138	6
More than regular yearly salary	72	17	40	9	112	12	57	10	60	9	117	9	229	11

a. N = number of samples. The percents ignore decimals. The percents are the closest in round numbers, and, hence, in the totals may not appear as the average of the East and the West percents. Where the percents do not total 100, the discrepancy is due to questions left unanswered.

52

TABLE 7Aᵃ

Choice of Remuneration

| | WEST | | | | | | EAST | | | | | | TOTAL | |
| | 1-5 years | | Over 10 years | | Total | | 1-5 years | | Over 10 years | | Total | | Number | |
	N = 431	Per-cent	N = 459	Per-cent	N = 890	Per-cent	N = 593	Per-cent	N = 659	Per-cent	N = 1252	Per-cent	N = 2142	Per-cent
Highest possible salary without other benefits	64	15	59	13	123	14	121	20	105	16	226	18	349	16
Lower than highest salary with a pension system	295	68	349	76	644	72	128	22	200	30	328	26	972	45
Still lower salary with provisions for housing, health insurance, and a pension system	52	12	35	8	87	10	197	33	198	30	395	32	482	22
Minimum salary with all the benefits mentioned above, plus others, such as life insurance, credit and loan arrangements, recreational facilities	12	3	5	1	17	2	137	23	152	23	289	23	306	14

a. N = number of samples. The percents ignore decimals, are the closest in round numbers, and, hence, in the totals may not appear as the average of the East and the West percents. Where the percents do not total 100, the discrepancy is due to questions left unanswered.

other forms of social assistance, such as medical care or old age assistance of various kinds, feel the pressures of retirement less keenly than teachers in countries where such benefits are usually not present.

In general, older teachers were more inclined to ask for a pension system after retirement than were younger ones. In other matters concerning salary, there was very slight variation between older and younger teachers in both East and West.

Table 8A indicates that there was considerable unanimity in the two areas concerning the proper proportion of female teachers in the primary school. Forty-one percent in the West were in favor of having from 40 to 59 percent women teachers; while 45 percent in the East said this was the proper proportion. When it came to a higher proportion of women teachers — 60 to 79 percent — half the teachers in the West and over one-fourth in the East favored this.

When it came to choice of head of school, the West was more conservative than the East with 63 percent preferring a male as against 58 percent in the East. Very few teachers in the West (only 4 percent) definitely preferred a female as head of the school. This sort of sex prejudice is an interesting phenomenon in the West. The younger teachers in the East preferred more women as head than did the older ones; while in the West the opposite was true. The older teachers in the East and the younger teachers in the West definitely preferred a man as head. About one-fourth of the old and the young in the East and the young in the West and more than one-third of the old in the West said they had no preference.

Teachers were asked to rank in order of prestige each of fifteen different vocations. The results are presented in Table 9A. For the group as a whole, the vocations receiving the highest ranking (1 to 3) are as follows: Medicine 60 percent, government official 51 percent, university professor 41 percent, lawyer 37 percent, priest 30 percent, businessman 13 percent, banker 10 percent, civil servant 8 percent, artist 7 percent, primary school head 6 percent, primary school teacher 6 percent, secondary school teacher 4 percent, farmer 3 percent, craftsman 2 percent, and shopkeeper 1 percent.

Differences in the rankings are to be noted between East and West. A higher proportion of teachers in the West gave greater prestige to doctors of medicine, lawyers, priests and clergymen; while teachers in the East held government officials, university professors, businessmen, civil servants and teachers in all categories in higher esteem. It should be noted, however, that teachers in the East ranked government

TABLE 8A[a]
Proportion of Male and Female Personnel

| | WEST | | | | | | EAST | | | | | | TOTAL |
| | 1-5 years | | Over 10 years | | Total | | 1-5 years | | Over 10 years | | Total | | Number |
	N = 431	Per-cent	N = 459	Per-cent	N = 890	Per-cent	N = 593	Per-cent	N = 659	Per-cent	N = 1252	Per-cent	N = 2142	Per-cent
Proper Proportion of Female Teachers														
0–19	1	—	2	—	3	1	3	1	17	3	20	2	23	1
20–39	17	4	10	2	27	3	54	9	83	13	137	11	164	8
40–59	193	45	168	37	361	41	250	42	310	47	560	45	921	43
60–79	196	45	239	52	435	49	198	33	160	24	358	29	793	37
80–100	9	2	20	4	29	3	36	6	42	6	78	6	107	5
Preferred Principal or Head														
Female	11	3	23	5	34	4	113	19	52	8	165	13	199	9
Male	296	69	261	57	557	63	307	52	417	63	724	58	1281	60
No preference	121	28	167	36	288	32	164	28	182	28	346	28	634	30

a. N = number of samples. The percents ignore decimals, are the closest in round numbers, and, hence, in the totals may not appear as the average of the East and the West percents. Where the percents do not total 100, the discrepancy is due to questions left unanswered.

55

TABLE 9A[a]

Ranking of Fifteen Vocations as to Prestige

| | WEST | | | | | | EAST | | | | | | TOTAL | |
| | 1–5 years | | Over 10 years | | Total | | 1–5 years | | Over 10 years | | Total | | Number | |
	N = 331	Per-cent	N = 359	Per-cent	N = 690	Per-cent	N = 561	Per-cent	N = 559	Per-cent	N = 1120	Per-cent	N = 1810	Per-cent
Government Official														
1–3[b]	122	28	148	32	270	39	319	54	343	52	662	59	932	51
4–6	112	26	109	24	221	32	118	20	77	12	195	17	416	23
7–9	49	11	49	11	98	14	46	8	56	8	102	9	200	11
10–12	11	3	20	4	31	4	31	5	33	5	64	6	95	5
13–15[c]	10	2	6	1	16	2	22	4	15	2	37	3	53	3
Government Worker or Civil Servant														
1–3	7	2	3	1	10	1	70	12	69	10	139	12	149	8
4–6	8	2	5	1	13	2	118	20	93	14	211	19	224	12
7–9	55	13	52	11	107	16	130	22	137	21	267	24	374	21
10–12	116	27	132	29	248	36	135	23	155	24	290	26	538	30
13–15	118	27	140	31	258	37	78	13	68	10	146	13	404	22
Doctor of Medicine														
1–3	256	59	252	55	508	74	284	48	302	46	586	52	1094	60
4–6	43	10	72	16	115	17	162	27	169	26	331	30	446	25
7–9	5	1	7	2	12	2	76	13	41	6	117	10	129	7
10–12	—	—	1	—	1	1	8	1	9	1	17	2	18	1
13–15	—	—	—	—	—	—	3	1	2	—	5	1	5	<1
Lawyer														
1–3	175	41	163	36	338	49	185	31	148	24	333	30	671	37
4–6	107	25	133	29	240	35	199	34	176	27	375	33	615	34
7–9	16	4	23	5	39	6	78	13	105	13	183	16	221	12
10–12	5	1	10	2	15	2	41	7	51	7	92	8	107	6
13–15	1	—	3	1	4	1	27	5	39	5	66	6	70	4

| | WEST | | | | | | EAST | | | | | | TOTAL | |
| | 1–5 years | | Over 10 years | | Total | | 1–5 years | | Over 10 years | | Total | | Number | |
	N = 331	Per-cent	N = 359	Per-cent	N = 690	Per-cent	N = 561	Per-cent	N = 559	Per-cent	N = 1120	Per-cent	N = 1810	Per-cent
Shopkeeper														
1–3	—	—	4	1	4	1	2	—	9	1	11	1	15	1
4–6	—	1	12	3	16	2	24	4	23	2	47	4	63	3
7–9	21	5	37	8	58	8	72	12	55	9	127	11	185	10
10–12	58	13	58	13	116	17	93	16	111	18	204	18	320	18
13–15	221	51	221	48	442	64	338	57	321	48	659	59	1101	61
Artist, Musician, or Actor														
1–3	14	3	28	6	42	6	53	9	27	3	80	7	122	7
4–6	55	13	72	16	127	18	100	17	90	15	190	17	317	18
7–9	77	18	97	21	174	25	156	26	152	24	308	28	482	27
10–12	83	19	82	18	165	24	153	26	152	24	305	27	470	26
13–15	75	17	53	12	128	19	71	12	99	15	170	15	298	16
Priest or Clergyman														
1–3	135	31	155	34	290	42	116	20	131	20	247	22	537	30
4–6	116	27	114	25	230	33	124	21	125	18	249	22	479	26
7–9	33	8	43	9	76	11	105	18	96	15	201	18	277	15
10–12	18	4	15	3	33	5	107	18	77	11	184	16	217	12
13–15	2	—	5	1	7	1	78	13	93	14	171	15	178	10
Farmer														
1–3	2	—	3	1	5	1	32	5	23	2	55	5	60	3
4–6	6	1	9	2	15	2	31	5	26	2	57	5	72	4
7–9	17	4	36	8	53	8	48	8	47	7	95	8	148	8
10–12	62	14	60	13	122	18	124	21	104	13	228	20	350	19
13–15	217	50	224	49	441	64	292	49	322	51	614	55	1055	58

| | WEST | | | | | | EAST | | | | | | TOTAL | |
| | 1–5 years | | Over 10 years | | Total | | 1–5 years | | Over 10 years | | Total | | Number | |
	N = 331	Per-cent	N = 359	Per-cent	N = 690	Per-cent	N = 561	Per-cent	N = 559	Per-cent	N = 1120	Per-cent	N = 1810	Per-cent
Banker														
1–3	47	11	67	15	114	17	38	6	38	6	76	7	190	10
4–6	111	26	154	34	265	38	116	20	140	21	256	23	521	29
7–9	82	19	73	16	155	22	156	26	165	26	321	29	476	26
10–12	49	11	33	7	82	12	164	28	130	21	294	26	376	21
13–15	15	3	5	1	20	3	56	9	49	7	105	9	125	7
Secondary School Teacher														
1–3	—	—	2	—	2	1	44	7	31	3	75	7	77	4
4–6	49	11	32	7	81	12	110	19	142	21	252	23	333	18
7–9	147	34	152	33	299	43	186	31	168	26	354	32	653	36
10–12	90	21	121	26	211	31	145	24	150	23	195	17	406	22
13–15	18	4	25	5	43	6	49	8	32	4	81	7	124	7
Business Man														
1–3	19	4	35	8	54	8	84	14	105	13	189	17	243	13
4–6	85	20	67	15	152	22	106	18	105	13	211	19	363	20
7–9	101	23	108	24	209	30	100	17	102	13	202	18	411	23
10–12	71	16	77	17	148	21	129	22	108	13	237	21	385	21
13–15	28	6	45	10	73	11	110	19	100	12	210	19	283	16
Primary School Principal or Head														
1–3	8	2	8	1	16	2	51	9	44	4	95	8	111	6
4–6	68	16	56	12	124	18	137	23	121	18	258	23	382	21
7–9	159	37	164	36	323	47	171	29	198	30	369	33	692	38
10–12	64	15	88	19	152	22	125	21	128	18	253	23	405	22
13–15	5	1	16	3	21	3	51	9	31	3	82	7	103	6

TABLE 9A—continued

| | WEST | | | | | | EAST | | | | | | TOTAL | |
| | 1–5 years | | Over 10 years | | Total | | 1–5 years | | Over 10 years | | Total | | Number | |
	N = 331	Per-cent	N = 359	Per-cent	N = 690	Per-cent	N = 561	Per-cent	N = 559	Per-cent	N = 1120	Per-cent	N = 1810	Per-cent
University Professor														
1–3	125	29	121	26	246	36	257	43	244	37	501	45	747	41
4–6	129	30	140	31	269	39	168	28	192	29	360	32	629	35
7–9	40	9	64	14	104	15	67	11	59	7	126	11	130	7
10–12	9	2	6	1	15	2	26	4	19	2	45	2	60	3
13–15	1	—	1	—	2	<1	14	2	8	1	22	2	24	1
Primary School Teacher														
1–3	1	—	1	—	2	<1	58	10	45	4	103	9	105	6
4–6	11	3	9	2	20	3	38	6	51	7	89	8	109	6
7–9	72	17	64	14	136	20	117	20	115	18	232	21	368	20
10–12	167	39	185	40	352	51	175	30	192	29	367	33	719	40
13–15	53	12	73	16	126	18	147	25	119	18	266	24	393	22
Skilled Craftsman														
1–3	1	—	6	1	7	1	18	3	20	3	38	3	45	2
4–6	8	2	12	3	20	3	50	8	38	4	88	8	108	6
7–9	38	9	27	6	65	9	82	14	68	9	150	13	215	12
10–12	109	25	108	24	217	31	133	22	142	24	275	25	492	27
13–15	148	34	179	39	327	47	247	42	253	39	500	45	827	46

a. N = number of samples. The percents ignore decimals, are the closest in round numbers, and, hence, in the totals may not appear as the average of the East and the West percents. Where the percents do not total 100, the discrepancy is due to questions left unanswered.
b. Denotes highest rank.
c. Denotes lowest rank.
d. Questionnaire omitted Finland and Pakistan.

59

officials, doctors of medicine and university professors as having highest prestige.

In the West, the secondary school teacher was held in slightly higher esteem than in the East, receiving most votes in the middle categories of the prestige rank. The same situation holds true for the primary school principal or head. The primary school teacher was consigned to the 10th to the 15th rank by 69 percent of the teachers in the West and by 57 percent of the teachers in the East. In contrast, 75 percent of teachers in the West and 77 percent of teachers in the East placed the university professor in the 1st to the 6th ranks.

Teachers in this study believed that all teachers with the exception of university professors are held in extremely low esteem in their countries. It would seem thus that raising the self-image of teachers is one of the most challenging problems facing both East and West at the present time. Nations have not convinced their teachers that their roles are of vital importance to the national welfare. So long as they are not made to feel that they have a valued status, it is questionable whether they can or will perform the important roles expected of them in the modern world. Between age groups in both East and West there were few discrepancies in the values assigned. Younger teachers in the East gave slightly more prestige to the banker, to the business-man and to the university professor than did the older group, while the older group held the farmer and the shopkeeper in slightly higher regard. In the West no marked differences in the two age groups appeared.

Table 10A indicates further the low esteem in which teachers of the primary school hold their profession. Half of them believed their status has deteriorated from that of former times, while the rest were almost equally divided between the feeling that prestige of the profession has improved or has remained stationary. While a higher proportion of older teachers in both East and West believed that their status has deteriorated in recent times, the younger ones were slightly more sanguine about their status. Teachers in the West, both young and old, were slightly more optimistic than teachers in the East.

On the question concerning possible reasons why the best young people may not be attracted to teaching as a lifework, nearly half of the teachers gave the little respect shown the teacher as a primary reason. However, the most important deterrents were too low salary, too little opportunity for advancement, and unattractive working conditions, in that rank order. Such factors as shortage of positions,

TABLE 10A[a]

Present Status of Primary Teachers

| | WEST | | | | | | EAST | | | | | | TOTAL | |
| | 1–5 years | | Over 10 years | | Total | | 1–5 years | | Over 10 years | | Total | | Number | |
	N = 431	Per-cent	N = 459	Per-cent	N = 890	Per-cent	N = 593	Per-cent	N = 659	Per-cent	N = 1252	Per-cent	N = 2142	Per-cent
Direction of Change of Status														
No change	125	29	120	26	245	28	100	17	104	16	204	16	449	21
Improved a great deal	99	23	100	22	199	22	179	30	157	24	336	27	535	25
Deteriorated	195	45	232	51	427	48	301	51	395	60	696	56	1123	52
Reasons Why Young People Hesitate to Choose This Profession														
Shortage of positions	16	4	7	2	23	3	102	17	120	18	222	18	245	11
Working conditions in schools too unattractive and difficult	217	50	265	57	482	54	273	46	361	55	634	51	1116	52
Too little intellectual stimulation in working with children	115	27	119	26	234	26	140	24	101	15	241	19	475	22
Too few teachers who have intellectual interests and tastes	55	13	54	12	109	12	82	14	59	9	141	11	250	12
Too little respect shown to teachers	211	49	212	46	423	48	237	40	310	47	547	44	970	45
Weak teachers' organizations	17	4	8	2	25	3	51	9	67	10	118	9	143	7
Too little opportunity for advancement	236	55	290	63	526	59	302	51	316	48	618	49	1144	53
Too much interference from government and superiors	31	7	58	13	89	10	88	15	141	21	229	18	318	15
Too low salary	323	75	273	59	596	67	345	58	364	55	709	57	1305	61
Living conditions in rural areas and villages too difficult	54	13	71	15	125	14	149	25	133	20	282	23	407	19

a. N = number of samples. The percents ignore decimals, are the closest in round numbers, and, hence, in the totals may not appear as the average of the East and the West percents. Where the percents do not total 100, the discrepancy is due to questions left unanswered.

weak teachers' organizations and governmental interference were not considered as of great importance in deterring prospective teachers. There was little disagreement between East and West on any of these points, except for shortage of positions. Teachers in the West thought the reasons of too little opportunity for advancement and too low salary more significant. This is interesting, since salaries in the West are notably higher than in the East and there are relatively more opportunities for in-service education. Teachers in the East were more conscious of weak teachers' organizations, difficult living conditions in villages, and too much interference from government and superiors.

More older than younger teachers, in both East and West, thought a major deterrent to attracting young people was that working conditions in schools were difficult. A low salary was noted as a cause by younger teachers more often than by the older ones. More older teachers than younger ones in the West felt there was too little opportunity for advancement. Younger teachers in the East were more certain than older teachers that lack of intellectual stimulation was likewise a deterrent.

Since a teacher shortage exists almost universally, teachers were asked how they felt the shortage could best be met. The most acceptable way in both East and West, as shown in Table 11A, was to use only qualified teachers but to divide the children into shifts, each attending only a part of the day. The second most acceptable way was to tolerate extremely large classes (much more acceptable in the East than in the West). Using unqualified teachers as needed was acceptable to relatively one-third in both East and West. Such methods as relaxing attendance laws or closing schools were not acceptable to any large part of either group. Fifty-nine percent of the teachers in the East and 42 percent of those in the West were in favor of shortening the period of training so that more teachers would become quickly available. There was almost complete agreement between the older and the younger teachers in finding means of meeting teacher shortages. The older teachers were slightly more inclined toward using only qualified teachers, even though children might not be able to attend school full time.

One of the important factors in the total working conditions of teachers is the amount of time which must be spent on activities outside of school. Two of the more time consuming were transportation to and from school and checking papers. Table 12A indicates that considerably more than half (69 percent in the West and 61 percent in the

TABLE 11A[a]

Ways of Meeting Teacher Shortages

| | WEST | | | | | | EAST | | | | | | TOTAL | |
| | 1-5 years | | Over 10 years | | Total | | 1-5 years | | Over 10 years | | Total | | Number | |
	N = 431	Per-cent	N = 459	Per-cent	N = 890	Per-cent	N = 593	Per-cent	N = 659	Per-cent	N = 1252	Per-cent	N = 2142	Per-cent
Using only qualified teachers, however large classes may have to be	188	44	203	44	391	44	334	56	386	59	720	58	1111	52
Using only qualified teachers, but dividing large classes into double or triple shifts each day	257	60	292	64	549	62	344	58	426	65	770	62	1319	62
Using only qualified teachers but limiting the number of days per week that each child may attend school	194	45	249	54	443	50	203	34	230	35	433	35	876	41
Using unqualified teachers as required	177	41	162	35	339	38	184	31	208	32	392	31	731	34
Relaxing compulsory attendance laws to cut down on the number of children in school	34	8	55	12	89	10	53	9	75	11	128	10	217	10
Closing as many schools as necessary until a sufficient number of qualified teachers are trained	25	6	33	7	58	7	63	11	61	9	124	10	182	8
Shortening the period of teacher training so that more teachers become quickly available	183	42	191	42	374	42	353	60	390	59	743	59	1117	52

a. N = number of samples. The percents ignore decimals, are the closest in round numbers, and, hence, in the totals may not appear as the average of the East and the West percents. Where the percents do not total 100, the discrepancy is due to questions left unanswered.

TABLE 12A[a]

Minutes Spent in Daily Activities Other Than Teaching

| | WEST | | | | | | EAST | | | | | | TOTAL | |
| | 1–5 years | | Over 10 years | | Total | | 1–5 years | | Over 10 years | | Total | | Number | |
	N = 431	Per-cent	N = 459	Per-cent	N = 890	Per-cent	N = 593	Per-cent	N = 659	Per-cent	N = 1252	Per-cent	N = 2142	Per-cent
Travelling To and From School														
Less than 20	61	14	67	15	128	14	91	15	133	20	224	18	352	16
20–39	160	37	168	37	328	37	126	21	201	31	327	26	655	31
40–59	66	15	96	21	162	18	108	18	111	17	219	17	381	18
60–79	67	16	78	17	145	16	88	15	91	14	179	14	324	15
80–99	40	9	24	5	64	7	41	7	36	5	77	6	141	7
100–119	8	2	10	2	18	2	20	3	14	2	34	3	52	2
120–139	22	5	7	2	29	3	46	8	31	5	77	6	106	5
140–159	—	—	3	1	4	*	8	1	3	—	11	1	15	1
160–179	—	—	—	—	—		13	2	2	—	15	1	15	1
Over 180	3	1	1	—	4	*	20	3	16	2	36	3	40	2
Checking Papers														
Less than 20	43	10	20	4	63	7	25	4	22	3	47	4	110	5
20–39	76	18	77	17	153	17	57	10	99	15	156	12	309	14
40–59	22	5	36	8	58	7	42	7	54	8	96	8	154	7
60–79	105	24	113	25	218	24	144	24	173	26	317	25	535	25
80–99	45	10	47	10	92	10	37	6	42	6	79	6	171	8
100–119	4	1	5	1	9	1	13	2	11	2	24	2	33	2
120–139	64	15	54	12	118	13	122	21	116	18	238	19	356	17
140–159	12	3	16	3	28	3	25	4	7	1	32	3	60	3
160–179	1	—	—	—	1	*	7	1	6	1	13	1	14	1
Over 180	39	9	37	8	76	9	75	13	87	13	162	13	238	11

a. N = number of samples. The percents ignore decimals, are the closest in round numbers, and, hence, in the totals may not appear as the average of the East and the West percents. Where the percents do not total 100, the discrepancy is due to questions left unanswered.

64

East) spent an hour or less each day in traveling to and from school. About a fifth spent up to an hour and forty minutes each day and a smattering spent a longer time. Seemingly, adequate housing in the proximity of the school was not available to a fair number of teachers and some type of fairly efficient transportation was likewise not available to them.

In checking papers at home, more time was needed. About one-third of the teachers in the West spent an hour or less a day, while one-fourth of those in the East indicated the same amount of time. One-third in both East and West used from one hour to an hour and forty minutes for this activity. In general, teachers in the West indicated they spent more time in traveling to and from school and those in the East had a heavier load of correcting papers. It is significant that there is almost complete agreement among both ages, East and West, in the amount of time spent in travel and clerical duties by both older and younger teachers in East and West in each type of activity.

Table 13A indicates that either the teachers sampled were a very healthy lot or the policy regarding absence from school for illness was a very strict one, for about three-fourths of them in both areas had missed five or fewer days during the course of the year. The proportion missing a month or more was almost negligible. This applied to the older as well as to the younger teachers in both East and West. The older teachers had a slightly better attendance record due to good health than had the younger teachers, particularly for those missing not a single day of school during the previous year.

One of the conditions of work which teachers value highly is the time, the opportunity and the resources to enjoy certain cultural and leisure time activities. Table 14A indicates the activities which these teachers said were usual with them. Newspaper reading was by far the most popular, being almost universal. Next were listening to the radio and reading professional journals. Activities which were more common to teachers in the West were reading popular magazines, TV viewing, taking a yearly trip, attending a concert or play at least once a year, and visiting a library at least once a month. Teachers in the East were more apt to go to a movie once a month. A little more than one-half in both regions professed to reading at least one book a month.

These data show that generally teachers in the West lead a much fuller and more varied cultural life than do teachers in the East. In some cases, such as TV viewing and reading popular magazines,

TABLE 13A[a]

Number of Days Absent for Illness During the Past Year

| | WEST | | | | | | EAST | | | | | | TOTAL | |
| | 1–5 years | | Over 10 years | | Total | | 1–5 years | | Over 10 years | | Total | | Number | |
	N = 431	Per-cent	N = 459	Per-cent	N = 890	Per-cent	N = 593	Per-cent	N = 659	Per-cent	N = 1252	Per-cent	N = 2142	Per-cent
None	169	39	184	40	353	40	210	35	285	43	495	40	848	40
1–5	140	32	148	32	288	32	181	31	218	33	399	32	687	32
6–10	64	15	51	11	115	13	53	9	53	8	106	8	221	10
11–15	20	5	20	4	40	4	24	4	18	3	42	3	82	4
16–20	11	3	8	2	19	2	51	9	6	1	57	5	76	4
Over 20	13	3	22	5	35	4	30	5	27	4	57	5	92	4

a. N = number of samples. The percents ignore decimals, are the closest in round numbers, and, hence, in the totals may not appear as the average of the East and the West percents. Where the percents do not total 100, the discrepancy is due to questions left unanswered.

66

TABLE 14A[a]
Regular Cultural Activities

| | WEST | | | | | | EAST | | | | | | TOTAL | |
| | 1–5 years | | Over 10 years | | Total | | 1–5 years | | Over 10 years | | Total | | Number | |
	N = 431	Per-cent	N = 459	Per-cent	N = 890	Per-cent	N = 593	Per-cent	N = 659	Per-cent	N = 1252	Per-cent	N = 2142	Per-cent
Reading general newspaper	411	95	452	98	863	97	556	94	616	93	1172	94	2035	95
Reading professional newspapers or journals	326	76	411	90	737	83	320	54	386	59	716	57	1453	68
Daily radio listening	378	88	396	86	774	87	432	73	506	77	938	75	1712	80
Reading popular magazines and journals	326	76	350	76	676	76	356	60	342	52	698	56	1374	64
Daily television viewing	260	60	289	63	549	62	123	21	140	21	263	21	812	38
Taking one yearly trip of at least 200 miles from your home	337	78	348	76	685	77	164	28	164	25	328	26	1013	47
Attending at least one professional or cultural meeting each month	154	36	203	44	357	40	179	30	188	29	367	29	724	34
Seeing at least one motion picture a month[b]	200	46	90	20	290	33	298	50	240	36	538	43	828	39
Attending at least one concert or play during the year[b]	286	66	317	69	603	68	207	35	187	28	394	31	997	47
Visiting a library at least once each month[b]	202	47	197	43	399	45	187	32	187	28	374	30	773	36
Reading at least one book each month[b]	231	54	255	56	486	55	354	50	353	54	707	56	1193	56
None of the above[b]	—	—	—	—	—	—	28	5	24	4	52	4	52	2

a. N = number of samples. The percents ignore decimals, are the closest in round numbers, and, hence, in the totals may not appear as the average of the East and the West percents. Where the percents do not total 100, the discrepancy is due to questions left unanswered.
b. These items were omitted from the Vietnam questionnaire.

the availability of the media no doubt accounted for some difference in their cultural opportunities.

There were no great differences in the cultural practices of older and younger teachers in either East or West. In the East, a higher proportion of younger teachers read popular magazines, saw a movie at least once a month, attended a concert or theatre performance, and visited the public library. More of the older teachers read professional journals, listened to the radio and read a book a month. In the West more of the younger teachers went to movies, while the older teachers were more disposed toward reading professional journals and attending professional meetings.

Table 15A reports the types of community activity teachers participated in. Over half in the West were engaged in some sort of community work involving adults, as against 89 percent in the East. Nearly two-thirds in the West and over one-half in the East were involved in work with children and youth, while about one-half in each region were active in some sort of project to improve the community. One-third of teachers in the West and one-fourth in the East were not involved in any sort of community work outside their regular school duties. For younger and older groups there was almost complete agreement. A higher proportion of older teachers than younger ones in the East believed that it was legitimate to engage teachers in literacy programs.

Table 16A contains information concerning the activities of these teachers in professional and political organizations. For some of the teachers these were "touchy" questions, for in some countries they are forbidden by law to hold membership in political parties or to stand for political office. Their true position on membership in teachers' organizations is likewise difficult to determine, since a variety of patterns exist. Some have no local, some no regional, organizations. The term "other professional organization or association" can be construed in a number of different ways, such as organizations of purely cultural activity. The table indicates that a much higher proportion of teachers in the West than in the East were members of local teachers' organizations. About half in each group belonged to a national organization. Nearly one-third in the East belonged to a regional professional group as against a little more than one-fourth in the West.

In matters of political activity, teachers in the West seem to take their responsibilities much more seriously: 92 percent in the West

TABLE 15Aᵃ

Participation in Community Activities Related to Education

| | WEST | | | | | | EAST | | | | | | TOTAL | |
| | 1–5 years | | Over 10 years | | Total | | 1–5 years | | Over 10 years | | Total | | Number | |
	N = 431	Per-cent	N = 459	Per-cent	N = 890	Per-cent	N = 593	Per-cent	N = 659	Per-cent	N = 1252	Per-cent	N = 2142	Per-cent
Teaching adults to read and write	158	37	146	32	304	34	304	51	385	58	689	55	993	46
Teaching adults such skills as sewing, cooking, animal care, crop raising, sanitary measures, etc.	98	23	98	21	196	22	203	34	218	33	421	34	617	29
Directing children and youth in projects to improve the community	267	62	285	62	552	62	342	58	388	59	730	58	1282	60
Working in projects to improve the community	226	52	255	56	481	54	298	50	313	47	611	49	1092	51
No community work except that closely connected to the regular work of the school	139	32	174	38	313	35	135	23	161	24	296	24	609	28

a. N = number of samples. The percents ignore decimals, are the closest in round numbers, and, hence, in the totals may not appear as the average of the East and the West percents. Where the percents do not total 100, the discrepancy is due to questions left unanswered.

69

TABLE 16A[a]

Professional and Political Activities

| | WEST | | | | | | EAST | | | | | | TOTAL | |
| | 1–5 years | | Over 10 years | | Total | | 1–5 years | | Over 10 years | | Total | | Number | |
	N = 431	Per-cent	N = 459	Per-cent	N = 890	Per-cent	N = 593	Per-cent	N = 659	Per-cent	N = 1252	Per-cent	N = 2142	Per-cent
Membership in Teachers' Organizations														
Local teachers' organization[b]	296	69	340	74	636	71	243	41	305	46	548	44	1184	55
Regional or provincial teachers' organization	105	24	128	28	233	26	154	26	228	35	382	31	615	29
National teachers' organization	205	48	257	56	462	52	286	48	379	58	665	53	1127	53
Other professional organization	73	17	134	29	207	23	59	10	68	10	127	10	334	16
None	44	10	30	7	74	8	89	15	62	9	151	12	225	11
Political Activities														
Holding public office at the local level	4	1	9	2	13	1	41	7	70	11	111	9	124	6
Holding public office at higher than local level	1	—	4	1	5	1	24	4	20	3	44	4	49	2
Voting regularly	372	86	444	97	816	92	403	68	491	75	894	71	1710	80
Holding membership in a political party	41	10	66	14	107	12	12	2	21	3	33	3	140	7
Participating in public rallies, protest demonstrations, etc.	25	6	39	8	64	7	88	15	96	15	184	15	248	12
Not at all	49	11	13	3	62	7	143	24	134	20	277	22	339	16

a. N = number of samples. The percents ignore decimals, are the closest in round numbers, and, hence, in the totals may not appear as the average of the East and the West percents. Where the percents do not total 100, the discrepancy is due to questions left unanswered.
b. Seoul has no local teachers' organization.

as against 71 percent in the East said they voted regularly. Very few teachers in either region held any political office or had membership in a political party. More teachers in the East had participated in public rallies: only 7 percent in the West but 15 percent in the East. However, 22 percent in the East and 7 percent in the West said they had participated not at all in any form of political activity.

From these responses, it is quite clear that teachers in both East and West are, for the most part, not actively engaged in the professional and political life of their countries. They seem more like a group of onlookers than molders of the kind of society they are endeavoring to create through education.

In modern educational theory, it is considered important that teachers have a clear understanding of the goals of education which are generally deemed desirable for fulfilling the aspirations of the nation. It is also considered important that teachers have an active voice in helping to formulate these goals, to guarantee that they understand and are in accord with them. Furthermore, it is generally considered essential that teachers be encouraged to use some initiative in the methods to be used in arriving at these goals. Teachers must have an active share in the development of curriculum, in deciding the time allotted to various subjects, in promotion policies, and in general school management. Tables 17–19 indicate the responses given by the teachers as to what they believe their role now is.

Table 17A deals with a number of commonly accepted goals for primary education. Those goals which half or more of the teachers considered to be of prime importance were moral values, skills of reading and writing, social skills, facts and habits of health, to reason and think. Those goals which were rated of much less importance were skill in group thinking, obedience, religious values, the facts of geography and history, and vocational skills. (Approximately only one-fourth of all the teachers gave these high priority.) Midway between these two extremes, voted high by 41 percent of the combined East and West, was teaching civic skills necessary to democratic government.

Differences are apparent between East and West. Teachers in the West gave higher place to teaching skills such as reading and writing, social skills, to reason and think (very much higher for this item) and religious values and ideals than did teachers in the East. On the other hand, teachers in the East gave higher position to teaching moral values, civic skills, vocational skills, and good health habits.

71

TABLE 17A[a]

Chief Goals of Primary Education

| | WEST | | | | | | EAST | | | | | | TOTAL | |
| | 1–5 years | | Over 10 years | | Total | | 1–5 years | | Over 10 years | | Total | | Number | |
	N = 431	Per-cent	N = 459	Per-cent	N = 890	Per-cent	N = 593	Per-cent	N = 659	Per-cent	N = 1252	Per-cent	N = 2142	Per-cent
Moral values	291	68	283	62	574	64	456	77	506	77	962	77	1536	72
Basic skills, such as reading, writing, and numbers	400	93	442	96	842	95	426	72	501	76	927	74	1769	83
Social skills of learning how to get along with other people	339	79	383	83	722	81	402	68	380	58	782	62	1504	70
Facts of history, geography, mathematics	93	22	127	28	220	25	160	27	202	31	362	29	582	27
Civic skills necessary to democratic government	112	26	92	20	204	23	317	53	347	53	664	53	868	41
Vocational skills to be used later in earning a living	59	14	74	16	133	15	204	34	262	40	466	37	599	28
Facts and habits of good health	164	38	185	40	349	39	329	55	373	57	702	56	1051	49
To reason and think	350	81	377	82	727	82	221	37	257	39	478	38	1205	56
Religious values and ideals	134	31	207	45	341	38	108	18	143	22	251	20	592	28
Obedience in obeying orders	120	28	119	26	239	27	130	22	161	24	291	23	530	25
Skill in group thinking	51	12	43	9	94	11	176	30	157	24	333	27	427	20

a. N = number of samples. The percents ignore decimals, are the closest in round numbers, and, hence, in the totals may not appear as the average of the East and the West percents. Where the percents do not total 100, the discrepancy is due to questions left unanswered

Differences between younger and older teachers in East and West were minimal in their beliefs concerning the chief goals of primary education. Younger teachers in the East showed stronger preference for teaching the social skills of getting along with others and for teaching skills in group thinking than did older teachers, who placed slightly more emphasis on teaching basic skills, facts, vocational skills and religious values. In the West, the younger teachers gave slightly more weight to moral values and civic skills, while the older teachers placed slightly more emphasis on basic skills, social skills, learning facts and religious values.

Table 18A indicates the matters in which the teachers wished to be self-directing, in which matters they would rather relinquish the responsibility for decisions to higher authority. Regarding the time teachers were to arrive and leave school, 58 percent of all teachers felt it best to relinquish decisions to higher authority. The matters in which some direction was desired by at least half of both groups were disciplining a disobedient child, deciding the schedule of classes, and deciding on the content of the subject matter taught. The one matter in which at least half or more wanted to use their own judgment was in contacting parents.

As the table indicates, teachers in the West were much more consistent in favoring less direction from above than were teachers in the East. This trend was particularly pronounced in such matters as handling a child who does not work well, deciding when to come and when to leave school, handling a child who is late, deciding the schedule of classes and deciding the content of the subject matter.

This difference in need for authority is particularly interesting in that teachers in the West usually have the advantage of more supervisory help than do teachers in the East. Surprisingly, no differences of any importance were noted between younger and older teachers in either East or West. Apparently length of service does little or nothing to change the teachers' basic attitude toward authority in both types of culture.

Traditionally teachers have been little involved in formal curriculum making. Textbooks and curriculum guides have usually been handed to them, prepared by officials in the higher echelons of ministers of education or by "experts" commissioned to such work. The extent to which teachers actually have followed the guidelines given to them invariably have been checked by various means: by the success of pupils on external examinations, by supervisors from outside the

TABLE 18A[a]
Teacher's Responsibility in the Conduct of School Matters

	WEST						EAST						TOTAL	
	1–5 years		Over 10 years		Total		1–5 years		Over 10 years		Total		Number	
	N = 431	Per-cent	N = 459	Per-cent	N = 890	Per-cent	N = 593	Per-cent	N = 659	Per-cent	N = 1252	Per-cent	N = 2142	Per-cent
Handling a child who does not work well														
A	9	2	—	—	9	1	111	19	118	18	229	18	238	11
B	151	35	200	44	351	39	239	40	270	41	509	41	860	40
C	269	62	256	56	525	59	221	37	246	37	467	37	992	46
Disciplining a child who is disobedient														
A	15	3	16	3	31	3	170	29	147	22	317	25	348	16
B	253	59	302	66	555	62	247	42	274	42	521	42	1076	50
C	162	38	137	30	299	34	154	26	216	33	370	30	669	31
Deciding methods of classroom Teaching														
A	9	2	17	4	26	3	78	13	92	14	170	14	196	9
B	265	61	286	62	551	62	326	55	311	47	637	51	1188	55
C	157	36	153	33	310	35	167	28	232	35	399	32	709	33

TABLE 18A—continued

| | WEST | | | | | | EAST | | | | | | TOTAL | |
| | 1–5 years | | Over 10 years | | Total | | 1–5 years | | Over 10 years | | Total | | Number | |
	N = 431	Per-cent	N = 459	Per-cent	N = 890	Per-cent	N = 593	Per-cent	N = 659	Per-cent	N = 1252	Per-cent	N = 2142	Per-cent
Deciding the Time Teachers should Arrive and Leave School														
A	178	41	199	43	377	42	393	66	464	70	857	68	1234	58
B	169	39	189	41	358	40	139	23	138	21	277	22	635	30
C	83	19	66	14	149	17	38	6	34	5	72	6	221	10
Handling a Child Who is Late														
A	46	11	26	6	72	8	114	19	107	16	221	18	293	14
B	224	52	219	48	443	50	235	40	252	38	487	39	930	43
C	159	37	209	46	368	41	220	37	270	41	490	39	858	40
Deciding the Schedule of Classes														
A	89	21	120	26	209	23	204	34	260	39	464	37	673	31
B	281	65	305	66	586	66	286	48	289	44	575	46	1161	54
C	61	14	29	6	90	10	78	13	85	13	163	13	253	12

TABLE 18A—*continued*

| | WEST | | | | | | EAST | | | | | | TOTAL | |
| | 1–5 years | | Over 10 years | | Total | | 1–5 years | | Over 10 years | | Total | | Number | |
	N = 431	Per-cent	N = 459	Per-cent	N = 890	Per-cent	N = 593	Per-cent	N = 659	Per-cent	N = 1252	Per-cent	N = 2142	Per-cent
Contacting Parents														
A	53	12	25	5	78	9	82	14	93	14	175	14	253	12
B	180	42	191	42	371	42	195	33	173	26	368	29	739	35
C	196	45	238	52	434	49	297	50	371	56	668	53	1102	51
Deciding on Methods of Reporting to Parents														
A	148	34	129	28	277	31	180	30	184	28	364	29	641	30
B	215	50	240	52	455	51	200	34	244	37	444	35	899	42
C	65	15	84	18	159	18	188	32	206	31	394	31	553	26
Deciding on the Content of Subject Matter														
A	84	19	110	24	194	22	160	27	220	33	380	30	574	27
B	314	73	328	71	642	72	339	57	320	49	659	53	1301	61
C	33	8	16	3	49	6	67	11	88	13	155	12	204	10

KEY: A: Teachers to follow strict rules laid down by higher authority.
B: Teachers to follow general rules but to allow for the situation.
C: No set rules; teachers to use their own judgment.

a. N = number of samples. The percents ignore decimals, are the closest in round numbers, and, hence, in the totals may not appear as the average of the East and the West percents. Where the percents do not total 100, the discrepancy is due to questions left unanswered.

school, and by supervisors from within the school, ordinarily the school principal. In general, teachers have accepted guidelines and directions for deciding their proper behavior in carrying forward both extremely simple and complex activities.

Newer theories in education hold that it is quite difficult, if not impossible, to impose curriculums on teachers. If the content of the subject matter to be taught is not derived at through their participation, they either do not understand what is demanded of them or they disagree with what is required and find many ways to sabotage the guidelines given them. Or, they may find it quite impossible to fulfill the expectations of the curriculum makers because of special conditions pertaining to their unique situations, of which the curriculum makers could not be aware. For this reason, modern practice leans more and more toward the involvement of teachers in planning the content of the curriculum.

Table 19A shows the reactions of teachers to certain proposals concerning methods for determining curriculum. Clearly the teachers feel the responsibility should be a shared one among experts, officials, and the local school staff. Teachers in the East placed much heavier reliance on following the content of a textbook than did teachers in the West (58 percent as against 37 percent). Two-thirds in each region wanted guidelines from a higher authority such as a ministry of education, but also wanted a good deal of freedom in deciding upon time schedules to be devoted to various subjects during the day. Here again the East relied more heavily on authority than did the West. Both East and West were strongly in favor of giving the local school staff, including the principal and teachers, a voice in deciding how the curriculum should be worked out. There was considerable difference of opinion in each region concerning how much authority should be given the individual teacher in deciding matters of curriculum. A number of the questionnaires were returned without a response to this question, a sign of indecision in the thinking of the respondents.

There was rather decided agreement, however, that neither in the East nor in the West did teachers wish their curriculum tied to the requirements of an external examination. This is interesting, since in a number of countries the demand of an external examination is a reality which must be faced by the teachers of the primary school.

In the East, older teachers are uniformly more content to rest on authority than are the younger teachers, although both groups wanted some voice in making adaptations to any set curriculum. In the West,

77

TABLE 19Aᵃ

Guides for Determining Content of Curriculum

| | WEST | | | | | | EAST | | | | | | TOTAL | |
| | 1–5 years | | Over 10 years | | Total | | 1–5 years | | Over 10 years | | Total | | Number | |
	N = 431	Per-cent	N = 459	Per-cent	N = 890	Per-cent	N = 593	Per-cent	N = 659	Per-cent	N = 1252	Per-cent	N = 2142	Per-cent
Textbook														
Agree	125	29	200	44	325	37	329	55	403	61	732	58	1057	49
Undecided	64	15	55	12	119	13	113	19	103	16	216	17	335	16
Disagree	239	55	184	40	423	48	127	21	127	19	254	20	677	32
The Curriculum Guide sent by School Authorities such as Ministry of Education														
Agree	268	62	306	67	574	64	389	66	453	69	842	67	1416	66
Undecided	65	15	63	14	128	14	104	18	100	15	204	16	332	15
Disagree	94	22	73	16	167	19	83	14	78	12	161	13	328	15
The Time Schedule Sent by School Authorities														
Agree	131	30	135	29	266	30	270	46	323	49	593	47	859	40
Undecided	104	24	84	18	188	21	150	25	161	24	311	25	499	23
Disagree	157	36	139	30	296	33	148	25	141	21	289	23	585	27

TABLE 19A—*continued*

	WEST						EAST						TOTAL
	1–5 years		Over 10 years		Total		1–5 years		Over 10 years		Total		Number
	N = 431	Per-cent	N = 459	Per-cent	N = 890	Per-cent	N = 593	Per-cent	N = 659	Per-cent	N = 1252	Per-cent	N = 2142	Per-cent
The Curriculum Guide Worked Out by Teachers and Principal of the School													
Agree	304	71	289	63	593	67	416	70	474	72	890	71	1483	69
Undecided	50	12	54	12	104	12	98	17	91	14	189	15	293	14
Disagree	70	16	95	21	165	19	51	9	70	11	121	10	286	13
The Curriculum Plan Worked Out by the Individual Teacher													
Agree	218	51	187	41	405	46	239	40	303	46	542	43	947	44
Undecided	56	13	64	14	120	13	128	22	119	18	247	20	367	17
Disagree	152	35	186	41	338	38	196	33	178	27	374	30	712	33
The Content of the Examinations which have been given in recent years by School Authorities for Entrance to the Next Class or the Next Higher School													
Agree	88	20	112	24	200	22	139	23	203	31	342	27	542	25
Undecided	82	19	80	18	162	18	138	23	150	23	288	23	450	21
Disagree	250	58	244	65	494	56	273	46	259	39	532	42	1026	48

a. N = number of samples. The percents ignore decimals, are the closest in round numbers, and, hence, in the totals may not appear as the average of the East and the West percents. Where the percents do not total 100, the discrepancy is due to questions left unanswered.

greater differences of opinion were given. Older teachers definitely placed more reliance on a textbook and on prepared curriculums than did younger teachers. The younger ones more definitely wanted a voice in making adaptations to fit specific situations. Particularly did they favor, over their older colleagues, a curriculum plan worked out by the individual teacher. The content of examinations as a guide for determining curriculum was more strongly rejected by both older and younger teachers in the West than was true in the East.

Because it is generally recognized that the intellectual powers of most children can function well only if their physical and emotional needs are first met, a number of countries have come to feel that supplementary social aids, such as health care, must be given children if the goals of education are to bear fruit. For this reason, a number of countries, particularly in Europe, provide school feeding and school health services and give extra financial help to families which cannot adequately provide for the basic needs of their children. The teachers' attitudes toward such aids are indicated in Table 20A.

The aids which a considerable proportion of teachers in both regions combined agreed were legitimate were free medical and dental check-ups and care, free textbooks and school supplies; free psychological counselling and clinics; special schools for atypical children; and grants to poor parents. The kinds of help which fewer than half of them did not wish to see incorporated were free meals, grants to parents with large families; and free birth control clinics.

Teachers in the West were more strongly in favor of psychological clinics and special schools than were teachers in the East. The reason for this may be that in many countries of the East the atypical children drop out of school and the teachers are not so aware of their needs. Also, teachers in the West were more disposed toward free birth control clinics. Teachers in the East were more strongly in favor of free medical and dental care and of grants to very poor parents and to parents with large families.

In general, it might be said from these data that teachers generally are rather conservative in their demands for supplementary social services for children. The reason for this may be that they feel that all available moneys are urgently needed for strictly school activities. In a number of cities, governmental policy seems more liberal than teacher attitude.

Examination of the data shows that while older and younger teachers tended to take similar positions in both East and West, the older

Supplementary Aids to Regular Instruction

| | WEST | | | | | | EAST | | | | | | TOTAL | |
| | 1–5 years | | Over 10 years | | Total | | 1–5 years | | Over 10 years | | Total | | Number | |
	N = 431	Per-cent	N = 459	Per-cent	N = 890	Per-cent	N = 593	Per-cent	N = 659	Per-cent	N = 1252	Per-cent	N = 2142	Per-cent
Free Meals in School for all Children														
Agree	120	28	113	25	233	26	220	37	227	34	447	36	680	32
Undecided	19	4	27	6	46	5	96	16	116	18	212	17	258	12
Disagree	285	66	297	65	582	65	235	40	270	41	505	40	1087	51
Free Medical and Dental Checkups in School														
Agree	317	74	329	72	646	73	480	81	562	85	1042	83	1688	79
Undecided	28	6	32	7	60	7	42	7	45	7	87	7	147	7
Disagree	80	19	86	19	166	19	37	6	25	4	62	5	228	11
Free Medical and Dental Services in School														
Agree	197	46	222	48	419	47	455	77	537	88	992	79	1411	66
Undecided	53	12	52	11	105	12	63	11	60	9	123	10	228	11
Disagree	172	40	173	38	345	39	45	8	34	5	79	6	424	20
Grants to Parents With Many Children														
Agree	250	58	170	37	320	36	278	47	356	54	634	51	954	45
Undecided	73	17	64	14	137	15	132	22	110	17	242	19	379	18
Disagree	201	47	209	46	410	46	157	26	162	25	319	25	729	34
Free Textbooks and School Supplies														
Agree	340	79	255	56	595	67	400	67	458	69	858	69	1453	68
Undecided	42	10	35	8	77	9	102	17	98	15	200	16	277	13
Disagree	44	10	163	36	207	23	72	12	75	11	147	12	354	17

81

TABLE 20A—continued

| | WEST | | | | | | EAST | | | | | | TOTAL | |
| | 1–5 years | | Over 10 years | | Total | | 1–5 years | | Over 10 years | | Total | | Number | |
	N = 431	Per-cent	N = 459	Per-cent	N = 890	Per-cent	N = 593	Per-cent	N = 659	Per-cent	N = 1252	Per-cent	N = 2142	Per-cent
Grants to Widows for Support of Children														
Agree	250	58	275	60	525	59	262	44	378	57	640	51	1165	54
Undecided	82	19	78	17	160	18	142	24	125	19	267	21	427	20
Disagree	94	22	85	19	179	20	156	26	114	17	270	22	449	21
Free Psychological Clinics and Counselling for Children														
Agree	361	84	378	82	739	83	431	73	483	73	914	73	1653	77
Undecided	40	9	41	9	81	9	76	13	96	15	172	14	253	12
Disagree	27	6	34	7	61	7	55	9	42	6	97	8	158	7
Free Birth Control Clinics														
Agree	221	51	231	50	452	51	197	33	238	36	435	35	887	41
Undecided	76	18	58	13	134	15	166	28	175	27	341	27	475	22
Disagree	127	29	151	33	278	31	192	32	195	30	387	31	665	31
Special Schools for Children not Fitted to Attend Regular Schools														
Agree	414	96	434	95	848	95	441	74	502	76	943	75	1791	84
Undecided	5	1	8	2	13	1	74	12	67	10	141	11	154	7
Disagree	8	2	11	2	19	2	58	10	54	8	112	9	131	6
Grants to Very Poor Parents														
Agree	217	50	235	51	452	51	358	60	426	65	784	63	1236	58
Undecided	87	20	83	18	170	19	87	15	91	14	178	14	348	16
Disagree	121	28	126	27	247	28	117	26	109	17	226	18	473	22

a. N = number of samples. The percents ignore decimals, are the closest in round numbers, and, hence, in the totals may not appear as the average

teachers in the East and the younger teachers in the West tended to be somewhat more liberal than their colleagues. In the East there was great difference regarding grants to parents and to widows. In the West, the younger group was more liberal in desiring grants to parents and free texts and supplies.

Table 21A reveals the factors which teachers believe contributed to poor achievement in the primary school. Factors which both regions agreed had very high significance were too many children in classes, too many duties for the teacher outside the classroom, too many dull children, and poor home training. Factors which were rated high in the East and not in the West were poor buildings and equipment, not enough books and teaching materials. The majority in both regions felt they had adequate help from the outside and that they were not greatly burdened by the demands of external examinations.

Younger and older teachers in both East and West were in almost perfect accord in their assessment of the handicaps which they were asked to judge. Younger teachers in the East and older teachers in the West were more conscious of heterogeneous grouping of bright and dull children than their colleagues of different ages. More older teachers in the East and more younger teachers in the West complained about the children's poor training at home.

Because a considerable amount of discussion centers currently around the need for pre-school education, there was a question on it (Table 22A). Here the teachers were extremely ambivalent. While nearly two-thirds of them disagreed with the statement that parents should be urged to keep their children at home until they reach proper school age, there was little agreement about how pre-school education should be provided. About half of the teachers in the West and nearly two-thirds in the East felt that such schools should be provided at government expense. Twice the proportion of teachers in the East (63 percent as opposed to 31 percent in the West) wanted to make attendance compulsory. Both regions were undecided about their position regarding private agencies assuming the responsibility for pre-school education. It would seem fair to say that primary school teachers have formed no strong opinions on pre-school experiences for children. Generally speaking, teachers in the East were more favorably disposed toward this level of schooling than were teachers in the West.

There was little disagreement between older and younger groups in assessing the importance of nursery schools. In the East, older

TABLE 21A[a]

Reasons for Poor Achievement by Children

	WEST						EAST						TOTAL	
	1–5 years		Over 10 years		Total		1–5 years		Over 10 years		Total		Number	
	N = 431	Per-cent	N = 459	Per-cent	N = 890	Per-cent	N = 593	Per-cent	N = 659	Per-cent	N = 1252	Per-cent	N = 2142	Per-cent
Too Many Children in the Classes														
Agree	373	87	402	88	775	87	513	87	554	84	1067	85	1842	86
Undecided	23	5	25	5	48	5	28	5	44	7	72	6	120	6
Disagree	30	7	23	5	53	6	43	7	48	7	91	7	144	7
Too Many Duties for the Teacher Outside the Classroom														
Agree	195	45	242	53	437	49	384	65	445	68	829	66	1266	59
Undecided	67	16	83	18	150	17	82	14	80	12	162	13	312	15
Disagree	162	38	120	26	282	32	105	18	103	16	208	17	490	23
Too Little Help for the Teacher from Inspectors and Heads or Principals														
Agree	99	23	98	21	197	22	183	31	205	31	388	31	585	27
Undecided	89	21	107	23	196	22	190	32	194	29	384	31	580	27
Disagree	234	64	237	52	471	53	179	30	221	34	400	32	871	41
Too Many Dull Children in the Same Classes with Bright Children														
Agree	226	52	271	59	497	56	330	56	334	51	664	53	1161	54
Undecided	81	19	63	14	144	16	134	23	122	19	256	20	400	19
Disagree	119	28	110	24	229	26	110	19	165	25	275	22	504	24

TABLE 21A—continued

	WEST						EAST						TOTAL	
	1–5 years		Over 10 years		Total		1–5 years		Over 10 years		Total		Number	
	N = 431	Per-cent	N = 459	Per-cent	N = 890	Per-cent	N = 593	Per-cent	N = 659	Per-cent	N = 1252	Per-cent	N = 2142	Per-cent
Poor Buildings and Equipment														
Agree	141	33	156	34	297	33	382	64	425	68	807	64	1104	52
Undecided	95	22	95	21	190	21	89	15	93	14	182	15	372	17
Disagree	188	44	187	41	375	42	98	17	107	18	205	16	580	27
Not Enough Books and Teaching Materials														
Agree	208	48	202	44	410	46	393	66	446	68	839	67	1249	58
Undecided	52	12	76	17	128	14	94	16	75	13	169	13	297	14
Disagree	162	38	162	35	324	36	78	13	104	18	182	15	506	24
For Home Training of the Children														
Agree	311	72	301	66	612	69	343	58	431	68	774	62	1386	65
Undecided	61	14	67	15	128	14	123	21	116	18	239	19	367	17
Disagree	53	12	77	17	130	15	103	17	81	13	184	15	314	15
Too Much Time Required for Preparing for Examinations to the Next Higher School														
Agree	117	27	68	15	185	21	171	29	192	29	363	29	548	26
Undecided	105	24	131	29	236	27	171	29	171	26	342	27	578	27
Disagree	203	47	240	52	443	50	203	34	249	38	452	36	895	42

a. N = number of samples. The percents ignore decimals, are the closest in round numbers, and, hence, in the totals may not appear as the average of the East and the West percents. Where the percents do not total 100, the discrepancy is due to questions left unanswered.

85

TABLE 22A[a]
Importance of Nursery School Education

	WEST						EAST						TOTAL	
	1–5 years		Over 10 years		Total		1–5 years		Over 10 years		Total		Number	
	N = 431	Per-cent	N = 459	Per-cent	N = 890	Per-cent	N = 593	Per-cent	N = 659	Per-cent	N = 1252	Per-cent	N = 2142	Per-cent
Required of All Children Before They Enter Regular Schools														
Agree	129	30	143	31	272	31	369	62	418	63	787	63	1059	49
Undecided	68	16	48	10	116	13	105	18	105	16	210	17	326	15
Disagree	228	53	260	57	488	55	107	18	116	18	223	18	711	33
Provided by the Government for Parents Who Wish Their Children to Have These Experiences														
Agree	223	52	227	49	450	51	363	61	432	66	795	63	1245	58
Undecided	48	11	50	11	98	11	111	19	106	16	217	17	315	15
Disagree	155	36	172	37	327	37	102	17	86	13	188	15	515	24
Provided for Parents by Private Agencies														
Agree	151	35	149	32	300	34	215	36	277	42	492	39	792	37
Undecided	117	27	97	21	214	24	237	40	208	32	445	36	659	31
Disagree	155	36	202	44	357	40	118	20	130	20	248	20	605	28
Strongly Discouraged and Parents Urged to Keep Their Children at Home Until They Reach School Age														
Agree	63	15	96	21	159	18	111	19	108	16	219	17	378	18
Undecided	51	12	65	14	116	13	100	17	150	23	250	20	366	17
Disagree	311	72	283	62	594	67	355	60	358	54	713	57	1307	61

a. N = number of samples. The percents ignore decimals, are the closest in round numbers, and, hence, in the totals may not appear as the average of the East and the West percents. Where the percents do not total 100, the discrepancy is due to questions left unanswered.

teachers were a shade more liberal in feeling this form of education is needed; in the West, the younger teachers were a bit more liberal.

Because procedures for promotion to the next level above primary education vary widely from country to country, a question was included to learn the teachers' attitudes toward some of the procedures commonly followed. Table 23A gives the results obtained.

The promotion procedures favored most strongly by teachers in the West were satisfactory school record in the primary school and the recommendation of the teachers and the principal or school head. While teachers in the East also approved these methods, they did not do so as strongly. Moreover, they gave greater support to intelligence tests and governmental examinations than did teachers in the West. Neither region thought highly of so-called standardized achievement tests as a possible basis for promotion. There was but one point of rather sharp disagreement among the age groups. Older teachers in the East did not wish to rely on a satisfactory school record as the basis of promotion, whereas most of the younger teachers did. For other methods, both groups in the East and the West were in close agreement. Older teachers in the West were slightly more skeptical of intelligence tests than were their younger colleagues. They also would rely to a slightly lesser degree on recommendations of teachers for promotion.

While teachers ordinarily have little voice in legal matters involving members of their profession, they were asked to state what kind of control they preferred concerning the regulations under which they operate (Table 24A). Both regions voted strongly for a middle ground between high centralized control and local control — for a control in which certain features such as licensing, placement, and salary were administered under central control and in which curriculum, textbooks, and pupil advancement came under local control. There was almost complete agreement among younger and older teachers in the East and the West concerning the degree of decentralization of school administration they deemed expedient for best results in the schools.

On the question of the type of teacher organization they considered best for them, the teachers as a whole were sharply divided (Table 25A). The West slightly favored an organization which catered exclusively to primary teachers, but the East was more in favor of an all-inclusive organization for all members of the profession. No question was raised concerning separate organizations for men and women, although

TABLE 23Aᵃ

Admission Procedures to Higher Schools

	WEST 1-5 years (N = 431)		WEST Over 10 years (N = 459)		WEST Total (N = 890)		EAST 1-5 years (N = 593)		EAST Over 10 years (N = 659)		EAST Total (N = 1252)		TOTAL Number (N = 2142)	
	N	Per-cent	N	Per-cent	N	Per-cent	N	Per-cent	N	Per-cent	N	Per-cent	N	Per-cent
Intelligence Tests														
Agree	182	42	154	34	336	38	375	63	442	67	817	65	1153	54
Undecided	76	18	79	17	155	17	117	20	111	17	228	18	383	18
Disagree	167	39	208	45	375	42	90	15	81	12	171	14	546	25
Examinations Made and Administered by the Government														
Agree	154	36	156	34	310	35	310	52	366	56	676	54	986	46
Undecided	63	15	47	10	110	12	138	23	123	19	261	21	371	17
Disagree	207	48	239	52	446	50	131	22	139	21	270	22	716	33
Satisfactory Record of Work in the Primary School														
Agree	369	86	391	85	760	85	424	72	108	16	532	42	1292	60
Undecided	22	5	35	8	57	6	112	19	150	23	262	21	319	15
Disagree	36	8	22	5	58	7	49	8	358	54	407	33	465	22
Recommendation of Teachers and Principal or Head of the Primary School														
Agree	319	74	315	69	634	71	375	63	442	67	817	65	1451	68
Undecided	38	9	51	11	89	10	117	20	111	17	228	18	317	15
Disagree	70	16	84	18	154	17	90	15	81	12	171	14	325	15
Examinations Made by Professional Organizations Based on Research														
Agree	157	36	176	38	333	37	267	45	272	41	539	43	872	41
Undecided	88	20	94	20	182	20	155	26	171	26	326	26	508	24
Disagree	180	42	168	37	348	39	149	25	182	28	331	26	679	32

a. N = number of samples. The percents ignore decimals, are the closest in round numbers, and, hence, in the totals may not appear as the average

88

TABLE 24A[a]

Degree of Centralization for Schools

	WEST						EAST						TOTAL	
	1–5 years		Over 10 years		Total		1–5 years		Over 10 years		Total		Number	
	N = 431	Per-cent	N = 459	Per-cent	N = 890	Per-cent	N = 593	Per-cent	N = 659	Per-cent	N = 1252	Per-cent	N = 2142	Per-cent
Highly centralized system of licensing and placing of teachers, with a uniform salary scale, uniform curriculum, textbooks, and common standards of achievement for pupils	70	16	81	18	151	17	151	25	160	24	311	25	462	22
A centralized system of licensing and placing teachers, uniform salary scale, but local variations in curriculum, textbooks, and standards of achievement for pupils	306	71	322	70	628	71	322	54	361	55	683	55	1311	61
Completely de-centralized system with local regulations and variations for teachers and for pupils	49	11	49	11	98	11	108	18	129	20	237	19	335	16

a. N = number of samples. The percents ignore decimals, are the closest in round numbers, and, hence, in the totals may not appear as the average of the East and the West percents. Where the percents do not total 100, the discrepancy is due to questions left unanswered.

TABLE 25A[a]
Type of Teacher Organization

	WEST			EAST			TOTAL
	1–5 years	Over 10 years	Total	1–5 years	Over 10 years	Total	Number
	N = 431 Per cent	N = 459 Per cent	N = 890 Per cent	N = 593 Per cent	N = 659 Per cent	N = 1252 Per cent	N = 2142 Per cent
For primary teachers only	199 46	212 46	411 46	185 31	275 42	460 37	871 41
For secondary and primary teachers	76 18	70 15	146 16	102 17	98 15	200 16	346 16
For all levels of teachers: primary, secondary, university, technical	151 35	173 38	324 36	297 50	279 42	594 47	918 43

a. N = number of samples. The percents ignore decimals, are the closest in round numbers, and, hence, in the totals may not appear as the average of the East and the West percents. Where the percents do not total 100, the discrepancy is due to questions left unanswered.

these now exist in several of the cities surveyed. Table 25A shows no great disparity between older and younger teachers in their ideas about the best form of teacher organization to meet their needs. In the East a slightly greater proportion of older teachers would prefer the more exclusive type, devoted particularly to primary teachers.

The question of how teachers can best be disciplined for neglect of duty or for other violations of their professional code is a touchy one. There are those who contend that such discipline should be the prerogative of professional organizations, which in the interests of building prestige and status for their profession should have the power to maintain the standards which have been set for the individual members. Table 26A shows that both East and West did not generally hold with this point of view, for only one-fifth in the West and one-third in the East indicated that discipline should be in the hands of teachers' organizations. Roughly one-half in each region felt that the rules should be made by the ministry of education or by the principal or head of the school. They did not generally favor democratic procedures whereby teachers of the school themselves decided on disciplinary measures, but they did suggest that the individual teacher has the responsibility for self-discipline.

Teachers in the West were more strongly in favor of permanent dismissal for just cause than were those in the East. However, concerning the temporary reduction of salary as a disciplinary measure, the position was reversed. A letter of apology was considered important, particularly by teachers in the East, while teachers in the West overwhelmingly believed that matters of discipline could best be cared for as a private matter between teacher and principal or other school official. One type of disciplinary measure not often resorted to in the West received commendation in the East; namely, removal of a teacher to an undesirable location. Forty-one percent voted for this practice.

Certain official policies regarding teachers are presented in Table 27A. Discrimination against women, especially in employment policies, has been present in nearly all countries of the world. The teachers in the present study believed strongly that women should not terminate their teaching careers because of marriage, but roughly about 50 percent felt that paid maternity leaves should be provided (the East 56 percent as against 45 percent in the West on the latter point). They did indicate that salaries should be equal for men and women (the West 74 percent as against 62 percent in the East).

91

TABLE 26A[a]

Control and Discipline of Teachers

| | WEST | | | | | | EAST | | | | | | TOTAL | |
| | 1–5 years | | Over 10 years | | Total | | 1–5 years | | Over 10 years | | Total | | Number | |
The Best Means of Control	N = 431	Per-cent	N = 459	Per-cent	N = 890	Per-cent	N = 593	Per-cent	N = 659	Per-cent	N = 1252	Per-cent	N = 2142	Per-cent
Laws passed by the government	77	18	94	20	171	19	210	35	267	41	477	38	648	30
Rules made by the ministry of education	176	41	245	53	421	47	287	48	293	44	580	46	1001	47
Regulations by supervisors and inspectors	207	48	230	50	437	49	164	28	138	21	302	24	739	35
Regulations by the principal or head of the school	268	62	245	53	513	58	244	41	315	48	559	45	1072	50
Regulations made by teachers' organizations	74	17	96	21	170	19	197	33	204	31	401	32	571	27
Regulations made by organizations of parents	12	3	4	1	16	2	39	7	54	8	93	7	109	5
Regulations made by the teachers of the school	154	36	135	29	289	32	218	37	244	37	462	37	751	35
Individual teacher's own self-discipline	284	66	287	63	571	64	336	57	359	54	695	56	1266	59

92

TABLE 26A—continued

Type of Discipline (Depending on Seriousness of Offense)	WEST						EAST						TOTAL	
	1–5 years		Over 10 years		Total		1–5 years		Over 10 years		Total		Number	
	N = 431	Per-cent	N = 459	Per-cent	N = 890	Per-cent	N = 593	Per-cent	N = 659	Per-cent	N = 1252	Per-cent	N = 2142	Per-cent
Permanent dismissal	213	49	218	47	431	48	163	27	171	26	334	27	765	36
Temporary dismissal with loss of pay	103	24	124	27	227	26	171	29	168	25	339	27	566	26
Permanent reduction of salary	7	2	7	2	14	2	80	13	95	14	175	14	189	9
Temporary reduction of salary	34	8	58	13	92	10	252	42	266	40	518	41	610	28
Removal to an undesirable position or area	22	5	50	11	72	8	218	37	292	44	510	41	582	27
Letter of apology to the principal, head, or other administrative officer	150	35	162	35	312	35	277	47	301	46	578	46	890	42
Public reprimand from principal, head, or other officer	23	5	19	4	42	5	177	30	174	26	351	28	393	18
Private reprimand from principal, head, or other official	382	89	423	92	805	90	322	54	413	63	735	59	1540	72

a. N = number of samples. The percents ignore decimals, are the closest in round numbers, and, hence, in the totals may not appear as the average of the East and the West percents. Where the percents do not total 100, the discrepancy is due to questions left unanswered.

TABLE 27A[a]

Special Regulations for Teachers

	WEST						EAST						TOTAL	
	1–5 years		Over 10 years		Total		1–5 years		Over 10 years		Total		Number	
	N = 431	Per-cent	N = 459	Per-cent	N = 890	Per-cent	N = 593	Per-cent	N = 659	Per-cent	N = 1252	Per-cent	N = 2142	Per-cent
When a Woman Marries She Should be Required to Stop Teaching														
Agree	19	4	32	7	51	6	75	13	114	17	189	15	240	11
Undecided	8	2	29	6	37	4	64	11	72	11	136	11	173	8
Disagree	401	93	388	85	789	89	424	72	436	66	860	69	1649	77
Men Teachers Should Have a Higher Salary than Women														
Agree	103	24	69	15	172	19	110	19	165	25	275	22	447	21
Undecided	28	6	21	5	49	6	80	13	63	10	143	11	192	9
Disagree	297	69	360	78	657	74	386	65	393	60	779	62	1436	67
Teachers Should Not be Paid Salaries According to the Years They Teach, But According to Merit														
Agree	91	21	53	12	144	16	220	37	232	35	452	36	596	28
Undecided	64	15	66	14	130	15	151	25	147	22	298	24	428	20
Disagree	272	63	324	71	596	67	207	35	252	38	459	37	1055	49

TABLE 27A—continued

| | WEST | | | | | | EAST | | | | | | TOTAL | |
| | 1–5 years | | Over 10 years | | Total | | 1–5 years | | Over 10 years | | Total | | Number | |
	N = 431	Per-cent	N = 459	Per-cent	N = 890	Per-cent	N = 593	Per-cent	N = 659	Per-cent	N = 1252	Per-cent	N = 2142	Per-cent
If Teachers Discontinue Teaching to Take Other Positions, They Should Not be Permitted to Return to Teaching														
Agree	18	4	33	7	51	6	130	22	156	24	286	23	337	16
Undecided	15	3	28	6	43	5	130	22	119	18	249	20	292	14
Disagree	396	92	387	84	783	88	314	53	353	54	667	53	1450	68
Women Should be Allowed Liberal Maternity Leaves With Full Pay														
Agree	185	43	218	47	403	45	435	73	272	41	707	56	1110	52
Undecided	40	9	44	10	84	9	52	9	171	26	223	18	307	14
Disagree	203	47	187	41	390	44	89	15	182	28	271	22	661	31
Teachers Should Receive Liberal Allowances for Sick Leave and Disability														
Agree	369	86	376	82	745	84	478	81	566	86	1044	83	1789	84
Undecided	31	7	44	10	75	8	62	10	40	6	102	8	177	8
Disagree	27	6	32	7	50	7	39	7	38	6	77	6	136	6

a. N = number of samples. The percents ignore decimals, are the closest in round numbers, and, hence, in the totals may not appear as the average of the East and the West percents. Where the percents do not total 100, the discrepancy is due to questions left unanswered.

95

The West strongly rejected the idea of merit pay (two-thirds were against it) while as many teachers in the East were for as against it. Both regions agreed that teachers should be permitted to return to the profession, if for any reason they left it to try other work, and that liberal allowances should be provided for sick leave and disability.

How to reward the outstanding performance of teachers is a difficult question and one of great importance. In Table 28A the preferences are indicated. The methods receiving highest approval in the West were simple promotion, promotion to teach in a higher school (presumably a secondary school), and self-satisfaction. (Virtue is its own reward!) Teachers in the East were much more in favor of increased pay or allowances above regular scale and promotion, but were less interested in promotion to teach at a higher level, perhaps because they could not be qualified on the basis of past training. They valued citations and medals much more than teachers in the West (47 percent as against 18 percent). Both East and West thought little of holding office in a teachers' organization as a form of recognition for service well performed.

In the East, older teachers were slightly more in favor of promotions, added pay, citations, choice of teaching position than were the younger. The younger were more interested in promotion to teach in a higher school and to serve in a teachers' organization than were the older. In the West, the older teachers felt promotion to teach in a higher school was more important than did the younger teachers. The younger tended to favor merit pay, citations and choice of teaching position. Both old and young in the West were more content with self-satisfaction than they were in the East.

Tenure has traditionally been one of the most prized fringe benefits of the teaching profession. With it teachers have felt reasonably safe from the pressures of government or from local whims which may be at variance with their professional knowledge or commitment. In the present study, the teachers were asked to react to several possibilities as grounds for their dismissal (Table 29A). Three-fourths in both regions felt that immoral conduct (not defined) should be grounds for dismissal. Sixty percent of teachers in the West believed that failure to meet their responsibilities could also be considered adequate grounds. Teachers in the East were more willing to accept teaching ideas contrary to government policy (46 percent) as a valid reason than were teachers in the West (29 percent). With the issue of Communism considered crucial in the West at the present time, it is

TABLE 28A[a]

Methods of Recognizing and Rewarding Good Teachers

| | WEST | | | | | | EAST | | | | | | TOTAL | |
| | 1-5 years | | Over 10 years | | Total | | 1-5 years | | Over 10 years | | Total | | Number | |
	N = 431	Per-cent	N = 459	Per-cent	N = 890	Per-cent	N = 593	Per-cent	N = 659	Per-cent	N = 1252	Per-cent	N = 2142	Per-cent
Simple Promotion														
Agree	211	49	257	56	468	53	343	58	437	66	780	62	1248	58
Undecided	78	18	84	18	162	18	122	21	129	20	251	20	413	19
Disagree	136	32	97	21	233	26	101	17	72	11	173	14	406	19
Increased Pay or Allowances, Above Regular Scale														
Agree	181	42	162	35	343	39	438	74	520	79	958	77	1301	61
Undecided	58	13	62	14	120	13	76	13	56	8	132	11	252	12
Disagree	184	43	212	46	396	44	65	11	68	10	133	11	529	25
Promotion to a Higher School														
Agree	263	61	303	66	566	64	242	41	214	32	456	36	1022	48
Undecided	76	18	89	19	165	19	142	24	197	30	339	27	504	24
Disagree	162	38	158	34	320	36	182	31	219	33	401	32	721	34
Citations, Medals, Honors														
Agree	91	21	71	15	162	18	270	46	324	49	594	47	756	35
Undecided	59	14	68	15	127	14	147	25	158	24	305	24	432	20
Disagree	267	62	298	65	565	63	142	24	151	23	293	23	858	40

97

TABLE 28A—continued

| | WEST | | | | | | EAST | | | | | | TOTAL | |
| | 1–5 years | | Over 10 years | | Total | | 1–5 years | | Over 10 years | | Total | | Number | |
	N = 431	Per-cent	N = 459	Per-cent	N = 890	Per-cent	N = 593	Per-cent	N = 659	Per-cent	N = 1252	Per-cent	N = 2142	Per-cent
Choice of Teaching Position[b]														
Agree	210	49	205	45	415	47	195	33	243	37	438	40	853	50
Undecided	93	22	92	20	185	21	122	21	129	20	251	23	436	23
Disagree	117	27	138	30	255	29	133	22	141	21	274	26	529	25
Selection to Office in Teachers' Organization[b]														
Agree	70	16	52	11	122	14	132	22	145	22	277	26	399	23
Undecided	125	29	98	21	223	25	132	22	150	23	282	27	505	24
Disagree	226	52	282	61	508	57	185	63	213	32	398	35	906	42
Self-satisfaction of Work Well Done; No Other Reward Needed														
Agree	260	60	286	62	546	61	233	39	224	34	457	37	1003	51
Undecided	50	12	56	12	106	12	117	20	135	20	252	20	358	20
Disagree	114	26	110	24	224	25	218	37	264	40	482	38	706	38

a. N = number of samples. The percents ignore decimals, are the closest in round numbers, and, hence, in the totals may not appear as the average of the East and the West percents. Where the percents do not total 100, the discrepancy is due to questions left unanswered.
b. Omitted from the Japanese questionnaire. The percents have been adjusted to allow for these omissions.

98

TABLE 29A[a]

Grounds for Dismissal of Teachers

| | WEST | | | | | | EAST | | | | | | TOTAL | |
| | 1–5 years | | Over 10 years | | Total | | 1–5 years | | Over 10 years | | Total | | Number | |
	N = 431	Per-cent	N = 459	Per-cent	N = 890	Per-cent	N = 593	Per-cent	N = 659	Per-cent	N = 1252	Per-cent	N = 2142	Per-cent
Immoral Conduct														
Agree	301	70	354	77	655	74	388	65	498	76	886	71	1541	72
Undecided	52	12	49	11	101	11	103	17	70	11	173	14	274	13
Disagree	71	16	37	8	108	12	91	15	75	11	166	13	274	13
Harsh Discipline of Children														
Agree	118	27	150	33	268	30	213	36	242	37	455	36	723	34
Undecided	109	25	125	27	234	26	170	29	183	28	353	28	587	27
Disagree	200	46	165	36	365	41	179	30	191	28	370	30	735	34
Laziness or Failure to Meet Their Responsibilities in Teaching and Maintaining Discipline														
Agree	261	61	276	60	537	60	284	48	301	46	585	47	1122	52
Undecided	76	18	87	19	163	18	157	26	166	25	323	26	486	23
Disagree	90	21	84	18	174	20	127	21	166	25	293	23	467	22
Teaching Ideas Contrary to Government Policy														
Agree	128	30	131	29	259	29	270	46	305	46	575	46	834	39
Undecided	100	23	112	24	212	24	112	19	156	24	268	21	480	22
Disagree	196	45	193	42	389	44	181	31	169	26	350	28	739	35

TABLE 29A—*continued*

| | WEST | | | | | | EAST | | | | | | TOTAL | |
| | 1–5 years | | Over 10 years | | Total | | 1–5 years | | Over 10 years | | Total | | Number | |
	N = 431	Per-cent	N = 459	Per-cent	N = 890	Per-cent	N = 593	Per-cent	N = 659	Per-cent	N = 1252	Per-cent	N = 2142	Per-cent
Frequent or Prolonged Illness														
Agree	59	14	68	15	127	14	137	23	125	19	262	21	389	18
Undecided	85	20	95	21	180	20	168	28	192	29	360	29	540	25
Disagree	283	66	276	60	559	63	259	44	316	48	575	46	1134	53
Disagreement with Principal or Other School or Government Official														
Agree	21	5	26	6	47	5	73	12	72	11	145	12	192	9
Undecided	36	8	48	10	84	9	115	19	118	18	233	19	317	15
Disagree	269	62	364	79	733	82	370	62	427	65	797	64	1530	71
Lack of Sufficient Knowledge of Their Subject Matter														
Agree	151	35	159	35	310	35	185	31	200	30	385	31	695	32
Undecided	101	23	129	28	230	26	176	30	198	30	374	30	604	28
Disagree	176	41	149	32	325	37	201	34	228	35	429	34	754	35

a. N = number of samples. The percents ignore decimals, are the closest in round numbers, and, hence, in the totals may not appear as the average of the East and the West percents. Where the percents do not total 100, the discrepancy is due to questions left unanswered.

surprising that so few teachers there were willing to admit that disagreement with government was a serious matter. Teachers of both regions were rather ambivalent about what to do about the matter of harsh discipline to children and about the teacher who did not know his subject matter sufficiently. Both regions were agreed that prolonged illness or disagreement with a school official should not constitute grounds for dismissal.

Older teachers, both in the East and in the West, were slightly more agreed that immoral conduct was a legitimate cause for dismissal. On other grounds for dismissal there was practically no disagreement among older and younger teachers.

Teachers have long considered retirement benefits of great importance in attracting good members into the profession. Most countries now make some sort of provision for teachers after a stated number of years of service, which varies widely from country to country, as do the benefits provided. Because of such wide variations only general questions regarding the teachers' opinions on retirement were asked. Their replies are included in Table 30A.

The East and the West were pretty well agreed that the same regulations should apply to men and women and that the widow and minor children of a teacher who dies before retirement should be provided for. (No question was included concerning the dependents of a female teacher who is deceased.) They were likewise agreed on full benefits for the teacher forced to retire early because of serious illness. They were, however ambivalent concerning the age of compulsory retirement. Generally, however, teachers in the West were not in favor of later retirement than is now permitted, while those in the East did not desire retirement earlier than is now compulsory. These wishes may be due in part to the expected life span of the average individual, which is at present longer in the West than in the East. In general, older teachers were more liberal in their point of view than were the younger ones. In the East the older teachers were more in favor of the same regulations for men and women, provision for spouses upon death of a teacher and early retirement with full benefits for serious illness. Teachers of the two age groups in the West were more in agreement. Older teachers wanted the same provisions for men and women to a greater degree, but did not want earlier retirement.

While the activities of professional organizations are partially regulated by law in all countries, there are spheres where they are not free to act as they see fit. The most often restricted activity is that of

101

TABLE 30A[a]

Retirement Regulations

| | WEST | | | | | | EAST[b] | | | | | | TOTAL | |
| | 1–5 years | | Over 10 years | | Total | | 1–5 years | | Over 10 years | | Total | | Number | |
	N = 431	Per-cent	N = 459	Per-cent	N = 890	Per-cent	N = 593	Per-cent	N = 659	Per-cent	N = 1252	Per-cent	N = 2142	Per-cent
Same Regulations for Men and Women														
Agree	358	83	422	92	780	88	386	64	464	70	850	68	1630	76
Undecided	31	7	15	3	46	5	42	8	25	3	67	5	113	5
Disagree	39	9	15	3	54	6	49	8	55	8	104	8	158	7
Provision for the Widow and Minor Children When a Teacher Dies Before Retirement														
Agree	371	86	389	85	760	85	418	69	506	76	924	74	1684	79
Undecided	43	10	43	9	86	10	41	7	28	4	69	5	155	7
Disagree	15	3	14	3	29	3	22	4	14	2	36	3	65	3
Retirement Made Compulsory at a Later Age Than Now Required														
Agree	58	13	75	16	133	15	206	34	231	35	437	35	570	27
Undecided	97	23	69	15	166	19	113	19	114	16	227	18	393	18
Disagree	273	63	300	65	573	64	149	25	189	28	338	27	911	43
Retirement Made Compulsory at an Earlier Age Than Now Required														
Agree	81	19	137	30	218	24	78	14	85	13	163	13	381	18
Undecided	113	26	95	21	208	23	101	17	70	11	171	14	379	18
Disagree	235	55	315	69	450	51	288	48	362	55	650	52	1100	51
Earlier Retirement with Full Medical Disability Benefits														
Agree	327	76	361	79	688	77	363	61	455	66	818	65	1506	70
Undecided	67	16	59	13	126	14	70	12	45	7	115	9	241	11
Disagree	35	8	31	7	66	7	48	8	44	7	92	7	158	7

a. N = number of samples. The percents ignore decimals, are the closest in round numbers, and, hence, in the totals may not appear as the average of the East and the West percents. Where the percents do not total 100, the discrepancy is due to questions left unanswered.

organizing strikes. Three-fourths of the teachers in the West and one-half in the East felt that strikes should not be organized, but those in the West were strongly in favor of putting other forms of pressure on the government (Table 31A). Both regions wanted their professional organizations to publish newspapers and professional journals, to set up workshops and to promote other means of professional growth. They favored, but not strongly, the promotion of social activities by the professional organizations.

In both East and West older and younger teachers think very much alike. The only matter of seeming greater importance to younger teachers in both East and West is that more of them would like their professional organizations to provide local meeting places and organize social groups.

Though most of the teachers of primary schools are at present trained in specialized institutions provided only for them, the teachers surveyed were very uncertain that this arrangement is the proper one for their training (Table 32A). Teachers in the East were somewhat more inclined to accept segregation of prospective teachers at this level, while those in the West were more in favor of common training institutions where students preparing to teach at both primary and secondary levels have opportunity for some study in common. Both older and younger teachers were in agreement concerning the type of teacher training institution they preferred for primary teachers. Older teachers in the East and younger teachers in the West showed slight preference for the institution set up specifically for training at the primary level. The older teachers in the West were more liberal than the younger teachers in feeling that multi-level training programs are preferable.

With the constant change in educational thinking and in the world in general, the demand for in-service education of teachers has increased tremendously in the last decades. Many countries now give beginning teachers only temporary licenses which must be periodically renewed. Some encourage in-service training through monetary rewards.

All of the means suggested in Table 33A received support in both East and West. There was more than 90 percent support of reading professional books and more than 80 percent support of professional meetings as means of in-service growth. Teachers in the West were more convinced than those in the East that returning to teacher training schools for additional work was important. Teachers in the East

103

TABLE 31A[a]

Proper Measures for Professional Organizations

	WEST						EAST[b]						TOTAL	
	1–5 years		Over 10 years		Total		1–5 years		Over 10 years		Total		Number	
	N = 431	Per-cent	N = 459	Per-cent	N = 890	Per-cent	N = 593	Per-cent	N = 659	Per-cent	N = 1252	Per-cent	N = 2142	Per-cent
Organizing and Leading Strikes to Get Needed Salary Raises or Other Benefits														
Agree	66	15	41	9	107	12	81	14	99	15	180	14	287	13
Undecided	59	14	44	10	103	12	99	17	125	19	224	18	327	15
Disagree	300	70	351	76	651	73	295	50	316	48	611	49	1262	59
Putting Pressures other Than Strikes on the Government for Better Salaries and other Benefits														
Agree	312	72	317	69	629	71	190	32	233	35	423	34	1052	49
Undecided	49	11	49	11	98	11	89	15	117	18	206	16	304	14
Disagree	60	14	73	16	133	15	198	33	194	29	392	31	525	25
Publishing Newspapers and Professional Journals														
Agree	368	85	380	83	748	84	350	59	400	61	750	60	1498	70
Undecided	41	10	45	10	86	10	83	14	93	14	176	14	262	12
Disagree	12	3	15	3	27	3	47	8	48	7	95	8	122	6

TABLE 31A—*continued*

| | WEST | | | | | | EAST | | | | | | TOTAL | |
| | 1–5 years | | Over 10 years | | Total | | 1–5 years | | Over 10 years | | Total | | Number | |
	N = 431	Per-cent	N = 459	Per-cent	N = 890	Per-cent	N = 593	Per-cent	N = 659	Per-cent	N = 1252	Per-cent	N = 2142	Per-cent
Setting Up Workshops and Discussion Groups, and Furthering other Means of Professional Growth														
Agree	369	86	391	85	760	85	365	62	410	62	775	62	1535	72
Undecided	41	10	36	8	77	9	62	10	82	12	144	12	221	10
Disagree	12	3	18	4	30	3	51	9	50	8	101	8	131	6
Providing Local Meeting Places and Organizing Social Groups														
Agree	230	53	228	50	458	51	270	46	241	37	511	41	969	45
Undecided	123	29	141	31	264	30	114	19	121	18	235	19	499	23
Disagree	71	16	71	15	142	16	57	10	78	12	135	11	277	13

a. N = number of samples. The percents ignore decimals, are the closest in round numbers, and, hence, in the totals may not appear as the average of the East and the West percents. Where the percents do not total 100, the discrepancy is due to questions left unanswered.
b. Thailand and Pakistan omitted a number of the questions. The percents have not been adjusted to account for the omissions.

105

TABLE 32Aᵃ

Type of Teacher Training Institution

	WEST						EAST						TOTAL	
	1–5 years		Over 10 years		Total		1–5 years		Over 10 years		Total		Number	
	N = 431	Per-cent	N = 459	Per-cent	N = 890	Per-cent	N = 593	Per-cent	N = 659	Per-cent	N = 1252	Per-cent	N = 2142	Per-cent
Training institutions set up specifically to prepare primary teachers	144	33	133	29	277	31	229	39	297	45	526	42	803	37
Common training institutions which prepare both primary and secondary teachers, but with separate curriculums	90	21	107	23	197	22	136	23	119	18	255	20	452	21
Common training institutions for both primary and secondary teachers, with some general curriculums in common	131	30	123	27	254	29	75	13	82	12	157	13	411	19
Almost identical training programs for primary and secondary teachers with a small amount of specialization for each group	56	13	93	20	149	17	142	24	152	23	294	23	443	21

a. N = number of samples. The percents ignore decimals, are the closest in round numbers, and, hence, in the totals may not appear as the average of the East and the West percents. Where the percents do not total 100, the discrepancy is due to questions left unanswered.

Methods of Inservice Training

| | WEST | | | | | | EAST | | | | | | TOTAL | |
| | 1–5 years | | Over 10 years | | Total | | 1–5 years | | Over 10 years | | Total | | Number | |
	N = 431	Per-cent	N = 459	Per-cent	N = 890	Per-cent	N = 593	Per-cent	N = 659	Per-cent	N = 1252	Per-cent	N = 2142	Per-cent
Reading Professional Books and Magazines														
Agree	397	92	439	96	836	94	542	91	613	93	1155	92	1991	93
Undecided	25	6	9	2	34	4	22	4	17	3	39	3	73	3
Disagree	8	2	4	1	12	1	18	3	17	3	35	3	47	2
Attending Professional Meetings and Discussion Groups														
Agree	339	79	411	90	750	84	470	79	589	89	1059	85	1809	84
Undecided	65	15	35	8	100	11	82	14	35	5	117	9	217	10
Disagree	27	6	6	1	33	4	31	5	19	3	50	4	83	4
Returning to Teacher Training Schools for Additional Courses														
Agree	315	73	320	70	635	71	310	52	352	53	662	53	1297	61
Undecided	66	15	73	16	139	16	115	19	135	20	250	20	389	18
Disagree	49	11	52	11	101	11	148	25	149	23	297	24	398	19
Studying to be Qualified for the Next Higher Level of Teaching														
Agree	194	45	202	44	396	44	391	66	431	65	822	66	1218	57
Undecided	109	25	124	27	233	26	116	20	131	20	247	20	480	22
Disagree	123	29	118	26	241	27	70	12	79	12	149	12	390	18
Carrying on Independent Research														
Agree	254	59	250	54	504	57	436	74	484	73	920	73	1424	66
Undecided	112	26	142	31	254	29	76	13	87	13	163	13	417	19
Disagree	63	15	53	12	116	13	68	11	68	10	136	11	252	12

a. N = number of samples. The percents ignore decimals. The percents are the closest in round numbers, and, hence, in the totals may not appear as the average of the East and the West percents. Where the percents do not total 100, the discrepancy is due to questions left unanswered.

were more interested in studying to qualify for the next higher level of teaching and in carrying on some kind of independent research. Since the questionnaire did not define the term "research," it is not known just what activity the teachers had in mind.

In both East and West older teachers were more interested in professional meetings than were the younger ones. To a slight degree, they read more professional materials. Younger teachers showed slightly more interest in independent research, particularly in the West.

The licensing of teachers by examination both in general subjects and in teaching methods was judged satisfactory by a majority of teachers in both East and West (Table 34A). A higher proportion of teachers in the West (91 percent) than in the East (64 percent) believed that a satisfactory record of work in the teacher training institution was important. Neither region placed much value on recommendations made by instructors in the teacher training institutions.

Table 34A denotes some differences of opinion between older and younger teachers in both East and West concerning methods of licensing teachers. Older teachers in the West were more in favor of subject matter examinations than were younger teachers. Older teachers, in both East and West, favored tests in pedagogical subjects. Demonstration teaching was thought proper by more older teachers in the East and more younger teachers in the West. Younger teachers in the West leaned more toward letters of recommendation from instructors than did older ones.

The final items of the questionnaire dealt with the degree of chauvinism which the teachers felt. Definite differences between the East and the West are apparent in Table 35A. While 70 percent of teachers in the West disagreed with the statement that their own culture is the superior way of life, only 13 percent of those in the East did so. Likewise is the difference great in the comparison of past history of one's country to the present: 76 percent in the West and 27 percent in the East disagreed with the statement that the past culture is superior to the present. There was divided opinion on the equality of cultural worth in all nations, but agreement on the notion that every nation has the potential to develop a high culture qualifying it to live in equality with all other nations. In both East and West no differences of opinion were noted among older and younger teachers concerning their ideas about their own and other nations' cultures.

While teachers in the East and in the West may disagree in assessing

108

Methods of Licensing Teachers

	WEST						EAST						TOTAL	
	1–5 years		Over 10 years		Total		1–5 years		Over 10 years		Total		Number	
	N = 431	Per-cent	N = 459	Per-cent	N = 890	Per-cent	N = 593	Per-cent	N = 659	Per-cent	N = 1252	Per-cent	N = 2142	Per-cent
Passing an Examination in General Subjects Such as History, Mathematics														
Agree	278	65	345	76	623	70	360	61	424	64	784	63	1407	66
Undecided	64	15	52	11	116	13	85	14	87	13	172	14	288	13
Disagree	85	20	54	12	139	16	133	22	127	19	260	21	399	19
Passing an Examination in Pedagogy, Psychology, Teaching Methods														
Agree	319	74	353	77	672	76	484	82	569	86	1053	84	1725	81
Undecided	46	11	50	11	96	11	53	9	41	6	94	8	190	9
Disagree	62	14	50	11	112	13	45	8	39	6	84	7	196	9
Passing an Examination by Demonstration Teaching														
Agree	365	85	367	80	732	82	338	57	412	63	750	60	1482	69
Undecided	27	6	40	9	67	8	134	23	134	20	268	21	335	16
Disagree	34	8	46	10	80	9	105	18	91	14	196	16	276	13
A Satisfactory Record of Work in Teacher Training Studies														
Agree	396	92	415	90	811	91	363	61	437	66	800	64	1611	75
Undecided	15	3	22	5	37	4	119	20	110	17	229	18	266	12
Disagree	14	3	17	4	31	3	98	17	97	15	195	16	226	11
Presenting Letters of Recommendation From Instructors in Teacher Training Schools														
Agree	167	39	149	32	316	36	135	23	162	25	297	24	613	29
Undecided	99	23	108	24	207	23	125	21	142	22	267	21	474	22
Disagree	162	38	189	41	351	39	317	53	326	49	643	51	994	46

a. N = number of samples. The percents ignore decimals, are the closest in round numbers, and, hence, in the totals may not appear as the average of the East and the West percents. Where the percents do not total 100, the discrepancy is due to questions left unanswered.

TABLE 35Aᵃ

Attitudes Toward Cultures

	WEST						EAST						TOTAL	
	1–5 years		Over 10 years		Total		1–5 years		Over 10 years		Total		Number	
	N = 431	Per-cent	N = 459	Per-cent	N = 890	Per-cent	N = 593	Per-cent	N = 659	Per-cent	N = 1252	Per-cent	N = 2142	Per-cent
The Culture of One's Own Country is the Superior Way of Life														
Agree	51	12	54	12	105	12	368	62	431	65	799	64	904	42
Undecided	58	13	72	16	130	15	119	20	112	17	231	18	361	17
Disagree	314	73	310	68	624	70	86	15	79	12	165	13	789	37
The Past Culture of One's Own Country was in Most Respects Superior to its Present Day Culture														
Agree	28	6	39	8	67	8	237	40	265	40	502	40	569	27
Undecided	46	11	69	15	115	13	180	30	180	27	360	29	475	22
Disagree	347	81	327	71	674	76	153	26	183	28	336	27	1010	47
The Cultures of All Nations are Equally Good														
Agree	145	34	139	30	284	32	259	44	251	38	510	41	794	37
Undecided	73	17	63	14	136	14	157	26	176	27	333	27	469	22
Disagree	201	47	230	50	431	48	154	26	204	31	358	29	789	37

TABLE 35A—*continued*

| | WEST | | | | | | EAST | | | | | | TOTAL | |
| | 1–5 years | | Over 10 years | | Total | | 1–5 years | | Over 10 years | | Total | | Number | |
	N = 431	Per cent	N = 459	Per cent	N = 890	Per cent	N = 593	Per cent	N = 659	Per cent	N = 1252	Per cent	N = 2142	Per cent
The Cultures of All Nations Including One's Own, Have Strengths and Weaknesses Which Have Historical Origins														
Agree	414	96	425	93	839	94	433	73	495	75	928	74	1767	82
Undecided	6	1	13	3	19	2	79	13	75	11	154	12	173	8
Disagree	4	1	5	1	9	1	45	8	41	6	86	7	95	4
Every Nation has the Potential for Developing a High Degree of Culture Which Fits its People to Live in Equality With All Other Peoples in the Modern World														
Agree	356	83	390	85	746	84	497	84	538	82	1035	83	1781	83
Undecided	44	10	28	6	72	8	52	9	56	8	108	9	180	8
Disagree	22	5	25	5	47	5	28	5	41	6	69	6	116	5

a. N = number of samples. The percents ignore decimals, are the closest in round numbers, and, hence, in the totals may not appear as the average of the East and the West percents. Where the percents do not total 100, the discrepancy is due to questions left unanswered.

the value of their own culture, they are agreed that teachers should use all means at their disposal for studying the modern world (Table 36A). Teachers in the West were more in favor of inviting teachers from other cultures to teach in their schools, while those in the East were more in favor of joining international organizations. Both regions were undecided about the value of compulsory foreign language training for teachers. Older teachers were somewhat more eager than younger ones in both East and West to study the modern world. They were more concerned about studying the work of the United Nations and in contacting foreigners in their own countries. However, younger teachers were more disposed toward inviting foreign teachers to work with them. In the East they were more in favor of membership in international organizations and in studying foreign languages. In the West, older teachers were more in favor of studying foreign languages.

In summary of the position taken by teachers in the West and in the East, it is clear that there is more general agreement than difference between the two areas.

There are relatively more male teachers in the East than in the West, although in both areas females predominate. A slightly higher proportion in the East are married.

Teachers in the West reported a longer period of training than those in the East. More in the East have been certified for teaching through examination rather than by completion of a regular training course. The West placed more emphasis on observation and teaching of children as part of the training course.

Teachers in the West appeared to be happier with their choice of vocation than were those in the East. Teachers in the East acknowledged, to a greater degree than did teachers in the West, that their ideas about education had changed considerably since they entered the profession.

While all of the teachers in the study are currently placed in large cities, more in the East had come originally from rural areas or small towns. Teachers in both areas favored remaining in a large city.

Religious training in the home was of far greater importance for the teachers in the West than for the East, but teachers of the latter area would impose stricter moral standards on teachers.

Although approximately one-half of the teachers in both areas said they did not supplement their income as teachers, more teachers in the West than in the East did so.

Teachers in the West were more inclined to vote for a salary scale

Methods and Means for Understanding the Modern World

	WEST			EAST			TOTAL
	1–5 years	Over 10 years	Total	1–5 years	Over 10 years	Total	Number
	N = 431 / Per-cent	N = 459 / Per-cent	N = 890 / Per-cent	N = 593 / Per-cent	N = 659 / Per-cent	N = 1252 / Per-cent	N = 2142 / Per-cent
Careful Study of the Work of the United Nations and its Agencies							
Agree	278 65	347 76	625 70	427 72	528 80	955 76	1580 74
Undecided	112 26	63 14	175 20	102 17	75 11	177 14	352 16
Disagree	33 8	26 6	59 7	43 7	27 4	70 6	129 6
Contact with Foreigners Living in One's Own Country							
Agree	284 66	315 69	599 67	370 62	437 66	807 64	1406 66
Undecided	96 22	95 21	191 21	146 25	144 22	290 23	481 22
Disagree	44 10	26 6	70 8	53 9	51 8	104 8	174 8
Inviting Teachers from Foreign Countries to Teach in the Schools							
Agree	337 78	328 71	665 75	339 57	362 55	701 56	1365 64
Undecided	59 14	76 17	135 15	146 25	174 26	320 26	455 21
Disagree	29 7	32 7	61 7	81 14	97 15	178 14	239 11

113

TABLE 36A—*continued*

| | WEST | | | | | | EAST | | | | | | TOTAL | |
| | 1–5 years | | Over 10 years | | Total | | 1–5 years | | Over 10 years | | Total | | Number | |
	N = 431	Per-cent	N = 459	Per-cent	N = 890	Per-cent	N = 593	Per-cent	N = 659	Per-cent	N = 1252	Per-cent	N = 2142	Per-cent
Study, Travel, and Teaching in Foreign Countries														
Agree	391	91	403	88	794	89	426	72	481	73	907	72	1701	79
Undecided	24	6	26	6	50	6	92	16	105	16	197	16	247	12
Disagree	11	3	10	2	21	2	51	9	49	7	100	8	121	6
Membership in Teachers' International Organizations														
Agree	250	58	277	60	527	59	441	74	452	69	893	71	1420	66
Undecided	124	29	112	24	236	27	84	14	122	19	206	16	442	21
Disagree	50	12	45	10	95	11	48	8	53	8	101	8	196	9
Compulsory Foreign Language Training														
Agree	122	28	191	42	313	35	276	47	243	37	519	41	832	39
Undecided	92	21	100	22	192	22	139	23	164	25	303	24	495	23
Disagree	197	46	145	32	342	38	151	25	221	34	372	30	714	33

a. N = number of samples. The percents ignore decimals, are the closest in round numbers, and, hence, in the totals may not appear as the average of the East and the West percents. Where the percents do not total 100, the discrepancy is due to questions left unanswered.

which included a pension after retirement, while those in the East definitely favored a salary scale which included more fringe benefits.

The West was more liberal than the East in feeling that a high proportion of teachers in the primary school might be women, but less liberal in allowing women to be the head of the school.

Teachers in both areas placed high prestige value on the professions of medicine, government official, university professor, and law. The majority of the teachers in both areas placed the primary teacher in a rank of low prestige. Furthermore, half of them believed their status had deteriorated in recent times. Low salary, too little opportunity for advancement and unattractive working conditions were given as the prime reasons for their low status.

Teachers in both areas spent, on the average, an hour or less a day in going to and from school, but more time than this on checking papers. Teachers in the East reported a heavier burden in this regard.

The cultural life of teachers in the West is fuller than that of teachers in the East, due perhaps to opportunities available to them. However, more teachers in the East assist in activities for community improvement than do teachers in the West.

Teachers generally were not involved in political activity, but a larger proportion of teachers in the West reported that they voted regularly.

There was considerable variation between East and West in the importance assigned to various goals for primary education. Teachers in the West gave higher place to teaching basic skills, to reason and think, and religious values than did teachers in the East. The latter gave greater importance to teaching moral values, civic skills, vocational skills and good health habits.

Teachers in the West were more inclined to want to use their own judgment rather than rely on outside authority in handling classroom matters than were teachers in the East. Teachers in the East placed heavier reliance on using the textbook as a guide for determining curriculum than did the others. Both areas were agreed, however, that curriculums should be worked out cooperatively between higher officials and local school staffs.

While all teachers were disposed to favor supplementary aids to education, teachers in the West were more strongly in favor of psychological clinics, special schools, and free birth control clinics. A greater proportion of teachers in the East favored the payment of grants to parents.

Too large classes were considered in both East and West as the prime deterrent to good learning by children. In addition, teachers in the East felt hindered by poor physical plant and lack of teaching aids.

Both areas wanted a combination of centralized and local control of schools, but were divided as to the type of teacher organization that could best serve their needs, the West being slightly in favor of one that included only primary teachers. However, the West was not in favor, as much as was the East, of putting much power in the hands of a teachers' organization.

Teachers in the East were more interested in merit pay and in medals and citations for outstanding performance in teaching than were teachers in the West.

Immoral conduct was the one basis for dismissal of a teacher which received universal support. Nearly half the teachers in the East, as opposed to slightly less than one-third in the West, believed that teaching ideas contrary to government policy was legitimate ground for dismissal.

Strikes were not condoned by either area, but less strongly by the East. Other forms of pressure in government were considered legitimate. However, the general feeling was that professional organizations should devote themselves primarily to academic affairs and not to political involvement.

Teachers in the East appeared to be more chauvinistic than teachers in the West, although both areas were definitely in favor of cooperation with international agencies.

In summarizing differences between the younger and the older teachers, it is likewise true that extreme differences did not appear in the study.

In the East, there is a higher proportion of females in the younger group than in the older one. The reverse is true in the West. The younger teachers have received longer training in both East and West. In the West, more older than younger teachers said they had materially changed their ideas about teaching. On this, in the East there was little difference between older and younger teachers.

In both East and West more of the younger teachers had been recruited from the large cities than was true for the older ones. The older teachers reported strict religious upbringing more frequently than the younger ones.

Younger teachers in the East were inclined to be more tolerant of large numbers of women teachers, but were less tolerant of a woman as head of the school.

Younger and older, in both East and West, agreed generally in the prestige value of various occupations, but younger teachers, in both East and West, were less pessimistic about the declining prestige of the primary teacher.

Low salary as a deterrent to the choice of teaching as a vocation by young people was mentioned more often by younger than by older teachers in both East and West.

In their cultural life, younger teachers are more apt, in both East and West, to go to movies, to attend a concert and to read popular magazines than are the older ones. Strictly professional matters interest the older ones more.

Older teachers were definitely more interested in membership in teachers' organizations than were the younger ones in both East and West. The differences between the ages were most marked in the matter of holding membership in a national organization, where the older ones predominated, although there was considerable difference between the two ages even at the local level. Fifteen percent of younger teachers in the East and 10 percent in the West indicated they wanted no affiliation with a professional organization of any sort.

About the same situation held for participation in political activities: older teachers felt more involved, even in so fundamental an activity as voting regularly. In fact, voting was the only type of activity which interested either age to any great degree. In the East, one-fourth of the younger teachers and one-fifth of the older teachers said they preferred to engage in no type of political activity. One-tenth of the younger teachers in the West held the same opinion. Only a very small proportion of the older teachers indicated they wanted no political activity at all.

In the matter of disciplining a child, younger teachers in the East were a little less confident of their judgment than older teachers. The same held true for deciding methods of classroom teaching and contacting parents. In the West, the younger teachers were more confident about relying on themselves when it came to handling a child who did not work well and disciplining a disobedient child. Older teachers felt more competent in handling tardy cases and in contacting parents.

There were slight variations in the attitude of older and younger teachers in regard to regulations governing them. In the East, older teachers were more disposed to favor laws passed by the government, while younger teachers would rely more on regulations from the ministry and supervisors or inspectors. Older teachers, rather than younger, favored supervision by the head of the school. In the matter of the disciplining of teachers, more older teachers felt that removal to an undesirable position and private reprimands were legitimate forms of discipline.

Younger teachers in both East and West showed themselves no more liberal than older teachers in designating their own culture as the superior way of life. While older teachers showed more interest in studying the modern world, the younger ones showed greater disposition to work with foreign teachers in their own schools.

IV
THE POSITION OF TEACHERS
IN INDIVIDUAL COUNTRIES

An educational system is something more than a mere organization for imparting knowledge to the rising generation. More adequately than any other phase of national life, an educational system expresses the innermost beliefs, ideals and aspirations of a people.

Peter Sandiford

CHANGES IN THE ROLE AND STATUS OF THE TEACHER MUST COME FROM two major sources: first, from the length and quality of his pre-service and in-service training; and second, from the conditions of work, including remuneration, which are imposed upon him. Some of the changes can result only from legal action, some from the activities of his professional organizations, and some from individual effort. All improvement in status and role must grow out of an increased aware-ness in the body politic, in the professional organizations, and by the individual teacher, of the vital place of the teacher in maintaining and building a good society.*

In general, primary school teachers in all societies are more closely supervised by the state than are teachers at higher levels. The reason

---

* The background material for this chapter is more or less ephemeral and was gleaned from various reports and directives of ministries of education, from handbooks and guides from teachers' organizations (many in mimeographed form) and from letters and interviews with officials from the cities surveyed.

for this is partly historic, partly the nearness of the primary school to local affairs. Because they are in constant public view, they themselves generally have remained neutral or indifferent to political and sociological affairs.

In general, also, the amount of training required for the teacher at the primary school level has closely paralleled the general economic level of the country in which he is employed (the lower the economic development, the shorter the period of training) and usually less training has been required of him than of the teacher at the secondary school level. The typical pattern of his training has been narrow in scope and has confined him to association with his own kind. In a number of countries of the West, this situation is rapidly changing so that the same length of training period is required of all teachers in the public schools. The pattern set in the West is gradually being accepted in countries of the Orient. The chief problem of setting training standards too high in any country is that it places teachers in direct competition with members of other professions where salary and other benefits may be more favorable, as recently in the U.S.A., where many teachers of science withdrew from the profession to enter more lucrative positions in industry.

Under present conditions, more women are entering teaching in most parts of the world. Women teachers create the special problems of maternity leaves, of protected periods of absence during which they as mothers care for young children, of training for those who enter the profession at a comparatively late age, and of retraining programs for those who return to the profession after long leaves of absence.

The need for teachers in rural areas is acute in a number of countries where the differences between urban and rural life are very marked. How life can be made attractive enough in villages and small communities to draw teachers is a major problem in many countries where schools are being established for all children.

In all countries some form of teaching organization exists. In some countries, primary teachers have their own groups, affiliated with organizations of teachers at other levels. In some places, like the Province of Ontario, Canada, membership is compulsory. The tendency is generally to combine levels and to use the teachers' organizations for the advancement of the position of the teacher. In some countries, organizations have legal status; in others they do not. The moot question in a number of countries is whether teachers ought to affiliate with labor unions and whether, when such affiliation occurs, the chief weapon of the labor unions — the strike — can legally be employed. In several states in the U.S.A. teachers' organizations are now legally recognized as unions with the right of collective bargaining with employing agencies — the school boards — for the writing of teacher contracts. In local communities strikes of teachers have been organized. Teachers' organizations have also declared sanctions against local school districts and against areas of the country in which employment practices considered unfair to teachers have prevailed. The influence of the International Labor Organization will probably make itself increasingly felt in many areas of the world where formerly teachers were in no way affiliated with organized labor.[1]

Two major groups have been organized at the international level: the World Confederation of the Organizations of the Teaching Profession, organized in 1952, and the International Council in Education for Teaching, an affiliate, founded in 1953. Both of these have been active in organizing conferences, carrying on surveys, disseminating information concerning the world picture in teaching, and representing the teaching profession in the formation of policy. UNESCO, while not directly affiliated with teachers' groups, is definitely concerned with the profession in all its aspects.

Present Status in Eastern Countries

The increasing demand for elementary school teachers in Asian countries because of expanding demands for education of children at this level has made it extremely difficult to increase the length of the training period, although many countries have gone on record as desiring higher academic and professional requirements for teachers in the elementary school. At the present time, the norm is a school certificate, with varying years of education completed, from eight to twelve and two to three years of preparation in a special training school. In some countries a rather large proportion of the teachers are not fully prepared, as in Vietnam, which reported in 1959–1960 that only 40 percent of its elementary teachers were fully qualified. (Those reporting in this study did not show this proportion of unqualified teachers in Saigon (Table 3B).) In the same year, Japan reported that 99.8 percent of its teachers were fully qualified. In some countries, such as Korea, teachers may be qualified through examination rather than through attendance at training institutions. In India, Pakistan,

Korea, Vietnam, and Thailand the great majority of teachers are men. In the Philippines the women greatly outnumber the men, while in Japan the sexes are nearly equal.

In most countries, the institutions providing teacher training are public. An exception is the Philippines, where private schools supply more than 90 percent of the teachers. Since there are no standards of admission which apply to these schools and no regulations for quality of work, it can be assumed from the results of the national examinations given by the Philippine Bureau of Civil Service that the quality of the teachers trained is low. In the year 1955–1956, the last year for which figures are available, of the 90,339 elementary teachers sitting for the national examination, only 27,788 passed it. Boys are exempt from taking entrance examinations since notably few men are in elementary teaching.

The survey made by the Bureau of Public Schools of the Philippines in 1960 criticized the nine public teacher training institutions, which have collegiate rank, because of the poor preparation of the faculty, the extremely large classes, the heavy teaching schedules, and the lack of library facilities and services. The survey also felt that the curriculum was too crowded, that the emphasis on purely professional subjects was too pronounced, that more electives should be offered — particularly in agriculture and practical arts — that modern textbooks and other instructional aids were lacking, and that too little attention was given to providing in-service courses for teachers in the area.[2]

Recognition of the rapid changes in education has led most of the countries to make provision for in-service education programs of various types. These are usually conducted by the ministry of education and by teachers' organizations. Vietnam, for example, has established a permanent center in Saigon for in-service seminars and short courses. In Japan, the Japanese Teachers' Union organizes district study programs, which culminate in a national assembly for the study of education. In India, special seminars for in-service education are attached to selected teacher education schools. Teachers' organizations are generally concerned with the upgrading of teachers through both formal and informal means.

Many of the teachers' organizations supply bulletins, magazines and journals to their members. Through these media teachers keep in touch with the latest developments in educational theory and practice. In a number of countries efforts are made by the departments and ministries of education to bring out special pamphlets and booklets for the guidance and information of teachers. In almost every country there are meetings and conferences of teachers at which, through personal contacts, discussions and sharing of experience, teachers are able to receive guidance in regard to the future lines of improvement in their work.

In most countries there is provision for the grant of special study leave to teachers, for study either in their own country or abroad. Such leave is granted on full pay. If the period exceeds a certain maximum, however, only half pay is allowed.[3]

The trend in the economic status of teachers in various countries is extremely difficult to assess because the adequacy of pay for teachers can be evaluated only in relationship to the general standard of living in each country and to the purchasing power of the currency. In conducting its survey of conditions in Asia in 1963, the WCOTP outlined a number of factors which must be considered in determining the total economic situation of teachers:

> Economic status consists of a number of components. Some of the major ones are as follows:
> Conditions of professional career: (1) probation, (2) confirmation, (3) security of tenure, (4) promotion and advancement.
> Salaries: (1) adequacy of payment, (2) regularity of payment, (3) equal pay for equal work, (4) salary schedules, (5) extra pay for extra duties, (6) participation of teachers in the development of salary schedules. These are some but not all of the factors involved in the problem of determining and implementing salary policies for teachers.
> Allowances: (1) cost of living, (2) dependents' allowances, (3) allowances for special duties and responsibilities.
> Retirement benefits: (1) structure of retirement plans, (2) pension provisions, (3) retirement age, (4) survivors' and invalidity benefits.
> Leave: (1) leaves of absence (including maternity and sick leave), (2) vacations, (3) study leave, (4) special leave.
> Other benefits: (1) housing, (2) insurance, (3) health insurance, (4) mutual aid, (5) free education for teachers' children.[4]

This survey revealed extremely wide variations on all these components. In general, salaries in Asia were low, when judged by Western standards, but when comparisons were made with the per capita annual income in the various countries the salaries of teachers were substantially higher. (The survey made no attempt at comparison with other professional groups.) In general, men and women received the same salary, but women were at a disadvantage in promotion to higher posts. In India, the Philippines, Thailand and Japan the teachers were represented in salary negotiations. Korea and Vietnam had no regular means of representation on legislative bodies.

The age at which retirement with pension is permitted and the age when it is compulsory varies greatly. The general age for the latter is sixty years, but with the increasing life span, there is a tendency to fix compulsory retirement at a later age. Pensions may be paid either as a fixed sum or as partial payments for varying lengths of time.

Fringe benefits vary widely but most countries permit paid leaves for limited periods of study, pregnancy, and illness. In a number of countries, including Thailand, Pakistan, India and Vietnam, teachers get medical treatment at reduced rates. In Japan, teachers have health insurance.

In a number of countries, the teachers' own organizations provide loans or set up mutual aid plans. This is true of Thailand, Japan, Pakistan, Korea and the Philippines.

Workers around the world have come to recognize the strength of cooperative action in presenting their claims to the body politic. Teachers have been no exception.

> The principle of freedom of association is recognized generally in almost all the countries. At the national level the rights of teachers who belong to the civil service are usually regarded as the rights of civil servants rather than those of teachers.... In some countries, teachers belonging to the public service are discouraged from forming associations. In others, the government sponsors the formation of such associations. Teachers the world over, however, are quite alive to their right to form associations and there is evidence that they are steadily winning greater rights for themselves as an organized profession.[5]

In all Asian countries represented in the present study, an active teachers' organization exists. It varies considerably in function and in the degree of influence it exercises on educational policy and programs.

In some Asian countries, committees of teachers have been formed to advise governmental agencies on educational policy. In Vietnam, for example, a thirty-six member National Education Council was elected in 1964 from a broad representation of teachers. This Council and the Commission for the Improvement of Education (composed of twenty-four department heads in the Ministry of Education) serve as a permanent advisory committee to the Minister of Education and to legislative committees dealing with educational matters.[6]

If teachers are not disbarred from any sort of political activity, they may participate in the political life of their nation, as decreed by law, in two possible ways:

1) By representation of teachers' organizations on law-making bodies.
2) By election or appointment as individuals to governmental posts.

In Korea, the Philippines and Pakistan, teachers are disbarred. In India, Japan and Thailand, they may serve in governmental posts. In Vietnam, they are represented by their teachers' organization. India has a guaranteed quota for teacher representatives on legislative bodies at all levels of government. In the countries represented in this study, except Japan, Pakistan and Vietnam, some form of award is presented for long and meritorious service.

Present Status in Western Countries

The current shortage of teachers in Europe and North America (i.e., England, Finland, Germany, U.S.A., Canada) has forced the employment of considerable numbers of those only partially qualified under present legal requirements. Nearly all teachers in the present study declared themselves fully qualified (Table 3B). The general trend in these countries is to require the primary school teachers' preparation to approximate that of the secondary teacher. This means training programs at the level of the university rather than of the secondary school, as was formerly usually the case. The one exception to this trend in the five cities surveyed is in Finland, where teacher training remains at the secondary level, although many recommendations have been placed before the government for raising the level. In the U.S.A., teachers for the elementary school are universally trained in institutions of university standing which prepare teachers for all levels of public school education and where baccalaureate degrees are necessary for the licensing of teachers. In Canada, elementary teachers are trained at different types of institutions, depending on provincial regulations. In Ontario, for example, they are trained at teacher training colleges where credits earned may be applied toward the completion of university degrees. In England, teacher training colleges are affiliated with university institutes, although they do not grant degrees at the present time. In Germany, teacher education varies from state to state, but in general requires the level of preparation required by the universities for entrance; the level of work at the *pädagogische hochschule* is recognized as of university standing, although transfer is usually not possible and baccalaureate degrees are not granted.

The initial preparation of teachers is usually divided into three general parts: education in broad cultural areas; education in the science of pedagogy; practical field experiences. The amount required in each part and the relationship of one part to another varies considerably from country to country. External examinations are now virtually unknown for licensing.

In-service education is encouraged in all five cities. In several states and provinces of the U.S.A. and Canada, a provisional license to teach is issued upon completion of the training period, which can be made permanent only by in-service courses at a teacher training institution. In Germany and England all in-service education is voluntary. However, in the five cities there are numerous opportunities and inducements for in-service education. In Finland paid leaves are granted for study, and government subsidies are granted to teachers' organizations to enable them to organize in-service courses for teachers. In Germany permanent centers for in-service training are subsidized by the government.

In Finland and Germany a period of probation following the initial licensing of the teacher is followed by an examination, the passing of which makes the license permanent. In Germany the examination is a combination of a prepared paper and demonstration teaching before school authorities.

The salary of teachers in the five cities is usually the same for men and women and by standards of the East is high. However, it is generally agreed that salaries for teachers are below those paid for comparable preparation and experience in other professions. The number of working hours is generally higher than the prevalent forty to forty-eight hour-work week. Teachers in Finland are required to participate in community activities enrolling children and young people. In Germany teachers are paid for after school classes and work in directing children's circles for leisure time activities. In the U.S.A., through the grants recently provided by the Federal Government, teachers are paid for an extended school day in certain types of schools.

Teachers' fringe benefits are generally good. In Germany teachers come under the civil service and are eligible for all benefits accorded to this service. The usual retirement age is sixty-five, with voluntary retirement possible at an earlier age, usually with lower pension rights.

Survivors' benefits may or may not be part of the retirement plan. Illness is usually recognized as grounds for granting partial pensions before retirement age. In the U.S.A., teachers generally make substantial contributions to their retirement programs. Generally, paid maternity leaves are not granted, but there is provision for paid sick leave for stated periods of time. Paid leave is usually granted in the U.S.A. for attendance at professional meetings, jury duty, illness or death in the family.

Other fringe benefits which teachers have set up in a number of Western countries are credit unions and group health and life insurance. Often the state government makes some contribution to insurance programs.

In all of the five countries, there are active national teachers' organizations. In none of these countries do the organizations have a legal voice in deciding policy concerning teachers, but they do have considerable influence in an advisory capacity. Representatives of the organizations serve on advisory legislative committees, give consultant services to departments or ministries of education, receive governmental subsidies for various purposes, recommend individuals for appointment by government agencies, and cooperate with legal authorities in enforcing regulations imposed upon the profession. Most of the associations have set up codes of ethics for teachers which they sometimes enforce through cooperation with legal agencies.

In general, teachers' organizations in Western countries are engaged in setting and maintaining professional standards in the training of teachers; in securing fair and reasonable standards of service, including salary and fringe benefits; in setting up diverse opportunities for in-service education; in maintaining morale within the profession by organizing professional meetings and publishing professional periodicals. Their power and influence seem to be on the increase, and if the trend in the U.S.A. is any indication of future development, it is probable that soon they will assume legal status, particularly in the setting of teachers' salaries and for conditions of employment.

Findings of The Present Study for Individual Countries

As already indicated in Chapter I, this study is based on a sampling of primary school teachers in metropolitan areas of twelve selected countries. It is assumed that the findings regarding the cities will be generally true for the countries. Throughout this chapter, thus, the reference to country is based on this assumption. To emphasize the fact that the findings are of teachers in cities, column headings in the B tables include city and country. (Percentage of responses was the basis for conclusions. Only total numbers are in tables.)

In Asian countries, the highest proportion of males occurred in S. Korea, Japan and Pakistan. In the West, the highest number was in Finland. The greatest proportion married was in Finland and the U.S.A. for the West; the highest was in the Philippines for the East, although the variation was not marked (Table B1).

In the West, teachers from England and Finland showed longest tenure in one place. In the East, the same was true for the Philippines, Thailand, and Vietnam (Table B2).

The only countries in the West reporting that teachers in any great proportion had received fifteen or more years of schooling were Finland and the U.S.A. Germany ranked lowest among the five countries. In the East, Japan was the only country where any considerable number of teachers reported this length of training (slightly less than one-half). England came first in number of clock hours spent in observing and teaching children, as one phase of teacher education, and Pakistan led the Eastern countries (Table 3B).

In the East, the highest number of teachers marking teaching as a second choice and the lowest number feeling it was a rewarding way of life were in Japan. In the West, German teachers were lowest in feeling that teaching was a rewarding way of life and Finland was highest in indicating that teaching was a second choice of profession (Table 4B).

The countries of the West where the highest proportion of teachers said that their ideas of education had changed very much were the U.S.A. and Canada, with England a poor third. In the East, Thailand and the Philippines indicated considerable numbers who said they had changed a great deal. Japan and Pakistan were lowest in this regard.

In the West, the highest proportion of teachers coming from a rural area was Germany (Table 5B). The highest proportion coming from a large city was the U.S.A. with Canada and Finland following. The greatest proportion of teachers from small towns or villages was in England. Teachers in the U.S.A., Canada and England, in that order, said religious training had been an important part of their family life. The country where the teachers thought teachers should have highest moral standards was England. The most liberal thinking in this matter was reported from Finland, followed by the U.S.A.

Korea, the Philippines and Vietnam reported considerable numbers

TABLE 1B[a]

Sex, Age, and Family Status

	London England N = 200	Helsinki Finland N = 200	WEST Munich Germany N = 112	Detroit U.S.A. N = 199	Windsor Canada N = 179
Sex					
Male	37	71	34	42	48
Female	163	129	78	157	131
Age					
20–29	94	46	27	55	91
30–39	20	65	36	53	38
40–49	34	48	25	37	16
50–59	45	29	20	44	27
60–69	7	12	1	7	5
Marital Status					
Unmarried	101	40	54	51	98
Married	90	148	49	121	73
Divorced or widowed	9	12	9	26	8
Number of Children					
None	151	56	59	88	125
1–3	46	119	39	96	35
4–6	2	19	2	7	7
Over 6	1	4	2	6	4

TABLE 1B—*continued*

EAST

	Seoul Korea N = 200	Manila, the Philippines N = 200	Yokohama Japan N = 200	Bangkok Thailand N = 200	Lahore Pakistan N = 132	Madras India N = 159	Saigon Vietnam N = 161
Sex							
Male	88	45	100	51	94	48	65
Female	112	155	100	148	38	111	96
Total	200	200	200	200	132	159	161
Age							
20–29	94	73	99	101	15	82	63
30–39	68	64	82	73	22	38	38
40–49	26	39	13	20	32	24	30
50–59	10	21	6	5	46	13	21
60–69	—	2	—	—	11	1	—
Marital Status							
Unmarried	82	70	92	77	20	72	36
Married	106	127	106	115	104	81	119
Divorced or widowed	12	3	2	3	6	5	3
Number of Children							
None	100	86	116	93	26	96	22
1–3	53	53	79	45	28	45	48
4–6	41	41	3	45	49	9	51
Over 6	6	20	—	8	29	8	17

a. As in Tables 1A–36A, where totals do not equal N, the discrepancy is due to questions left unanswered.

TABLE 2B[a]
Teaching Experience

	London England N = 200	Helsinki Finland N = 200	WEST Munich Germany N = 112	Detroit U.S.A. N = 199	Windsor Canada N = 179
Total Number of Years					
Less than five	100	100	31	100	100
More than ten	100	100	81	99	79
Years in Present Position					
Less than one	47	34	10	28	42
1– 2	48	30	26	55	34
3– 6	32	55	29	60	56
7–10	13	31	20	22	17
11–20	47	36	26	25	11
Over 20	12	13	1	8	19
Type of School					
Public	200	200	109	198	179
Private	—	—	3	—	—

TABLE 2B—*continued*

				EAST			
	Seoul Korea N = 200	Manila, the Philippines N = 200	Yokohama Japan N = 200	Bangkok Thailand N = 200	Lahore Pakistan N = 132	Madras India N = 159	Saigon Vietnam N = 161
Total Number of Years							
Less than five	100	100	100	100	32	100	61
More than ten	100	100	100	100	100	59	100
Years in Present Position							
Less than one	58	17	44	11	28	22	5
1– 2	56	46	44	49	41	42	38
3– 6	81	79	67	83	51	55	56
7–10	—	12	23	18	3	10	31
11–20	4	34	22	28	6	22	23
Over 20	—	12	—	7	—	6	8
Type of School							
Public	195	198	199	188	91	113	160
Private	2	2	1	1	39	34	1

a. As in Tables 1A–36A, where totals do not equal N, the discrepancy is due to questions left unanswered.

132

TABLE 3Bᵃ

Training and Qualifications for Teaching

	WEST				
	London England N = 200	Helsinki Finland N = 200	Munich Germany N = 112	Detroit U.S.A. N = 199	Windsor Canada N = 179
Qualification					
Fully qualified	197	191	110	195	174
Not fully qualified	3	9	2	4	4
Total Years of Education					
Less than 10	—	4	1	2	—
10	3	1	2	—	—
11	6	9	1	1	2
12	24	9	12	1	7
13	45	11	21	1	23
14	35	28	27	1	65
15	48	39	16	9	29
Over 15	32	99	29	183	51
Methods of Qualifying					
Regular government examination	99	10	104	8	24
Special examination	26	23	7	38	1
Completion of training course	189	161	20	193	164
Special arrangement	3	38	1	5	1
Clock Hours Spent in Observing or Teaching Children					
None	—	—	1	13	24
10– 50	3	10	18	31	16
51–100	9	45	13	33	22
101–200	30	83	24	53	52
Over 200	155	60	56	67	54

133

TABLE 3B—*continued*

	Seoul Korea N = 200	Manila, the Philippines N = 200	Yokohama Japan N = 200	Bangkok Thailand N = 200	Lahore Pakistan N = 132	Madras India N = 159	Saigon Vietnam N = 161
Qualification							
Fully qualified	197	197	195	141	132	155	151
Not fully qualified	3	3	1	55	—	3	4
Total Years of Education							
Less than 10	10	3	—	41	7	4	27
10	22	1	8	34	36	8	31
11	35	2	17	14	21	37	31
12	81	6	14	26	10	24	39
13	7	19	19	11	4	64	2
14	17	65	43	20	42	7	13
15	14	55	8	20	1	11	8
Over 15	14	49	90	27	1	4	6
Methods of Qualifying							
Regular government examination	20	135	9	98	92	145	149
Special examination	5	22	4	36	6	9	14
Completion of training course	185	126	165	97	75	44	12
Special arrangement	2	3	20	24	2	—	1
Clock Hours Spent in Observing or Teaching Children							
None	30	8	44	18	3	—	16
10– 50	50	113	42	28	16	10	31
51–101	31	21	33	22	7	29	32
101–200	38	24	33	27	8	49	28
Over 200	50	26	36	31	90	71	46

a. As in Tables 1A–36A, where totals do not equal N, the discrepancy is due to questions left unanswered.

134

Factors in the Choice of Teaching as a Profession

			WEST		
	London England N = 200	Helsinki Finland N = 200	Munich Germany N = 112	Detroit U.S.A. N = 199	Windsor Canada N = 179
Influences Affecting Choice					
Parent or close relative was a teacher	61	92	35	70	49
Chose to follow the example of an admired teacher	42	31	46	79	66
Felt that teaching was a rewarding way of life	165	111	66	149	133
Took teaching as a second choice	10	41	5	12	15
High scholastic average	45	52	45	53	23
No special reason	8	9	4	14	19
None of the above					
Present Attitude toward Choice of Vocation					
Positively would choose teaching	113	82	36	107	90
Probably would choose teaching	40	67	52	43	41
Uncertain; depends on opportunities	37	37	11	29	30
Possibly would choose another occupation	7	8	9	8	8
Positively would choose another occupation	2	6	4	10	8
Changes in Ideas Concerning Purposes of Education					
Changed very much	37	15	18	58	70
Changed a little	98	111	45	101	72
Hardly changed at all	61	65	43	34	24
Do not know	3	9	6	5	11

135

TABLE **4B**—*continued*

	Seoul Korea N = 200	Manila, the Philippines N = 200	Yokohama Japan N = 200	Bangkok Thailand N = 200	Lahore Pakistan N = 132	Madras India N = 159	Saigon Vietnam N = 161
				EAST			
Influences Affecting Choice							
Parent or close relative was a teacher	41	78	54	102	53	64	77
Chose to follow the example of an admired teacher	38	73	33	91	41	54	92
Felt that teaching was a rewarding way of life	92	132	20	162	78	85	104
Took teaching as a second choice	21	20	40	18	30	19	3
High scholastic average	43	24	12	49	36	28	17
No special reason	39	12	36	11	10	17	8
None of the above	18						
Present Attitude toward Choice of Vocation							
Positively would choose teaching	47	124	20	103	75	105	137
Probably would choose teaching	71	27	45	19	7	11	12
Uncertain; depends on opportunities	20	35	66	56	33	26	8
Possibly would choose another occupation	41	10	44	12	17	8	1
Positively would choose another occupation	21	3	21	9	—	8	3
Changes in Ideas Concerning Purposes of Education							
Changed very much	68	104	29	154	21	82	64
Changed a little	84	79	104	36	19	63	86
Hardly changed at all	41	14	61	8	12	6	2
Do not know	6	2	4	—	77	5	1

a As in Tables 1A, 26A, where

136

TABLE 5Bᵃ

Environmental Background and Choice of Teaching Environment

	London England N = 200	Helsinki Finland N = 200	WEST Munich Germany N = 112	Detroit U.S.A. N = 199	Windsor Canada N = 179
Environment of Childhood					
Rural area or small village	65	76	112	26	55
Small city or town	93	46	30	32	35
Large city	42	78	25	138	83
Parents' Regard for Religious Training					
Paid little attention to religion	23	33	9	9	10
Observed special rituals and ceremonies	15	67	2	11	9
Gave some emphasis to understanding basic meaning of religion	78	43	46	51	71
Considered religion very important	83	57	55	124	87
Attitude toward Morals for Teachers					
Standards should be higher than for other professional workers	54	36	30	27	31
Standards should be higher than for the general public	119	78	70	96	98
Standards should be the same as for the general public	26	86	10	72	43
Choice of Environment for Teaching					
Rural area or small village	61	17	3	2	1
Small city or town	114	29	12	56	49
Large city	23	154	97	138	124

TABLE 5B—*continued*

				EAST			
	Seoul Korea N = 200	Manila, the Philippines N = 200	Yokohama Japan N = 200	Bangkok Thailand N = 200	Lahore Pakistan N = 132	Madras India N = 159	Saigon Vietnam N = 161
Environment of Childhood							
Rural area or small village	74	67	54	45	60	46	52
Small city or town	27	102	47	84	47	44	69
Large city	98	31	99	70	25	68	37
Parents' Regard for Religious Training							
Paid little attention to religion	51	71	159	24	7	34	48
Observed special rituals and ceremonies	97	20	17	117	17	10	11
Gave some emphasis to understanding basic meaning of religion	17	33	18	23	35	39	48
Considered religion very important	35	75	3	35	70	72	42
Attitude toward Morals for Teachers							
Standards should be higher than for other professional workers	69	128	22	58	105	96	65
Standards should be higher than for the general public	109	66	133	127	19	47	73
Standards should be the same as for the general public	22	6	43	12	6	11	17
Choice of Environment for Teaching							
Rural area or small village	24	50	17	22	11	27	17
Small city or town	14	112	42	80	26	50	42
Large city	160	38	141	96	94	81	100

of teachers coming from rural areas or small communities. Japan had by far the highest proportion of its teachers coming from families which paid little or no attention to religious training in the family, while teachers in the Philippines, Pakistan, and India said their parents considered religious training important.

Teachers in the Philippines (64 percent) and in Pakistan (80 percent) insisted on the highest moral standards for teachers, while teachers in Japan were the most liberal in feeling that no special demands should be placed on the profession. The teachers in the Philippines evinced the greatest willingness to teach in rural areas or small towns. The teachers least willing to teach there were in Korea and Pakistan.

Only in England would any considerable number of teachers consent to teach in a small town or rural area.

In the West, England and Canada showed the largest number reporting no supplementary income (Table 6B). Working at jobs outside education was by far more common in the U.S.A. One-fourth or more of the teachers in England, Finland, and the U.S.A. said they supplemented income by the paid work of the spouse. Over one-fourth of those reporting additional income in the U.S.A. and slightly over one-eighth of those in England indicated that the extra salary amounted to more than one year's regular salary.

The country in the East reporting the lowest proportion of teachers supplementing their salaries was Vietnam. The one with the greatest proportion working outside the field of education was Thailand. Tutoring pupils was most prevalent in Pakistan and India. The Philippines had the largest number reporting extra income from the paid work of the spouse. The countries reporting the greatest amounts earned as supplemental income (more than one year's regular salary) were Japan, Vietnam and India, in this order.

Teachers from all countries in the West were slightly in favor of a retirement scheme which gave them a somewhat reduced salary with a pension plan. Teachers from the East were less agreed, with more teachers from Korea and Thailand asking for additional benefits such as housing and health insurance, in addition to a pension. More from the Philippines and Vietnam asked for maximum fringe benefits (Table 7B).

In the East, the countries where higher proportions of women in the teaching staff was thought desirable were the Philippines and India (Table 8B). Those wanting lower proportions of women were Korea and Japan. Definite preferences for male principals were expressed by

139

TABLE 6B[a]

Adequacy of Income

	London England N = 200	Helsinki Finland N = 200	WEST Munich Germany N = 112	Detroit U.S.A. N = 199	Windsor Canada N = 179
Method of Supplementing Income					
Not at all	130	102	59	69	119
Teaching in other schools	2	25	5	8	1
Tutoring pupils privately	11	10	7	14	1
Writing educational books or articles	1	8	10	1	1
Working jobs outside of education	7	27	3	40	13
By the paid work of spouse	48	51	21	68	33
Other ways	9	29	21	36	15
Annual Amount of Supplement to Income					
Less than one month of regular teaching salary	17	31	24	22	15
One to three months	17	34	14	51	20
Four to nine months	7	17	3	15	9
Ten to eleven months	—	—	—	12	—
More than regular yearly salary	27	4	11	56	14

TABLE 6B—*continued*

		EAST				
	Seoul Korea N = 200	Manila, the Philippines N = 200	Yokohama Japan N = 200	Bangkok Thailand N = 200	Lahore Pakistan N = 132	Madras India N = 159	Saigon Vietnam N = 161
Method of Supplementing Income							
Not at all	85	74	104	91	52	76	93
Teaching in other schools	1	2	—	9	—	1	2
Tutoring pupils privately	11	8	29	15	35	50	6
Writing educational books or articles	4	3	2	3	5	8	11
Working jobs outside of education	10	11	3	34	16	3	2
By the paid work of spouse	37	69	55	38	11	22	42
Other ways	56	60	12	32	18	10	2
Annual Amount of Supplement to Income							
Less than one month of regular teaching salary	37	74	5	46	33	26	31
One to three months	36	27	31	39	28	28	33
Four to nine months	13	7	5	14	13	6	29
Ten to eleven months	10	—	15	—	—	—	—
More than regular yearly salary	16	15	30	7	6	18	25

a. As in Tables 1A–36A, where totals do not equal N, the discrepancy is due to questions left unanswered.

TABLE 7B[a]

Choice of Remuneration

	London England N = 200	Helsinki Finland N = 200	WEST Munich Germany N = 112	Detroit U.S.A. N = 199	Windsor Canada N = 179
Highest possible salary without other benefits	30	12	13	40	28
Lower than highest salary with a pension system	146	159	75	129	135
Still lower salary with provisions for housing, health insurance, and a pension system	20	27	16	16	8
Minimum salary with all the benefits mentioned above, plus others, such as life insurance, credit and loan arrangements, recreation facilities	1	2	1	10	3

TABLE 7B—*continued*

				EAST			
	Seoul Korea N = 200	Manila, the Philippines N = 200	Yokohama Japan N = 200	Bangkok Thailand N = 200	Lahore Pakistan N = 132	Madras India N = 159	Saigon Vietnam N = 161
Highest possible salary without other benefits	35	50	63	22	25	23	8
Lower than highest salary with a pension system	59	37	62	74	44	21	31
Still lower salary with provisions for housing, health insurance, and a pension system	96	21	61	91	57	45	24
Minimum salary with all the benefits mentioned above, plus others, such as life insurance, credit and loan arrangements, recreation facilities	10	92	12	12	4	67	92

a. As in Tables 1A–36A, where totals do not equal N, the discrepancy is due to questions left unanswered.

143

TABLE 8Bᵃ

Proportion of Male and Female Personnel

	London England N = 200	Helsinki Finland N = 200	WEST Munich Germany N = 112	Detroit U.S.A. N = 199	Windsor Canada N = 179
Proper Percentage of Female Teachers					
0– 19	1	—	—	2	—
20– 39	2	1	10	7	7
40– 59	90	60	73	90	48
60– 79	101	134	29	69	102
80–100	4	3	—	8	14
Preferred Principal or Head					
Female	7	3	5	14	5
Male	107	140	70	102	138
No preference	86	56	36	74	36

TABLE 8B—*continued*

EAST

	Seoul Korea N = 200	Manila, the Philippines N = 200	Yokohama Japan N = 200	Bangkok Thailand N = 200	Lahore Pakistan N = 132	Madras India N = 159	Saigon Vietnam N = 161
Proper Percentage of Female Teachers							
0– 19	2	—	1	2	13	2	—
20– 39	22	10	37	9	23	16	20
40– 59	88	60	147	101	60	37	67
60– 79	71	118	12	40	14	57	46
80–100	15	9	1	7	5	22	19
Preferred Principal or Head							
Female	9	24	35	12	19	54	12
Male	138	142	119	83	88	63	91
No preference	52	32	44	102	21	40	55

a. As in Tables 1A–36A, where totals do not equal N, the discrepancy is due to questions left unanswered.

145

all teachers. Only in Thailand did any considerable number say they had no distinct preference.

In the West, the countries where the teachers felt it acceptable to have more than 60 percent of the teaching force women were England, Finland and Canada. Germany and the U.S.A. voted for a higher proportion of men. Here, also, the preference for a male head was first in all countries. In England and the U.S.A. the highest number of teachers indicated no preference as to sex.

In the East (Table 9B), Japan rated government officials higher in prestige than any other country; the Philippines and Thailand, the doctor of medicine; Korea, the lawyer. For second place, the Philippines rated the priest; Korea, Thailand and Japan, the university professor. Thailand gave lower status to the lawyer; Korea to the shopkeeper; the Philippines to the artist; Japan to the farmer; Thailand to the businessman; India to the primary school teacher than did the other countries. In the West, the professions receiving highest ratings were doctor of medicine in England, U.S.A. and Canada; lawyer, England and Canada; university professor, Germany and England. A primary school head received a median rating, with more status in England, the U.S.A. and Canada than in Germany. A secondary school teacher received a median rating, with more status in Canada than in the other countries. The primary school teacher had a universally low rating, with less prestige in England and the U.S.A. than in the other three Western countries.

Table 10B concerns the teachers' appraisal of their own status and the reasons why young people hesitate to choose teaching as a career. In the East, the teachers who felt most strongly that the position of the primary teacher has deteriorated were in Korea, Japan, Pakistan and Vietnam. The only teachers who felt that status has improved were those in Thailand.

Teachers in the Philippines and Japan listed unfavorable working conditions as a prime deterrent to young people choosing teaching as a profession; Pakistan, India and Vietnam, too little respect shown the teacher; Korea, too little opportunity for advancement. All but the Philippines and Vietnam listed too low salary as a high deterrent; Thailand, difficult living conditions in villages. Only in Japan did any considerable number of teachers complain about interference from the government and superiors.

In the West, teachers in the U.S.A. and England believed most strongly that the position of the elementary teacher has deteriorated

Ranking of Fifteen Vocations as to Prestige

	London England N = 200	Helsinki[d] Finland N = 200	WEST Munich Germany N = 112	Detroit U.S.A. N = 199	Windsor Canada N = 179
Government Official					
1– 3[b]	66		53	90	61
4– 6	72		33	59	57
7– 9	24		14	30 [a]	30
10–12	13		5	2	11
13–15[c]	9		—	2	5
Government Worker or Civil Servant					
1– 3	4		2	3	1
4– 6	6		2	3	2
7– 9	49		22	20	16
10–12	70		46	71	61
13–15	55		33	86	84
Doctor of Medicine					
1– 3	135		55	158	160
4– 6	45		43	24	3
7– 9	4		6	1	1
10–12	—		1	—	—
13–15	—		—	—	—

TABLE 9B—*continued*

	London England N = 200	Helsinki[d] Finland N = 200	WEST—*continued* Munich Germany N = 112	Detroit U.S.A. N = 199	Windsor Canada N = 179
Lawyer					
1– 3	127		18	87	106
4– 6	48		62	80	50
7– 9	7		16	11	5
10–12	1		6	5	3
13–15	1		3	—	—
Shopkeeper					
1– 3	—		4	—	—
4– 6	—		14	—	2
7– 9	6		31	10	11
10–12	15		43	29	29
13–15	163		13	144	122
Artist, Musician, or Actor					
1– 3	12		17	11	2
4– 6	37		39	40	11
7– 9	56		22	63	33
10–12	45		14	44	62
13–15	34		13	25	56

TABLE 9B—*continued*

WEST—*continued*

	London England N = 200	Helsinki[d] Finland N = 200	Munich Germany N = 112	Detroit U.S.A. N = 199	Windsor Canada N = 179
Priest or Clergyman					
1– 3	62		48	90	90
4– 6	83		27	65	55
7– 9	24		25	16	11
10–12	12		5	9	7
13–15	3		—	3	1
Farmer					
1– 3	2		—	1	2
4– 6	11		1	1	2
7– 9	36		9	5	3
10–12	51		15	24	32
13–15	84		80	152	125
Banker					
1– 3	42		25	36	11
4– 6	76		44	83	62
7– 9	41		21	44	49
10–12	16		13	16	37
13–15	9		2	4	5

149

TABLE 9B—*continued*

	London England N = 200	Helsinki[d] Finland N = 200	WEST—*continued* Munich Germany N = 112	Detroit U.S.A. N = 199	Windsor Canada N = 179
Secondary School Teacher					
1– 3	—		2	—	—
4– 6	9		16	10	46
7– 9	77		60	71	91
10–12	78		21	90	22
13–15	20		6	12	5
Businessman					
1– 3	18		5	21	10
4– 6	45		6	54	47
7– 9	69		21	65	54
10–12	39		34	33	42
13–15	13		39	10	11
Primary School Principal or Head					
1– 3	2		—	5	9
4– 6	29		9	44	42
7– 9	89		40	108	86
10–12	56		47	24	25
13–15	8		9	2	2

150

TABLE 9B—continued

WEST—continued

	London England N = 200	Helsinki[d] Finland N = 200	Munich Germany N = 112	Detroit U.S.A. N = 199	Windsor Canada N = 179
University Professor					
1– 3	80		84	45	37
4– 6	78		14	75	102
7– 9	21		6	54	23
10–12	5		1	8	1
13–15	—		—	1	1
Primary School Teacher					
1– 3	—		—	—	2
4– 6	3		2	7	8
7– 9	29		17	36	54
10–12	92		52	121	87
13–15	60		34	19	13
Skilled Craftsman					
1– 3	2		2	2	1
4– 6	10		3	4	3
7– 9	20		5	15	25
10–12	59		12	73	73
13–15	93		83	89	62

a. As in Tables 1A–36A, where totals do not equal N, the discrepancy is due to questions left unanswered.
b. Denotes highest rank.
c. Denotes lowest rank.
d. Questionnaire omitted Finland and Pakistan.

151

TABLE 9B[a]—continued

<table>
<tr><th></th><th></th><th></th><th></th><th>EAST</th><th></th><th></th><th></th></tr>
<tr><th></th><th>Seoul Korea N = 200</th><th>Manila, the Philippines N = 200</th><th>Yokohama Japan N = 200</th><th>Bangkok Thailand N = 200</th><th>Lahore[d] Pakistan N = 132</th><th>Madras India N = 159</th><th>Saigon Vietnam N = 161</th></tr>
<tr><td colspan="8">Government Official</td></tr>
<tr><td>1– 3[b]</td><td>110</td><td>92</td><td>169</td><td>99</td><td></td><td>84</td><td>108</td></tr>
<tr><td>4– 6</td><td>31</td><td>58</td><td>21</td><td>40</td><td></td><td>26</td><td>19</td></tr>
<tr><td>7– 9</td><td>25</td><td>29</td><td>5</td><td>16</td><td></td><td>25</td><td>2</td></tr>
<tr><td>10–12</td><td>19</td><td>12</td><td>2</td><td>17</td><td></td><td>9</td><td>5</td></tr>
<tr><td>13–15[c]</td><td>13</td><td>4</td><td>3</td><td>7</td><td></td><td>10</td><td>—</td></tr>
<tr><td colspan="8">Government Worker or Civil Servant</td></tr>
<tr><td>1– 3</td><td>13</td><td>13</td><td>34</td><td>34</td><td></td><td>27</td><td>18</td></tr>
<tr><td>4– 6</td><td>46</td><td>44</td><td>17</td><td>48</td><td></td><td>38</td><td>18</td></tr>
<tr><td>7– 9</td><td>51</td><td>39</td><td>40</td><td>51</td><td></td><td>40</td><td>46</td></tr>
<tr><td>10–12</td><td>62</td><td>68</td><td>72</td><td>23</td><td></td><td>27</td><td>38</td></tr>
<tr><td>13–15</td><td>26</td><td>31</td><td>37</td><td>16</td><td></td><td>22</td><td>14</td></tr>
<tr><td colspan="8">Doctor of Medicine</td></tr>
<tr><td>1– 3</td><td>59</td><td>150</td><td>70</td><td>110</td><td></td><td>94</td><td>103</td></tr>
<tr><td>4– 6</td><td>83</td><td>31</td><td>102</td><td>53</td><td></td><td>36</td><td>26</td></tr>
<tr><td>7– 9</td><td>43</td><td>12</td><td>26</td><td>11</td><td></td><td>22</td><td>3</td></tr>
<tr><td>10–12</td><td>9</td><td>2</td><td>1</td><td>3</td><td></td><td>2</td><td>—</td></tr>
<tr><td>13–15</td><td>2</td><td>—</td><td>1</td><td>—</td><td></td><td>—</td><td>2</td></tr>
</table>

TABLE 9B—*continued*

EAST—*continued*

	Seoul Korea N = 200	Manila, the Philippines N = 200	Yokohama Japan N = 200	Bangkok Thailand N = 200	Lahore[d] Pakistan N = 132	Madras India N = 159	Saigon Vietnam N = 161
Lawyer							
1– 3	123	88	37	6		36	43
4– 6	53	52	105	38		60	67
7– 9	12	39	46	41		32	13
10–12	7	9	9	44		15	8
13–15	2	7	3	40		11	3
Shopkeeper							
1– 3	—	—	—	6		3	2
4– 6	2	4	1	19		15	6
7– 9	1	25	10	31		33	27
10–12	11	27	41	39		41	45
13–15	182	139	148	75		61	54
Artist, Musician, or Actor							
1– 3	20	2	17	11		27	3
4– 6	40	9	64	28		40	9
7– 9	70	31	73	48		44	42
10–12	57	84	30	64		23	47
13–15	10	69	16	22		20	33

153

EAST—*continued*

	Seoul Korea N = 200	Manila, the Philippines N = 200	Yokohama Japan N = 200	Bangkok Thailand N = 200	Lahore[d] Pakistan N = 132	Madras India N = 159	Saigon Vietnam N = 161
Priest or Clergyman							
1– 3	38	121	13	33		21	21
4– 6	59	47	45	27		27	44
7– 9	48	11	56	30		29	27
10–12	32	13	48	29		41	21
13–15	20	3	38	54		35	21
Farmer							
1– 3	8	7	—	10		27	3
4– 6	3	5	—	25		19	5
7– 9	12	10	3	38		20	12
10–12	25	50	15	59		40	39
13–15	149	123	182	39		46	75
Banker							
1– 3	12	12	15	14		16	7
4– 6	57	38	53	43		34	31
7– 9	57	63	69	40		46	46
10–12	66	68	43	52		34	31
13–15	6	14	20	23		23	19

TABLE 9B—*continued*

EAST—*continued*

	Seoul Korea N = 200	Manila, the Philippines N = 200	Yokohama Japan N = 200	Bangkok Thailand N = 200	Lahore[d] Pakistan N = 132	Madras India N = 159	Saigon Vietnam N = 161
Secondary School Teacher							
1– 3	5	7	—	30		19	14
4– 6	33	51	11	64		20	73
7– 9	89	100	55	50		27	33
10–12	68	32	114	27		42	12
13–15	2	5	20	7		45	2
Businessman							
1– 3	37	8	115	4		23	2
4– 6	58	21	60	17		40	15
7– 9	42	42	18	21		39	40
10–12	38	78	6	40		31	44
13–15	22	46	1	87		21	33
Primary School Principal or Head							
1– 3	11	24	2	38		17	3
4– 6	52	77	37	52		19	21
7– 9	66	58	110	49		29	57
10–12	61	27	45	30		45	45
13–15	8	9	6	7		44	8

TABLE 9B—*continued*

EAST—*continued*

	Seoul Korea N = 200	Manila, the Philippines N = 200	Yokohama Japan N = 200	Bangkok Thailand N = 200	Lahore [d] Pakistan N = 132	Madras India N = 159	Saigon Vietnam N = 161
University Professor							
1– 3	137	47	121	103		30	63
4– 6	48	99	56	42		60	55
7– 9	12	40	17	17		32	8
10–12	—	6	6	5		23	5
13–15	1	3	—	6		9	3
Primary School Teacher							
1– 3	10	12	3	43		27	8
4– 6	11	44	3	20		3	8
7– 9	34	73	27	47		12	39
10–12	97	42	111	40		34	43
13–15	46	24	56	26		78	36
Skilled Craftsman							
1– 3	12	2	4	5		11	4
4– 6	17	5	25	11		25	5
7– 9	31	13	45	22		32	7
10–12	40	67	57	38		54	19
13–15	97	108	69	95		32	99

a. As in Tables 1A–36A, where totals do not equal N, the discrepancy is due to questions left unanswered.
b. Denotes highest rank.
c. Denotes lowest rank.
d. Questionnaire omitted Finland and Pakistan.

TABLE 10B[a]

Present Status of Primary School Teachers

	London England N = 200	Helsinki Finland N = 200	WEST Munich Germany N = 112	Detroit U.S.A. N = 199	Windsor Canada N = 179
Direction of Change of Status					
No change	64	69	13	50	49
Improved a great deal	23	39	34	35	68
Deteriorated	108	92	62	107	58
Reasons Why Young People Hesitate to Choose this Profession					
Shortage of positions	1	9	—	5	8
Working conditions in schools too unattractive and difficult	155	27	72	147	81
Too little intellectual stimulation in working with children	38	96	16	26	58
Too few teachers who have intellectual interests and tastes	17	29	13	14	36
Too little respect shown to teachers	72	123	40	116	72
Weak teachers' organizations	6	—	1	8	10
Too little opportunity for advancement	122	168	62	85	89
Too much interference from government and superiors	8	2	39	13	27
Too low salary	173	89	48	176	110
Living conditions in rural areas and villages too difficult	4	47	48	7	19

157

TABLE 10B—continued

				EAST			
	Seoul Korea N = 200	Manila, the Philippines N = 200	Yokohama Japan N = 200	Bangkok Thailand N = 200	Lahore Pakistan N = 132	Madras India N = 159	Saigon Vietnam N = 161
Direction of Change of Status							
No change	14	86	31	19	7	18	29
Improved a great deal	42	61	25	119	4	65	20
Deteriorated	141	52	137	61	120	74	111
Reasons Why Young People Hesitate to Choose this Profession							
Shortage of positions	2	40	12	59	17	22	70
Working conditions in schools too unattractive and difficult	46	118	155	87	84	68	76
Too little intellectual stimulation in working with children	53	76	44	22	14	11	21
Too few teachers who have intellectual interests and tastes	12	32	30	20	15	21	11
Too little respect shown to teachers	87	43	56	70	91	92	108
Weak teachers' organizations	37	11	20	14	14	4	18
Too little opportunity for advancement	176	91	62	84	60	69	76
Too much interference from government and superiors	22	60	72	20	18	32	5
Too low salary	138	63	133	108	109	125	33
Living conditions in rural areas and villages too difficult	13	42	15	110	20	30	52

a. As in Tables 1A–36A, where totals do not equal N, the discrepancy is due to questions left unanswered.

158

in recent times. However, considerable numbers in Finland and Germany expressed the same opinion. The one country where a considerable number of teachers believed their condition had improved was Canada.

England and the U.S.A. placed high priority on difficult working conditions in schools as deterrents to young people choosing teaching as a profession; Finland and the U.S.A. stressed the little respect shown teachers; all countries named too little opportunity for advancement; and all but Finland and Germany blamed low salaries. Only in Finland and Germany were difficult living conditions in villages mentioned as important deterrents.

In the East, large numbers of Korean, Japanese and Pakistani teachers were in favor of shortening the period of training so that more teachers could be made available (Table 11B). Only in Korea was any marked sentiment expressed that unqualified teachers should be used as needed. In all countries except Korea and Japan, teachers expressed themselves in favor of multiple shifts of children during each day, in order to make maximum use of qualified teachers. Korea, the Philippines, Thailand and Vietnam said classes should be made as large as necessary before unqualified teachers should be hired.

In the West, teachers in England, the U.S.A. and Canada believed classes should be expanded and schools put on multiple shifts in order to keep only qualified teachers at work. These countries also condoned a practice seldom used in the West; namely, limiting the number of days of school attendance per week for each child. The only country in favour of using unqualified teachers to any extent was Finland. Only England and Canada showed much disposition toward shortening the period of training so that teachers could become more readily available.

One of the conditions of work often cited as unfavorable for the teaching profession is the amount of time spent in travel to and from school and in performing such clerical duties, as checking papers (Table 12B). Considerable numbers of teachers who spent an hour or more in daily transportation were Korean and Japanese. Countries where large numbers spent less than twenty minutes per day were the Philippines and Thailand. For most of the teachers in the East, transportation does not seem to present a major problem. The median time spent in correcting papers daily was from sixty to eighty minutes. Countries in which a considerable number of teachers spent more than two hours were Korea, the Philippines, Japan and Vietnam.

TABLE 11B[a]

Ways of Meeting Teacher Shortages

	London England N = 200	Helsinki Finland N = 200	WEST Munich Germany N = 112	Detroit U.S.A. N = 199	Windsor Canada N = 179
Using only qualified teachers, however large classes have to be	111	32	39	95	114
Using only qualified teachers, but dividing large classes into double or triple shifts each day	109	72	52	171	145
Using only qualified teachers but limiting the number of days per week that each child may attend school	104	63	52	135	89
Using unqualified teachers as required	73	124	48	49	45
Relaxing compulsory attendance laws to cut down on the number of children in school	29	16	20	14	10
Closing as many schools as necessary until a sufficient number of qualified teachers are trained	19	1	18	16	4
Shortening the period of teacher training so that more teachers become quickly available	103	56	43	72	100

TABLE 11B—*continued*

		EAST					
	Seoul Korea N = 200	Manila, the Philippines N = 200	Yokohama Japan N = 200	Bangkok Thailand N = 200	Lahore Pakistan N = 132	Madras India N = 159	Saigon Vietnam N = 161
Using only qualified teachers, however large classes have to be	118	148	82	120	80	67	105
Using only qualified teachers, but dividing large classes into double or triple shifts each day	72	140	89	126	102	115	126
Using only qualified teachers but limiting the number of days per week that each child may attend school	18	75	5	122	22	88	103
Using unqualified teachers as required	130	47	52	82	25	48	8
Relaxing compulsory attendance laws to cut down on the number of children in school	9	28	2	15	36	30	8
Closing as many schools as necessary until a sufficient number of qualified teachers are trained	30	51	1	6	20	13	3
Shortening the period of teacher training so that more teachers become quickly available	150	88	109	82	115	98	101

a. As in Tables 1A–36A, where totals do not equal N, the discrepancy is due to questions left unanswered.

161

TABLE 12B[a]

Minutes Spent in Daily Activities other than Teaching

	WEST				
	London England N = 200	Helsinki Finland N = 200	Munich Germany N = 112	Detroit U.S.A. N = 199	Windsor Canada N = 179
Traveling to and from School					
Less than 20	18	30	12	26	42
20– 39	64	43	35	91	95
40– 59	37	44	16	34	31
60– 79	45	39	24	31	6
80– 99	17	29	8	9	1
100–119	6	6	3	3	—
120–139	9	7	8	2	3
140–159	2	1	1	1	—
160–179	—	—	—	—	—
Over 180	1	—	2	1	—
Checking Papers					
Less than 20	13	17	—	20	13
20– 39	42	34	3	48	26
40– 59	26	15	1	6	10
60– 79	59	69	6	42	42
80– 99	16	28	7	24	17
100–119	—	2	3	—	4
120–139	25	22	29	17	25
140–159	6	2	16	2	2
160–179	—	—	—	—	1
Over 180	5	7	44	9	11

EAST

	Seoul Korea N = 200	Manila, the Philippines N = 200	Yokohama Japan N = 200	Bangkok Thailand N = 200	Lahore Pakistan N = 132	Madras India N = 159	Saigon Vietnam N = 161
Traveling to and from School							
Less than 20	17	44	13	52	24	37	37
20– 39	28	56	26	84	25	48	60
40– 59	48	69	38	16	12	16	20
60– 79	34	12	43	20	26	23	21
80– 99	35	6	18	4	5	4	5
100–119	7	3	17	2	4	—	1
120–139	12	2	25	9	16	8	5
140–159	3	—	5	—	3	—	—
160–179	2	—	2	1	10	—	—
Over 180	12	—	12	5	2	1	4
Checking Papers							
Less than 20	2	4	22	6	4	8	1
20– 39	6	17	37	42	27	26	1
40– 59	7	25	6	18	16	23	1
60– 79	41	45	65	63	42	51	10
80– 99	21	12	12	6	1	10	17
100–119	10	5	3	1	4	1	—
120–139	50	47	40	29	18	11	43
140–159	10	9	2	2	3	—	6
160–179	3	2	1	—	5	—	2
Over 180	46	22	8	12	1	5	68

a. As in Tables 1A–36A, where totals do not equal N, the discrepancy is due to questions left unanswered.

In Vietnam more than a third of the teachers reported spending more than three hours a day in checking papers. The country next in amount of time for this activity was Korea.

Teachers in Germany, the U.S.A., and Canada spent less time in traveling to and from school than did teachers in England and Finland. This may be due to the numbers of teachers in these countries possessing private automobiles. In checking papers, teachers in Germany spent far more time than did teachers in the other countries; more than one-third of them reporting more than three hours daily, as against only a negligible number in other countries. The great majority of teachers in all other countries finished their paper correcting in eighty minutes or less.

Table 13B shows that the teachers with the best health record in the East were from Korea, Japan and Vietnam. The country reporting most absence due to illness was India. In the West, the best record was reported by Finland and the poorest by the U.S.A.

Table 14B presents the data on the regular cultural activities of the teachers sampled. The only country reporting TV as a popular activity in the East was Japan, the only country where it is generally available. Professional meetings were popular only in India. Movie going was common in Korea and Thailand; theatre and concerts, in Thailand. Half or more of the teachers in the Philippines, Thailand and India visited a library at least once a month. Reading professional journals was not as common in Pakistan, India and Vietnam as in the other countries. Reading newspapers, reading professional periodicals, daily radio listening and reading a book a month were all common activities for teachers in the East.

In the five Western countries there were few differences in the cultural activities of teachers. Teachers in Germany reported less popular magazine reading, less TV, fewer visits to library than did teachers in the other countries. However, they attended a concert or the theatre more frequently.

The participation of teachers in community activities is presented in Table 15B. In the East, teachers in Korea, the Philippines, Pakistan, India and Vietnam favored engaging teachers in literacy programs. Japan and Thailand did not (Japan probably because there is little need for such work in that country). Teaching adults skills had most approval in the Philippines, India and Vietnam. Directing children and youth in activities to improve the community was sanctioned by large numbers, except in Thailand, Pakistan, India and Vietnam.

TABLE 13B[a]
Number of Days Absent for Illness During Past Year

WEST

	London England N = 200	Helsinki Finland N = 200	Munich Germany N = 112	Detroit U.S.A. N = 199	Windsor Canada N = 179
None	86	121	35	25	86
1– 5	57	40	27	93	71
6–10	24	10	10	59	12
11–15	13	5	9	9	4
16–20	9	3	2	4	1
Over 20	8	11	7	7	2

EAST

	Seoul Korea N = 200	Manila, the Philippines N = 200	Yokohama Japan N = 200	Bangkok Thailand N = 200	Lahore Pakistan N = 132	Madras India N = 159	Saigon Vietnam N = 161
None	116	98	82	60	38	26	75
1– 5	61	82	89	86	31	15	35
6–10	9	11	18	22	24	12	10
11–15	1	—	—	6	8	22	5
16–20	—	—	2	2	7	45	1
Over 20	2	7	8	1	6	27	6

a. As in Tables 1A–36A, where totals do not equal N, the discrepancy is due to questions left unanswered.

TABLE 14B[a]

Regular Cultural Activities

	London England N = 200	Helsinki Finland N = 200	WEST Munich Germany N = 112	Detroit U.S.A. N = 199	Windsor Canada N = 179
Reading general newspaper	187	198	106	196	176
Reading professional newspapers or journals	160	185	100	154	138
Daily radio listening	168	188	88	171	159
Reading popular magazines and journals	133	173	42	173	155
Daily television viewing	130	97	26	161	135
Taking one yearly trip of at least 200 miles	168	151	69	155	142
Attending at least one professional or cultural meeting each month	97		54	91	115
Seeing at least one motion picture a month	71		49	92	78
Attending at least one concert or play during the year	181		100	174	148
Visiting a library at least once each month	153		35	117	94
Reading at least one book each month	179		86	112	109
None of the above	—		—	—	—

EAST

	Seoul Korea N = 200	Manila, the Philippines N = 200	Yokohama Japan N = 200	Bangkok Thailand N = 200	Lahore Pakistan N = 132	Madras India N = 159	Saigon Vietnam N = 161
Reading general newspaper	189	174	188	185	124	152	160
Reading professional newspapers or journals	131	139	116	177	26	54	63
Daily radio listening	177	140	131	184	74	100	132
Reading popular magazines and journals	119	104	139	139	56	107	34
Daily television viewing	28	13	172	48	1	1	26
Taking one yearly trip of at least 200 miles	23	52	56	87	26	58	85
Attending at least one professional or cultural meeting each month[b]	21	71	62	22	11	95	
Seeing at least one motion picture a month[b]	155	84	40	158	21	80	
Attending at least one concert or play during the year[b]	85	53	83	104	13	56	
Visiting a library at least once each month[b]	20	99	13	118	42	82	
Reading at least one book each month[b]	146	78	127	157	73	126	
None of the above[b]	40	1	2	2	7	—	

a. As in Tables 1A–36A, where totals do not equal N, the discrepancy is due to questions left unanswered.
b. These items were omitted from the Vietnam questionnaire.

167

TABLE 15B[a]

Participation in Community Activities Related to Education

	London England N = 200	Helsinki Finland N = 200	WEST Munich Germany N = 112	Detroit U.S.A. N = 199	Windsor Canada N = 179
Teaching adults to read and write	84	38	25	82	75
Teaching adults such skills as sewing, cooking, animal care, crop raising, sanitary measures	54	18	17	73	34
Directing children and youth in projects to improve the community	138	128	35	133	118
Working in projects to improve the community	117	75	37	129	123
No community work except that closely connected to the regular work of the school	51	89	78	58	37

TABLE 15B—*continued*

	Seoul Korea N = 200	Manila, the Philippines N = 200	Yokohama Japan N = 200	EAST Bangkok Thailand N = 200	Lahore Pakistan N = 132	Madras India N = 159	Saigon Vietnam N = 161
Teaching adults to read and write	159	141	16	48	97	109	119
Teaching adults such skills as sewing, cooking, animal care, crop raising, sanitary measures	57	103	6	53	35	82	85
Directing children and youth in projects to improve the community	148	130	128	82	69	98	75
Working in projects to improve the community	86	136	84	87	102	54	62
No community work except that closely connected to the regular work of the school	70	30	50	19	25	68	34

a. As in Tables 1A–36A, where totals do not equal N, the discrepancy is due to questions left unanswered.

169

Only in the Philippines and Pakistan was it suggested that teachers should work on projects to improve the community.

In the West, the only activities receiving much support (except in Germany) were directing children and youth in community improvement and actually participating in such activity. Teachers in Germany led the group in disapproving all sorts of community work for teachers, with Finland second.

In the East, the countries where teachers were particularly interested in local teachers' organizations were the Philippines, Japan, Pakistan and India (Table 16B). Regional organizations were of importance to teachers in Korea and Japan. Except in India and Pakistan, a considerable number said they believed teachers should belong to a national teachers' organization. In no country did a considerable number of teachers belong to any other professional group. Few believed that teachers should have no professional affiliation. In all countries but Korea, the teachers were almost unanimously in favour of teachers' voting regularly. Most teachers in Korea believed that teachers should take no part in political affairs.

In the West, all teachers but in Germany expressed strong interest in local teachers' organizations. Regional organizations were popular only in Canada. There was strong sentiment in favor of national organizations except in the U.S.A. and Canada. A minority of teachers indicated they held membership in other professional organizations in all countries but Germany. In Finland and Canada, teachers seemed most certain that professional organizations are important to teachers. In no country did teachers wish to hold public office. They were all strongly in favor of voting regularly, but this was about the extent of their interest. One-tenth of teachers in England and Canada felt that teachers should engage in no form of political activity.

Table 17B reveals the values the cities (and hence, the countries) placed upon some commonly accepted goals for primary education. Teachers in the Eastern countries were quite well agreed on the values they considered most important. Pakistan, India and Vietnam put less stress in teaching children the social skills of getting along than did other countries. Vietnam rated learning facts of history and other subjects higher than did other countries. India and Pakistan played down civic skills. Vocational skills were emphasized most by Vietnam and the Philippines. Good health was rated high except in Thailand, Pakistan and Vietnam. Obedience was rated high by India. Learning

TABLE 16B[a]

Professional and Political Activities

	London England N = 200	Helsinki Finland N = 200	WEST Munich Germany N = 112	Detroit U.S.A. N = 199	Windsor Canada N = 179
Membership in Teachers' Organizations					
Local teachers' organization	125	195	—	165	151
Regional or provincial teachers' organization	41	26	—	46	120
National teachers' organization	173	112	81	62	34
Other professional organization	23	55	—	70	59
None	20	3	27	20	4
Political Activities					
Holding public office at the local level	5	6	2	—	—
Holding public office at higher than local level	—	4	1	—	—
Voting regularly	173	189	105	193	156
Holding membership in a political party	45	25	6	26	5
Participating in public rallies, protest demonstrations etc.	14	8	20	19	3
Not at all	21	11	1	7	22

TABLE 16B—*continued*

	Seoul Korea N = 200	Manila, the Philippines N = 200	Yokohama Japan N = 200	EAST Bangkok Thailand N = 200	Lahore Pakistan N = 132	Madras India N = 159	Saigon Vietnam N = 161
Membership in Teachers' Organizations							
Local teachers' organization[b]	—	169	115	31	101	107	25
Regional or provincial teachers' organization	134	79	100	3	6	31	29
National teachers' organization	134	124	97	191	1	18	100
Other professional organization	11	45	8	27	2	31	3
None	58	1	29	5	23	8	27
Political Activities							
Holding public office at the local level	—	17	9	4	3	7	71
Holding public office at higher than local level	—	5	1	1	—	2	35
Voting regularly	45	193	161	170	77	121	127
Holding membership in a political party	—	6	1	2	1	8	15
Participating in public rallies, protest demonstrations etc.	6	6	74	4	12	17	65
Not at all	142	5	18	23	58	26	5

a. As in Tables 1A–36A, where totals do not equal N, the discrepancy is due to questions left unanswered.
b. Seoul has no local teachers' organization.

TABLE 17B[a]

Chief Goals of Primary Education

	London England N = 200	Helsinki Finland N = 200	WEST Munich Germany N = 112	Detroit U.S.A. N = 199	Windsor Canada N = 179
Moral values	156	145	21	134	118
Basic skills such as reading, writing, and numbers	192	191	107	186	166
Social skills of learning how to get along with other people	146	161	102	166	147
Facts of history, geography, mathematics	24	49	59	49	39
Civic skills necessary to democratic government	4	67	56	51	26
Vocational skills to be used later in earning a living	19	32	18	36	28
Facts and habits of good health	91	53	43	93	69
To reason and think	180	135	80	162	170
Religious values and ideals	117	95	75	12	42
Obedience in obeying orders	53	62	1	44	79
Skill in group thinking	7	22	4	34	27

TABLE 17B—*continued*

EAST

	Seoul Korea N = 200	Manila, the Philippines N = 200	Yokohama Japan N = 200	Bangkok Thailand N = 200	Lahore Pakistan N = 132	Madras India N = 159	Saigon Vietnam N = 161
Moral values	155	167	135	163	107	95	140
Basic skills, such as reading, writing, and numbers	131	152	150	162	95	111	126
Social skills of learning how to get along with other people	107	152	163	142	43	92	83
Facts of history, geography, mathematics	50	50	43	30	56	47	86
Civic skills necessary to democratic government	169	106	111	101	45	26	106
Vocational skills to be used later in earning a living	46	97	20	90	64	59	90
Facts and habits of good health	168	98	123	69	65	101	78
To reason and think	71	76	107	95	31	51	47
Religious values and ideals	21	49	14	32	85	43	7
Obedience in obeying orders	18	34	5	31	64	118	21
Skill in group thinking	61	30	99	73	22	38	10

a. As in Tables 1A–36A, where totals do not equal N, the discrepancy is due to questions left unanswered.

to reason and think was rated low by Pakistan and Vietnam. Religion was rated lowest by Vietnam.

Teachers in the West likewise showed remarkable unanimity in their evaluation of goals, but again certain differences are to be noted. Germany rated teaching moral values low in contrast to all other countries. Teaching facts and habits of health received highest favor in England and the U.S.A. Teaching religious values was rated very low by the U.S.A.; high in England, Finland and Germany.

Table 18B shows the degree to which teachers felt they should rely on authority in dealing with certain school situations. The one matter in which teachers in the East wanted strict guidance was deciding the time teachers arrive and leave school (except for Japan). The countries where they wanted minimum direction from outside in handling a child who does not work well were Japan and Thailand; Japan, in deciding methods of classroom teaching; Japan, in handling a child who is late; all countries except Vietnam, in contacting parents. Matters in which most of the teachers said they wished some direction were disciplining children (except in India); deciding the schedule of classes (except in Pakistan and Vietnam).

Countries where teachers seemed most uncertain about their role and gave sharply divided opinions as to how matters of classroom control could best be handled were Pakistan, India, and Vietnam. The country where teachers seemed best agreed was Japan, with Korea second.

In the West, in general, teachers from England, Germany and the U.S.A. wished to rely more on their own judgment and less on authority than did teachers from Finland and Canada. English teachers wanted to do their own disciplining, whereas teachers of no other country indicated the same position. German teachers were more insistent on deciding for themselves methods of classroom teaching; on handling a child who is late, on contacting parents, and on reporting to parents. The only matters in which Finnish and Canadian teachers wanted to take much initiative were handling a child who does not work well, and contacting parents. Teachers from Finland were not generally agreed that they could handle tardiness on their own initiative. National differences may stem from the administrative set-up of the individual country.

Table 19B shows how the teachers reacted in the various cities to handling curriculum content and emphasis. The countries which indicated that teachers relied rather heavily on a textbook were

TABLE 18B[a]

Teacher's Responsibility in the Conduct of School Matters

	London England N = 200	Helsinki Finland N = 200	WEST Munich Germany N = 112	Detroit U.S.A. N = 199	Windsor Canada N = 179
Handling a Child who Does Not Work Well					
A	—	5	1	1	2
B	37	116	36	85	77
C	163	79	75	110	98
Disciplining a Child who is Disobedient					
A	4	11	1	6	9
B	84	152	58	136	125
C	111	37	53	55	43
Deciding Methods of Classroom Teaching					
A	3	15	1	7	—
B	114	141	37	127	132
C	83	44	74	63	46
Deciding the Time Teachers should Arrive and Leave School					
A	49	167	57	65	39
B	84	33	46	98	97
C	66	—	8	34	41
Handling a Child who is Late					
A	17	6	2	21	26
B	99	101	25	110	108

TABLE 18B—*continued*

WEST—*continued*

	London England N = 200	Helsinki Finland N = 200	Munich Germany N = 112	Detroit U.S.A. N = 199	Windsor Canada N = 179
Deciding the Schedule of Classes					
A	13	101	27	33	35
B	162	99	78	117	130
C	25	—	6	47	12
Contacting Parents					
A	39	3	1	18	17
B	97	61	20	105	88
C	64	135	90	72	73
Deciding on Methods of Reporting to Parents					
A	53	47	16	78	83
B	118	111	41	99	86
C	29	40	53	20	7
Deciding on the Content of Subject Matter					
A	16	47	26	43	62
B	169	145	80	134	114
C	15	8	5	20	1

KEY:
A: Teachers to follow strict rules laid down by higher authority.
B: Teachers to follow general rules, but to allow for the situation.
C: No set rules; teachers to use their own judgment.

a. As in Tables 1A–36A, where totals do not equal N, the discrepancy is due to questions left unanswered.

TABLE 18B—*continued*

| | | | | EAST | | | |
	Seoul Korea N = 200	Manila, the Philippines N = 200	Yokohama Japan N = 200	Bangkok Thailand N = 200	Lahore Pakistan N = 132	Madras India N = 159	Saigon Vietnam N = 161
Handling a Child who Does Not Work Well							
A	41	39	6	37	21	37	48
B	105	79	64	52	56	84	69
C	51	74	128	103	49	31	31
Disciplining a Child who is Disobedient							
A	18	41	49	68	19	81	41
B	117	75	88	74	47	31	89
C	62	76	63	51	58	41	19
Deciding Methods of Classroom Teaching							
A	22	16	9	17	12	30	64
B	126	125	87	99	55	75	70
C	49	51	104	76	59	47	13
Deciding the Time Teachers should Arrive and Leave School							
A	143	107	91	152	115	131	118
B	40	68	104	25	9	14	17
C	14	16	5	15	1	8	13
Handling a Child who is Late							
A	43	27	9	43	21	50	28
B	115	69	54	82	51	56	60
			127	67	53	48	51

EAST—continued

	Seoul Korea N = 200	Manila, the Philippines N = 200	Yokohama Japan N = 200	Bangkok Thailand N = 200	Lahore Pakistan N = 132	Madras India N = 159	Saigon Vietnam N = 161
Deciding the Schedule of Classes							
A	92	57	81	50	44	47	93
B	93	97	116	121	38	68	42
C	11	35	3	21	43	38	12
Contacting Parents							
A	18	24	9	19	25	20	60
B	85	51	58	46	20	49	59
C	95	116	133	127	81	84	32
Deciding on Methods of Reporting to Parents							
A	73	45	34	69	22	55	66
B	88	60	87	76	42	42	49
C	36	83	77	48	60	55	35
Deciding on the Content of Subject Matter							
A	83	35	37	53	46	57	69
B	101	122	153	111	48	65	59
C	12	31	8	27	27	32	18

KEY:
A: Teachers to follow strict rules laid down by higher authority.
B: Teachers to follow general rules, but to allow for the situation.
C: No set rules; teachers to use their own judgment.
a. As in Tables 1A–36A, where totals do not equal N, the discrepancy is due to questions left unanswered.

TABLE 19B[a]

Guides for Determining Content of Curriculum

	London England N = 200	Helsinki Finland N = 200	WEST Munich Germany N = 112	Detroit U.S.A. N = 199	Windsor Canada N = 179
Textbook					
Agree	6	143	73	67	36
Undecided	16	22	12	44	25
Disagree	117	32	24	80	110
The Curriculum Guide sent by School Authorities such as Ministry of Education					
Agree	83	166	68	112	145
Undecided	50	18	11	33	16
Disagree	66	12	28	49	12
The Time Schedule sent by School Authorities					
Agree	33	92	—	68	73
Undecided	58	35	—	44	51
Disagree	105	66	—	79	46

TABLE 19B—*continued*

| | | WEST—*continued* | | |
	London England N = 200	Helsinki Finland N = 200	Munich Germany N = 112	Detroit U.S.A. N = 199	Windsor Canada N = 179
The Curriculum Guide worked out by Teachers and Principal of the School					
Agree	196	85	42	147	123
Undecided	1	43	16	22	22
Disagree	2	66	44	24	29
The Curriculum Plan worked out by the Individual Teacher					
Agree	130	39	79	102	55
Undecided	22	31	5	32	30
Disagree	46	121	28	58	85
The Content of the Examinations which have been Given in Recent Years by School Authorities for Entrance to the Next Class or the Next Higher School					
Agree	39	62	10	57	32
Undecided	38	37	11	51	25
Disagree	121	94	86	82	111

a. As in Tables 1A–36A, where totals do not equal N, the discrepancy is due to questions left unanswered.

181

TABLE 19B[a]—continued

| | | | | EAST | | | |
	Seoul Korea N = 200	Manila, the Philippines N = 200	Yokohama Japan N = 200	Bangkok Thailand N = 200	Lahore Pakistan N = 132	Madras India N = 159	Saigon Vietnam N = 161
Textbook							
Agree	120	93	73	123	110	80	133
Undecided	50	41	43	38	6	24	14
Disagree	27	64	79	28	7	39	10
The Curriculum Guide sent by School Authorities such as Ministry of Education							
Agree	145	113	101	158	63	121	141
Undecided	37	41	56	13	32	18	7
Disagree	16	41	42	19	26	11	6
The Time Schedule sent by School Authorities							
Agree	117	74	78	79	76	52	117
Undecided	50	62	59	47	22	46	25
Disagree	29	59	61	60	23	41	16

TABLE 19B—*continued*

EAST—*continued*

	Seoul Korea N = 200	Manila, the Philippines N = 200	Yokohama Japan N = 200	Bangkok Thailand N = 200	Lahore Pakistan N = 132	Madras India N = 159	Saigon Vietnam N = 161
The Curriculum Guide worked out by Teachers and Principal of the School							
Agree	99	180	169	133	81	108	120
Undecided	57	14	17	30	24	19	28
Disagree	41	3	12	21	20	16	8
The Curriculum Plan worked out by the Individual Teacher							
Agree	61	105	138	31	103	48	56
Undecided	58	52	34	42	11	21	29
Disagree	75	40	26	102	9	71	51
The Content of the Examinations which have been Given in Recent Years by School Authorities for Entrance to the Next Class or the Next Higher School							
Agree	45	25	17	23	96	55	81
Undecided	50	73	53	30	8	27	47
Disagree	100	99	127	118	22	52	14

a. As in Tables 1A–36A, where totals do not equal N, the discrepancy is due to questions left unanswered.

Korea, Thailand, Pakistan and Vietnam. A guide sent out by higher authority was voted of great importance in all countries but Japan and Pakistan. Even in these countries, many teachers rated it high. But teachers in Korea and Vietnam gave highest place to the time schedule devised by authorities. Teachers giving less importance to the school's attempt to make its own curriculum were Korea and Pakistan. Only the Philippines, Japan and Pakistan thought the teacher's own guide of any great value. Pakistan and Vietnam rated the content of examinations as important.

In the West, English and Canadian teachers objected strongly to the use of a textbook as a guide for curriculum. Teachers in Finland and Germany expressed strong reliance on it. Teachers in the U.S.A. were ambivalent. On the matter of a guide sent out by educational authorities, English teachers were ambivalent. Finnish and Canadian teachers thought such help important. English teachers wanted no set time schedules. All but Germany and Finland wanted individual schools to have a voice in deciding on curriculum. Finland and Canada rejected the idea of the responsibility of the individual teacher. All the countries rejected the idea of being guided by a terminal examination. Clearly, teachers in England. manifest the greatest independence in determining curriculum content. Canada and the U.S.A. were ambivalent and teachers in Finland and Germany looked to outside authority in greater degree than other countries.

The data on certain supplementary helps as benefitting the work carried on by schools are given in Table 20B. In the East, teachers in Korea, the Philippines, Thailand and Vietnam generally opposed the idea of free meals in school, while those in Japan and India favored such a practice. All countries agreed on the need for dental and medical care; free texts and supplies; psychological counselling; and on special schools. Korea was definitely opposed to grants to parents with large families, although India would give grants to widows, and all countries but Korea would give aid to very poor parents. Only in Japan and Vietnam were any considerable number of teachers in favor of free birth control clinics.

In the West, all countries but Finland were strongly opposed to free meals in schools. Only the U.S.A. and Canada strongly opposed free medical and dental care for children. Teachers in the U.S.A. opposed even free check-ups. Only England and Finland voted in large numbers for free care. Only Finland wanted grants for parents with many children and only Germany rejected free textbooks. Teachers in the

Supplementary Aids to Regular Instruction

	London England N = 200	Helsinki Finland N = 200	WEST Munich Germany N = 112	Detroit U.S.A. N = 199	Windsor Canada N = 179
Free Meals in School for all Children					
Agree	11	193	9	16	4
Undecided	8	3	11	18	6
Disagree	177	3	88	157	157
Free Medical and Dental Checkups in School					
Agree	165	199	103	76	103
Undecided	9	1	3	25	22
Disagree	21	—	6	92	47
Free Medical and Dental Services in School					
Agree	123	186	34	43	33
Undecided	19	9	15	31	31
Disagree	55	4	61	117	108
Grants to Parents with Many Children					
Agree	64	141	66	25	24
Undecided	30	37	19	25	26
Disagree	103	19	26	143	119
Free Textbooks and School Supplies					
Agree	102	184	58	105	146
Undecided	11	6	13	33	14
Disagree	87	10	41	54	15

TABLE 20B—continued

WEST—continued

	London England N = 200	Helsinki Finland N = 200	Munich Germany N = 112	Detroit U.S.A. N = 199	Windsor Canada N = 179
Grants to Widows for Support of Children					
Agree	145	134	76	70	100
Undecided	26	44	13	49	28
Disagree	28	16	20	73	42
Free Psychological Clinics and Counselling for Children					
Agree	135	188	103	168	145
Undecided	32	8	6	18	17
Disagree	33	3	3	9	13
Free Birth Control Clinics					
Agree	92	179	33	68	80
Undecided	41	12	12	39	30
Disagree	65	7	61	85	60
Special Schools for Children Not Fitted to Attend Regular Schools					
Agree	198	197	103	182	168
Undecided	2	—	1	7	3
Disagree	—	2	7	5	5
Grants to Very Poor Parents					
Agree	121	130	87	58	56
Undecided	32	35	8	51	44
Disagree	47	31	15	84	70

186

TABLE 20B[a]—*continued*

	Seoul Korea N = 200	Manila, the Philippines N = 200	Yokohama Japan N = 200	Bangkok Thailand N = 200	Lahore Pakistan N = 132	Madras India N = 159	Saigon Vietnam N = 161
Free Meals in School for all Children							
Agree	71	44	135	39	36	97	25
Undecided	33	34	35	33	23	16	38
Disagree	89	114	28	94	64	29	87
Free Medical and Dental Checkups in School							
Agree	169	181	167	149	127	107	142
Undecided	18	12	15	22	4	10	6
Disagree	5	4	16	11	—	18	8
Free Medical and Dental Services in School							
Agree	151	188	154	148	125	91	135
Undecided	31	9	26	18	4	22	13
Disagree	12	2	17	17	1	22	8
Grants to Parents with Many Children							
Agree	12	97	126	137	92	65	105
Undecided	30	62	48	27	25	20	30
Disagree	150	37	24	24	14	51	19
Free Textbooks and School Supplies							
Agree	141	172	158	76	84	110	117
Undecided	27	25	27	51	26	22	22
Disagree	29	2	12	52	20	17	15

TABLE 20B—*continued*

EAST—*continued*

	Seoul Korea N = 200	Manila, the Philippines N = 200	Yokohama Japan N = 200	Bangkok Thailand N = 200	Lahore Pakistan N = 132	Madras India N = 159	Saigon Vietnam N = 161
Grants to Widows for Support of Children							
Agree	40	97	159	52	96	90	106
Undecided	58	59	20	51	27	20	32
Disagree	93	41	19	69	7	26	15
Free Psychological Clinics and Counselling for Children							
Agree	161	180	174	133	105	56	105
Undecided	22	14	13	33	21	33	36
Disagree	11	5	10	19	3	37	12
Free Birth Control Clinics							
Agree	66	30	87	68	62	35	87
Undecided	52	73	70	42	42	24	38
Disagree	75	95	41	59	24	63	30
Special Schools for Children Not Fitted to Attend Regular Schools							
Agree	153	136	181	146	110	94	123
Undecided	26	45	6	19	8	15	22
Disagree	14	19	10	20	10	25	14
Grants to Very Poor Parents							
Agree	28	146	159	148	107	83	113
Undecided	42	34	19	21	20	18	24
Disagree	120	16	21	17	3	31	18

188

U.S.A. were ambivalent about support for widows, whereas other countries supported the idea. Only in Finland were teachers strongly in favour of birth control clinics, with English teachers coming second. Teachers in all countries agreed that special psychological clinics and special schools should be provided for atypical children. England, Finland and Germany would provide grants to very poor parents. Without doubt, teachers in the West reflect rather accurately the degree to which welfare services are presently provided to children. It would seem that teachers are not given to questioning the status quo in matters of social welfare, but reflect it rather faithfully.

Teachers in the East (Table 21B) were pretty well in agreement as to the factors which hinder optimal learning in school. Teachers in Thailand were less positive that they were too burdened with extra teaching duties than were teachers in other countries. Filipino teachers complained about too little help from higher authority. Japanese, Thai, Pakistani and Vietnamese teachers thought there were too many dull children in classes with the bright children. All countries complained of poor buildings, inadequate materials and poor home training of children. Only Vietnamese teachers were seriously concerned about the time required for examinations.

Among the teachers in the West, there was some disagreement as well as some agreement. Teachers in Finland and Germany did not feel harried by too many duties outside the classroom; teachers from the three other countries did. All felt they received adequate help from higher authority. Only the Finnish and German teachers disagreed strongly with heterogeneous grouping of bright and dull children. Other teachers were ambivalent on this point. Teachers in Germany felt most keenly the handicap of poor buildings, while English teachers put stress on the lack of teaching materials. All teachers except the German deplored the poor home training of children and only the British felt to any degree the demands of examinations on the time of the children.

Table 22B shows that Korean teachers disapproved strongly of nursery schools while teachers in other Eastern countries strongly favored making them either compulsory or voluntary. Korean teachers were in favor of private agencies providing them. In no country was there marked feeling that nursery schools should be strongly discouraged.

In the West, England, the U.S.A. and Canada were all strongly opposed to compulsory nursery school education, whereas Finland

Reasons for Poor Achievement by Children

	London England N = 200	Helsinki Finland N = 200	West Munich Germany N = 112	Detroit U.S.A. N = 199	Windsor Canada N = 179
Too Many Children in the Classes					
Agree	187	195	104	166	123
Undecided	6	3	4	14	21
Disagree	5	2	4	15	27
Too Many Duties for the Teacher Outside the Classroom					
Agree	108	64	42	124	99
Undecided	34	41	23	25	27
Disagree	54	92	46	45	45
Too Little Help for the Teacher from Inspectors and Heads or Principals					
Agree	54	23	15	50	55
Undecided	41	43	22	57	33
Disagree	101	131	74	86	79
Too Many Dull Children in the Same Classes with Bright Children					
Agree	97	155	86	76	83
Undecided	37	28	10	45	24
Disagree	64	17	15	72	61

	London England N = 200	Helsinki Finland N = 200	WEST—*continued* Munich Germany N = 112	Detroit U.S.A. N = 199	Windsor Canada N = 179
Poor Buildings and Equipment					
Agree	78	72	60	54	33
Undecided	45	40	20	49	36
Disagree	74	83	31	89	98
Not Enough Books and Teaching Materials					
Agree	112	89	55	96	58
Undecided	26	32	17	24	29
Disagree	58	77	39	71	79
Poor Home Training of the Children					
Agree	144	144	48	146	130
Undecided	32	30	25	23	18
Disagree	20	24	38	25	23
Too Much Time Required for Preparing for Examinations to the Next Higher School					
Agree	92	47	7	8	31
Undecided	45	69	18	61	43
Disagree	60	80	87	121	95

a. As in Tables 1A–36A, where totals do not equal N, the discrepancy is due to questions left unanswered.

191

TABLE 21B^a—continued

	Seoul Korea N = 200	Manila, the Philippines N = 200	Yokohama Japan N = 200	EAST Bangkok Thailand N = 200	Lahore Pakistan N = 132	Madras India N = 159	Saigon Vietnam N = 161
Too Many Children in the Classes							
Agree	170	157	175	141	130	144	150
Undecided	11	27	12	16	1	4	1
Disagree	17	15	11	36	—	4	8
Too Many Duties for the Teacher Outside the Classroom							
Agree	104	169	184	85	82	89	116
Undecided	49	16	4	35	17	16	25
Disagree	44	13	10	63	29	35	14
Too Little Help for the Teacher from Inspectors and Heads or Principals							
Agree	29	110	47	49	70	42	41
Undecided	60	43	105	55	28	34	59
Disagree	105	44	46	70	33	51	51
Too Many Dull Children in the Same Classes with Bright Children							
Agree	78	89	135	100	99	72	91
Undecided	60	45	41	41	13	34	22
Disagree	57	61	23	43	18	33	40

				EAST—continued				
	Seoul Korea N = 200	Manila, the Philippines N = 200	Yokohama Japan N = 200	Bangkok Thailand N = 200	Lahore Pakistan N = 132	Madras India N = 159	Saigon Vietnam N = 161
Poor Buildings and Equipment							
Agree	146	130	160	69	110	85	107
Undecided	36	42	21	32	14	22	15
Disagree	15	25	17	79	5	31	33
Not Enough Books and Teaching Materials							
Agree	121	178	165	96	96	72	111
Undecided	46	13	17	35	18	26	14
Disagree	27	8	17	52	16	32	30
Poor Home Training of the Children							
Agree	154	106	97	91	113	83	130
Undecided	24	73	57	37	11	24	13
Disagree	17	18	45	53	6	32	13
Too Much Time Required for Preparing for Examinations to the Next Higher School							
Agree	78	54	62	21	51	28	69
Undecided	56	81	81	23	28	28	45
Disagree	61	63	56	126	51	63	32

a. As in Tables 1A–36A, where totals do not equal N, the discrepancy is due to questions left unanswered.

193

Importance of Nursery School Education

	London England N = 200	Helsinki Finland N = 200	WEST Munich Germany N = 112	Detroit U.S.A. N = 199	Windsor Canada N = 179
Required of all Children Before they Enter Regular Schools					
Agree	27	89	72	32	52
Undecided	16	41	6	36	17
Disagree	157	68	33	125	105
Provided by the Government for Parents who wish their Children to have these Experiences					
Agree	116	152	92	41	49
Undecided	27	22	8	22	19
Disagree	57	23	9	132	106
Provided for Parents by Private Agencies					
Agree	58	42	25	105	70
Undecided	59	57	23	37	38
Disagree	83	97	62	50	65
Strongly Discouraged and Parents Urged to Keep their Children at Home until they Reach School Age					
Agree	51	15	18	35	40
Undecided	28	29	11	24	24
Disagree	121	150	80	134	109

				EAST			
	Seoul Korea N = 200	Manila, the Philippines N = 200	Yokohama Japan N = 200	Bangkok Thailand N = 200	Lahore Pakistan N = 132	Madras India N = 159	Saigon Vietnam N = 161
Required of all Children before they Enter Regular Schools							
Agree	32	145	114	162	97	121	116
Undecided	40	36	56	20	18	15	25
Disagree	123	18	27	14	13	12	16
Provided by the Government for Parents who wish their Children to have these Experiences							
Agree	83	145	128	163	90	93	93
Undecided	36	35	42	16	23	25	40
Disagree	76	19	23	12	15	24	19
Provided for Parents by Private Agencies							
Agree	109	92	47	72	67	47	58
Undecided	46	81	99	69	39	47	64
Disagree	42	26	48	41	22	45	24
Strongly Discouraged and Parents Urged to Keep their Children at Home until they Reach School Age							
Agree	35	39	13	14	41	42	35
Undecided	47	42	39	22	34	17	49
Disagree	113	118	145	142	52	84	59

a. As in Tables 1A–36A, where totals do not equal N, the discrepancy is due to questions left unanswered.

and Germany mildly favored it. However, England, Finland and Germany were definitely in favor of voluntary schools, provided by the government, a scheme to which the U.S.A. and Canada were opposed. Teachers in the U.S.A. were most in favor of private agencies, but on this point Canadian teachers were ambivalent. Strangely enough, comparatively few teachers felt that the whole matter of nursery school education should be discouraged, although they gave no indication that they considered such education valuable.

In the East (Table 23B), all teachers were strongly in favor of the use of intelligence tests as a basis for promotion to higher schools. All except Japan wanted external examinations and all felt that a satisfactory record of work was important, with Korean teachers dissenting slightly more than the others. Thailand, Pakistan and Vietnam relied on principals' and teachers' recommendations. Korea, Japan and Vietnam were the only countries where teachers in considerable numbers liked standardized tests.

In the West, teachers in England, Finland and Germany liked intelligence tests; teachers in the U.S.A. and Canada did not. England, which has such a test, was strongly opposed to external examinations made and administered by the government, as were Canada and the U.S.A., which do not have them. Finland and Germany both indicated a liking for these tests, both of which have some form of this type of examination. Satisfactory records of work and recommendations by heads of schools were deemed important in all countries. Finland was the only country which expressed a strong liking for standardized tests.

Table 24B shows that in the East teachers in the Philippines were more in favor of high centralization than were the other countries, while Korean teachers favored complete decentralization. In the West, teachers in Finland and Canada showed slightly more preference for high centralization than did the other countries. Otherwise there was almost complete agreement that the middle ground was best, some matters being left to local authority and others to state authority.

In Eastern countries (Table 25B), Pakistan, India and Vietnam were not as enthusiastic about the overall type of teacher organization as were teachers in the other countries. In the West, Finland and Canada were definitely in favor of the primary teacher organization while England and the U.S.A. were definitely in favor of the all-inclusive organization. German teachers were divided in their opinion, with the largest number voting for the primary school organization.

196

TABLE 23B[a]

Admission Procedures to Higher Schools

	London England N = 200	Helsinki Finland N = 200	WEST Munich Germany N = 112	Detroit U.S.A. N = 199	Windsor Canada N = 179
Intelligence Tests					
Agree	104	97	68	25	42
Undecided	40	47	13	16	39
Disagree	55	52	29	151	88
Examinations Made and Administered by the Government					
Agree	36	151	64	17	42
Undecided	33	19	13	9	36
Disagree	131	25	33	165	92
Satisfactory Record of Work in the Primary School					
Agree	192	115	94	188	171
Undecided	4	33	12	5	3
Disagree	4	44	5	3	2
Recommendation of Teachers and Principal or Head of the Primary School					
Agree	161	80	82	152	159
Undecided	16	35	6	21	11
Disagree	23	80	24	22	5
Examinations Made by Professional Organizations Based on Research					
Agree	82	153	39	34	25
Undecided	52	21	17	53	39
Disagree	66	19	53	104	106

TABLE 23B—*continued*

				EAST			
	Seoul Korea N = 200	Manila, the Philippines N = 200	Yokohama Japan N = 200	Bangkok Thailand N = 200	Lahore Pakistan N = 132	Madras India N = 159	Saigon Vietnam N = 161
Intelligence Tests							
Agree	127	140	115	138	89	109	99
Undecided	35	43	55	31	26	9	29
Disagree	31	17	30	20	12	38	23
Examinations Made and Administered by the Government							
Agree	122	121	36	101	90	77	129
Undecided	39	46	61	48	23	32	12
Disagree	33	31	101	37	15	37	16
Satisfactory Record of Work in the Primary School							
Agree	88	183	143	128	99	117	109
Undecided	64	15	39	43	26	22	29
Disagree	41	2	18	21	4	12	16
Recommendation of Teachers and Principal or Head of the Primary School							
Agree	53	79	78	103	71	40	67
Undecided	59	53	64	36	29	24	31
Disagree	82	68	58	48	30	86	52
Examinations made by Professional Organizations Based on Research							
Agree	154	45	95	62	61	37	85
Undecided	24	71	56	57	41	34	43
Disagree	18	83	49	65	25	74	17

a. As in Tables 1A–36A, where totals do not equal N, the discrepancy is due to questions left unanswered.

TABLE 24B[a]

Degree of Centralization for Schools

	London England N = 200	Helsinki Finland N = 200	WEST Munich Germany N = 112	Detroit U.S.A. N = 199	Windsor Canada N = 179
Highly centralized system of licensing and placing teachers, with a uniform salary scale, uniform curriculum, textbooks, and common standards of achievement for pupils	13	42	14	37	45
A centralized system of licensing and placing teachers, uniform salary scale, but local variations in curriculum, textbooks, and standards of achievement for pupils	150	154	90	121	113
Completely de-centralized system with local regulations and variations for teachers and for pupils	37	4	6	35	16

TABLE 24B—*continued*

	Seoul Korea N = 200	Manila, the Philippines N = 200	Yokohama Japan N = 200	EAST Bangkok Thailand N = 200	Lahore Pakistan N = 132	Madras India N = 159	Saigon Vietnam N = 161
Highly centralized system of licensing and placing teachers, with a uniform salary scale, uniform curriculum, textbooks, and common standards of achievement for pupils	34	73	16	43	45	65	35
A centralized system of licensing and placing teachers, uniform salary scale, but local variations in curriculum, textbooks, and standards of achievement for pupils	90	89	153	109	74	78	90
Completely de-centralized system with local regulations and variations for teachers and for pupils	72	37	29	45	12	13	29

a. As in Tables 1A–36A, where totals do not equal N, the discrepancy is due to questions left unanswered.

TABLE 25Bᵃ

Preferred Type of Teacher Organization

	WEST					EAST						
	London England N = 200	Helsinki Finland N = 200	Munich Germany N = 112	Detroit U.S.A. N = 199	Windsor Canada N = 179	Seoul Korea N = 200	Manila, the Philippines N = 200	Yokohama Japan N = 200	Bangkok Thailand N = 200	Lahore Pakistan N = 132	Madras India N = 159	Saigon Vietnam N = 161
For primary teachers only	40	173	55	34	109	82	73	23	72	79	34	97
For secondary and primary teachers	43	2	23	51	27	8	18	77	20	5	61	11
For all levels of teachers: primary, secondary, university, technical	114	25	34	109	42	109	109	99	101	46	62	50

a. As in Tables 1A–36A, where totals do not equal N, the discrepancy is due to questions left unanswered.

In the East (Table 26B), Korea was the only country strongly in favor of control of teacher conduct through law. Korea, Thailand and Vietnam felt regulations by a ministry of education were legitimate. Pakistan, India and Vietnam wanted supervision by the principal of the school. Japan was the only country strongly in favor of regulations made by teachers' organizations and by teachers of the school. All countries favored strong self-discipline.

Temporary reduction of salary was thought a good disciplinary measure by teachers in Thailand; removal to an undesirable area by Korean and Vietnamese teachers. Letters of apology were favored by teachers in India. Japan and Korea had the fewest numbers satisfied with private reprimands.

In the West, teachers in Finland liked control by governmental laws and also, along with England and Germany, regulations by a ministry of education. Finland and Canada favored regulations by supervisors. England, U.S.A. and Canada were all strongly in favor of supervision by the head of the school. All countries felt self-discipline was important.

Only in England did a considerable number vote for permanent dismissal of teachers for grave offense. Finland was content with temporary dismissal with loss of pay. Only England felt a letter of apology was proper. In all countries, teachers would like to keep the discipline of teachers a quiet affair.

The only country in the East (Table 27B) to suggest that married teachers should not continue working when they marry and that men should be better paid than women was Pakistan. Teachers from Thailand were in favor of pay based on merit but not on years of service. Indian teachers were the only ones not favoring paid maternity leaves. All countries wanted liberal allowances for sick leave.

Teachers in the West were well agreed on continued service for married women and equal pay for the sexes. They affirmed their strong belief in a pay scale based on years of service and that teachers should be reinstated after absence for other employment. On the matter of paid maternity leave, England, Finland and Germany were strongly in favor; Canada and the U.S.A., not. All were agreed on liberal allowances for disability and sick leave.

In the East (Table 28B), teachers in all countries but Japan rated promotion high as a means of recognition and for rewarding good teaching. All were certain that increased pay was a good recognition for good work. They were divided on the idea of promotion to teach

TABLE 26B[a]

Control and Discipline of Teachers

	London England N = 200	Helsinki Finland N = 200	WEST Munich Germany N = 112	Detroit U.S.A. N = 199	Windsor Canada N = 179
The Best Means of Control					
Laws passed by the government	6	77	35	43	10
Rules made by the ministry of education	100	144	72	44	61
Regulations by supervisors or inspectors	48	152	46	78	113
Regulations by the principal or head of the school	171	56	22	148	116
Regulations made by teachers' organizations	27	6	39	44	54
Regulations made by organizations of parents	2	5	5	3	1
Regulations made by the teachers of the school	76	40	53	88	32
Individual teacher's own self discipline	162	120	44	127	118
Type of Discipline (Depending on Seriousness of Offense)					
Permanent dismissal	126	86	46	83	90
Temporary dismissal with loss of pay	41	103	29	32	22
Permanent reduction of salary	5	—	7	2	—
Temporary reduction of salary	17	25	29	13	8
Removal to an undesirable position or area	3	22	38	9	—
Letter of apology to the principal, head, or other administrative officer	128	34	40	41	69
Public reprimand from principal, head, or other officer	4	33	1	2	2
Private reprimand from principal, head, or other official	190	193	94	165	163

203

	Seoul Korea N = 200	Manila, the Philippines N = 200	Yokohama Japan N = 200	EAST Bangkok Thailand N = 200	Lahore Pakistan N = 132	Madras India N = 159	Saigon Vietnam N = 161
The Best Means of Control							
Laws passed by the government	124	89	41	57	72	41	53
Rules made by the ministry of education	122	73	68	163	16	49	89
Regulations by supervisors or inspectors	25	82	22	38	28	74	33
Regulations by the principal or head of the school	60	87	37	85	98	94	98
Regulations made by teachers' organizations	51	68	111	58	41	55	17
Regulations made by organizations of parents	8	24	3	11	6	16	25
Regulations made by the teachers of the school	64	45	137	83	44	53	36
Individual teacher's own self discipline	108	110	145	69	81	81	101
Type of Discipline (Depending on Seriousness of Offense)							
Permanent dismissal	63	91	81	53	10	17	19
Temporary dismissal with loss of pay	71	92	52	38	16	38	32
Permanent reduction of salary	6	22	37	85	3	14	8
Temporary reduction of salary	62	89	54	121	61	86	45
Removal to an undesirable position or area	119	69	21	82	61	46	112
Letter of apology to the principal, head or other administrative officer	95	86	69	84	53	129	62
Public reprimand from principal, head, or other officer	81	29	48	157	4	29	3
Private reprimand from principal, head, or other official	81	92	79	171	93	83	136

a. As in Tables 1A–36A, where totals do not equal N, the discrepancy is due to questions left unanswered.

204

TABLE 27B[a]

Special Regulations for Teachers

	London England N = 200	Helsinki Finland N = 200	WEST		Windsor Canada N = 179
			Munich Germany N = 112	Detroit U.S.A. N = 199	
When a Woman Marries she should be Required to Stop Teaching					
Agree	10	1	21	9	10
Undecided	9	1	9	1	17
Disagree	181	193	82	185	148
Men Teachers should have a Higher Salary than Women					
Agree	43	51	10	25	43
Undecided	5	19	5	5	15
Disagree	152	127	97	165	116
Teachers should Not be Paid Salaries According to the Years they Teach, but According to Merit					
Agree	37	9	17	37	44
Undecided	31	12	23	34	30
Disagree	132	173	70	124	97

	London England N = 200	Helsinki Finland N = 200	West—continued Munich Germany N = 112	Detroit U.S.A. N = 199	Windsor Canada N = 179
If Teachers Discontinue Teaching to take other Positions, they should Not be Permitted to Return to Teaching					
Agree	10	5	15	10	11
Undecided	13	7	14	4	5
Disagree	177	185	82	181	158
Women should be Allowed Liberal Maternity Leaves with Full Pay					
Agree	104	191	72	22	14
Undecided	34	3	14	23	10
Disagree	62	4	26	149	149
Teachers should Receive Liberal Allowances for Sick Leave and Disability					
Agree	179	196	67	165	138
Undecided	15	—	22	16	22
Disagree	6	3	20	14	16

a. As in Tables 1A–36A, where totals do not equal N, the discrepancy is due to questions left unanswered.

TABLE 27B[a]—*continued*

| | | EAST | | | | | |
	Seoul Korea N = 200	Manila, the Philippines N = 200	Yokohama Japan N = 200	Bangkok Thailand N = 200	Lahore Pakistan N = 132	Madras India N = 159	Saigon Vietnam N = 161
When a Woman Marries she should be Required to Stop Teaching							
Agree	49	7	8	9	63	41	12
Undecided	28	19	16	16	30	17	10
Disagree	118	168	176	151	36	80	131
Men Teachers should have a Higher Salary than Women							
Agree	44	15	47	18	83	52	16
Undecided	18	33	35	17	12	15	13
Disagree	133	147	118	141	36	79	125
Teachers should Not be Paid Salaries According to the Years they Teach, But According to Merit							
Agree	39	66	53	155	52	55	32
Undecided	39	67	59	21	32	17	63
Disagree	115	62	86	17	44	76	59

TABLE 27B—*continued*

EAST—*continued*

	Seoul Korea N = 200	Manila, the Philippines N = 200	Yokohama Japan N = 200	Bangkok Thailand N = 200	Lahore Pakistan N = 132	Madras India N = 159	Saigon Vietnam N = 161
If Teachers Discontinue Teaching to take other Positions, they should Not be Permitted to Return to Teaching							
Agree	15	45	22	37	34	77	56
Undecided	23	51	30	50	27	23	45
Disagree	157	101	146	95	69	47	52
Women should be Allowed Liberal Maternity Leaves with Full Pay							
Agree	174	162	180	165	113	67	142
Undecided	11	23	16	16	12	19	8
Disagree	13	12	21	11	6	59	7
Teachers should Receive Liberal Allowances for Sick Leave and Disability							
Agree	152	184	154	152	128	128	146
Undecided	29	9	22	21	1	16	4
Disagree	16	3	22	17	—	10	9

a. As in Tables 1A–36A, where totals do not equal N, the discrepancy is due to questions left unanswered.

208

TABLE 28B[a]

Methods of Recognizing and Rewarding Good Teachers

	London England N = 200	Helsinki Finland N = 200	WEST Munich Germany N = 112	Detroit U.S.A. N = 199	Windsor Canada N = 179
Simple Promotion					
Agree	139	68	80	78	103
Undecided	24	55	17	40	26
Disagree	35	70	13	75	40
Increased Pay or Allowances, above Regular Scale					
Agree	98	37	55	86	67
Undecided	26	23	12	32	27
Disagree	75	132	43	74	72
Promotion to a Higher School					
Agree	21	37	17	29	25
Undecided	39	46	26	49	41
Disagree	138	109	66	115	94
Citations, Medals, Honors					
Agree	7	38	16	69	32
Undecided	11	46	11	38	21
Disagree	180	106	82	85	112

TABLE 28B—*continued*

			WEST—*continued*		
	London England N = 200	Helsinki Finland N = 200	Munich Germany N = 112	Detroit U.S.A. N = 199	Windsor Canada N = 179
Choice of Teaching Position					
Agree	80	76	71	111	77
Undecided	61	43	14	34	33
Disagree	55	72	23	48	57
Selection to Office in Teachers' Organization					
Agree	18	58	5	19	22
Undecided	47	50	5	63	58
Disagree	133	83	101	108	83
Self-satisfaction of Work Well Done; No other Reward Needed					
Agree	131	142	47	109	117
Undecided	31	20	12	23	20
Disagree	37	38	51	63	35

a. As in Tables 1A–36A, where totals do not equal N, the discrepancy is due to questions left unanswered.

TABLE 28B—*continued*

				EAST			
	Seoul Korea N = 200	Manila, the Philippines N = 200	Yokohama Japan N = 200	Bangkok Thailand N = 200	Lahore Pakistan N = 132	Madras India N = 159	Saigon Vietnam N = 161
Simple Promotion							
Agree	105	171	82	102	99	109	112
Undecided	53	17	70	39	27	22	23
Disagree	38	11	48	37	3	15	21
Increased Pay or Allowances, above Regular Scale							
Agree	119	184	90	176	130	128	131
Undecided	38	10	56	8	1	8	11
Disagree	40	5	54	10	—	12	12
Promotion to a Higher School							
Agree	81	78	46	66	37	87	61
Undecided	55	58	64	52	36	34	40
Disagree	58	60	90	65	52	25	51
Citations, Medals, Honors							
Agree	102	96	48	111	72	85	80
Undecided	40	66	57	37	33	29	43
Disagree	53	35	95	33	22	27	28

	Seoul Korea N = 200	Manila, the Philippines N = 200	Yokohama Japan N = 200	EAST—*continued* Bangkok Thailand N = 200	Lahore Pakistan N = 132	Madras India N = 159	Saigon Vietnam N = 161
Choice of Teaching Position[b]							
Agree	138	86	103	35	61	48	70
Undecided	24	66	64	62	34	25	40
Disagree	33	45	32	83	30	53	30
Selection to Office in Teachers' Organization[b]							
Agree	31	57		48	38	45	58
Undecided	55	64		56	28	34	45
Disagree	107	74		66	57	54	40
Self-satisfaction of Work Well Done; No other Reward Needed							
Agree	59	86		70	28	48	63
Undecided	48	36		35	21	12	36
Disagree	85	76		75	80	79	55

a. As in Tables 1A–36A, where totals do not equal N, the discrepancy is due to questions left unanswered.

212

in a higher school. Citations and medals were strongly approved in Korea, the Philippines and Thailand but were rejected in Japan. Korean and Vietnamese teachers liked the idea of giving outstanding teachers their choice of teaching position. All rejected the reward of a position in a teachers' organization and, except in Japan, were divided on the matter of giving no extrinsic reward for meritorious service.

England, Germany and Canada liked the idea of promotion for good work; the other countries were divided. Finland strongly rejected increased pay, but England was disposed to accept it. All countries rejected the proposal of promotion to a higher school and citations or medals as rewards for good work. The U.S.A. and Germany were in favor of giving outstanding teachers their choice of teaching position, Canada and England leaned in that direction, but Finland was divided. All countries rejected the idea of serving in a teachers' organization and all but Germany felt that no extrinsic recognition was necessary.

In the East (Table 29B), all countries agreed that immoral conduct should be grounds for the dismissal of teachers. Teachers in the Philippines, Japan and Vietnam showed greatest concern about teachers who use harsh discipline. Korea, the Philippines, Thailand and Vietnam believed that teachers who failed to perform their duties because of lack of responsibility should be dismissed. On the matter of teaching ideas contrary to government policy, teachers were strongly divided: Korea, the Philippines, Thailand and Vietnam tended to believe it should be a cause for dismissal, while Japan strongly rejected this idea and Pakistan and India were undecided. All countries rejected prolonged illness or dispute with a government official as grounds for dismissal, but were ambivalent about teachers with insufficient background, though Vietnam tended to accept this ground for dismissal.

All countries in the West agreed that immoral conduct is proper grounds for dismissal. Harsh discipline of children was considered serious by more teachers in England and Finland than elsewhere. Failure in responsibility was voted a serious offense in the five countries. All but the U.S.A. and Canada strongly rejected the ground that teaching ideas contrary to the government was legitimate reason for the dismissal of a teacher, with more than half of the teachers in the U.S.A. indicating this as legitimate reason. Both prolonged illness and disagreement with officials were rejected as grounds for dismissal by

TABLE 29B[a]

Grounds for Dismissal of Teachers

	London England N = 200	Helsinki Finland N = 200	WEST Munich Germany N = 112	Detroit U.S.A. N = 199	Windsor Canada N = 179
Immoral Conduct					
Agree	145	148	98	135	129
Undecided	25	20	3	27	26
Disagree	26	28	6	32	16
Harsh Discipline of Children					
Agree	77	75	21	52	43
Undecided	48	52	30	58	46
Disagree	74	69	58	82	82
Laziness or Failure to Meet their Responsibilities in Teaching and Maintaining Discipline					
Agree	134	93	60	119	131
Undecided	31	59	23	37	13
Disagree	33	45	28	36	32
Teaching Ideas Contrary to Government Policy					
Agree	28	33	21	103	74
Undecided	55	54	22	37	44
Disagree	114	108	66	47	54

TABLE 29B—*continued*

	London England N = 200	Helsinki Finland N = 200	WEST—*continued* Munich Germany N = 112	Detroit U.S.A. N = 199	Windsor Canada N = 179
Frequent or Prolonged Illness					
Agree	24	20	20	27	36
Undecided	33	31	25	57	34
Disagree	138	146	65	110	100
Disagreement with Principal or other School or Government Official					
Agree	4	17	1	14	11
Undecided	14	22	4	23	21
Disagree	178	156	106	155	138
Lack of Sufficient Knowledge of their Subject Matter					
Agree	76	43	42	88	61
Undecided	45	52	35	55	43
Disagree	77	100	33	50	65

a. As in Tables 1A–36A, where totals do not equal N, the discrepancy is due to questions left unanswered.

215

TABLE 29B—*continued*

	Seoul Korea N = 200	Manila, the Philippines N = 200	Yokohama Japan N = 200	EAST Bangkok Thailand N = 200	Lahore Pakistan N = 132	Madras India N = 159	Saigon Vietnam N = 161
Immoral Conduct							
Agree	132	178	106	161	101	101	107
Undecided	34	9	64	17	10	12	27
Disagree	31	13	28	15	20	35	24
Harsh Discipline of Children							
Agree	48	94	91	70	29	40	83
Undecided	76	39	55	57	57	28	41
Disagree	70	66	31	57	43	74	29
Laziness or Failure to Meet their Responsibilities in Teaching and Maintaining Discipline							
Agree	94	106	73	137	45	43	87
Undecided	54	48	71	35	42	36	37
Disagree	47	45	54	20	43	53	31
Teaching Ideas Contrary to Government Policy							
Agree	111	136	14	101	42	53	118
Undecided	33	26	84	43	32	30	20
Disagree	53	37	101	42	55	46	16

EAST—continued

	Seoul Korea N = 200	Manila, the Philippines N = 200	Yokohama Japan N = 200	Bangkok Thailand N = 200	Lahore Pakistan N = 132	Madras India N = 159	Saigon Vietnam N = 161
Frequent or Prolonged Illness							
Agree	51	68	19	27	28	32	37
Undecided	62	51	81	61	35	33	37
Disagree	84	80	100	93	66	72	80
Disagreement with Principal or other School or Government Official							
Agree	17	13	9	31	22	40	13
Undecided	30	31	34	47	20	33	38
Disagree	147	154	156	95	87	58	100
Lack of Sufficient Knowledge of their Subject Matter							
Agree	75	60	45	62	29	44	70
Undecided	64	88	73	50	35	21	43
Disagree	57	49	81	68	64	69	41

a. As in Tables 1A–36A, where totals do not equal N, the discrepancy is due to questions left unanswered.

217

all. There was ambivalence about removing colleagues who did not know their subject matter, except for the Finnish teachers, who felt strongly that this should not be cause for dismissal.

Table 30B gives the teachers' reactions to certain retirement benefits. All countries in the East (except Japan, which was omitted) were agreed that the same benefits should apply to men and women; that provision be made for the dependents of deceased teachers; and that early retirements should be granted for medical disability. Teachers in Korea and Vietnam asked for later retirement than is now compulsory, while those from the Philippines would like earlier retirement.

Teachers in the West were in strong agreement concerning retirement policy. Only in Germany did teachers express a desire for earlier retirement.

Table 31B gives the reaction of the teachers to certain types of action which may legitimately be undertaken by professional organizations. In the East, all countries reported that they definitely opposed teachers' strikes, except Japan, where opinion was divided. Korean teachers were opposed to putting any sort of pressure on the government, as were teachers in Vietnam. Teachers in other countries were divided in their opinion, except Pakistan, which decidedly favored it. All were in favor of their organizations publishing professional journals, setting up in-service workshops, and providing local meeting centers.

All countries in the West agreed that strikes are illegitimate for teachers, but that other pressures should be put on governments for the betterment of teachers. They also felt that professional organizations should publish journals and promote professional growth. American, English and German teachers showed some enthusiasm for local centers as meeting places.

On type of teacher training institution, considerable differences among the countries of the East appeared (Table 32B), Japanese and Korean teachers voted strongly for almost identical training programs for primary and secondary teachers; Filipino and Vietnamese teachers wanted the single purpose institution, and opinion was divided in Pakistan and India.

In the West, teachers in Canada and Finland were most in favor of the school exclusively for primary school teachers; teachers in the U.S.A. and England were for common training programs and German teachers were undecided.

As a method of in-service training (Table 33B), in the East, there was general agreement that teachers read books and attended professional

TABLE 30Bᵃ

Retirement Regulation

	London England N = 200	Helsinki Finland N = 200	West — Munich Germany N = 112	Detroit U.S.A. N = 199	Windsor Canada N = 179
Same Regulations for Men and Women					
Agree	171	186	107	173	143
Undecided	14	8	2	4	18
Disagree	15	5	2	19	13
Provision for the Widow and Minor Children when a Teacher Dies before Retirement					
Agree	190	175	111	139	145
Undecided	8	19	—	40	19
Disagree	1	4	1	15	8
Retirement made Compulsory at a Later Age than now Required					
Agree	29	16	—	37	51
Undecided	43	45	3	41	34
Disagree	127	135	109	116	86
Retirement made Compulsory at an Earlier Age than now Required					
Agree	21	46	72	32	47
Undecided	43	59	17	45	44
Disagree	135	94	23	118	80
Earlier Retirement with Full Medical Disability Benefits					
Agree	181	178	74	145	110
Undecided	15	15	19	33	44
Disagree	4	6	17	18	21

219

TABLE 30B—continued

	Seoul Korea N = 200	Manila, the Philippines N = 200	Yokohama Japan[b] N = 200	Bangkok Thailand N = 200	Lahore Pakistan N = 132	Madras India N = 159	Saigon Vietnam N = 161
				EAST			
Same Regulations for Men and Women							
Agree	134	183		162	91	129	151
Undecided	31	8		11	8	8	1
Disagree	32	6		17	30	14	5
Provision for the Widow and Minor Children when a Teacher Dies before Retirement							
Agree	170	174		178	129	126	147
Undecided	23	16		9	1	15	5
Disagree	5	7		8	1	9	6
Retirement made Compulsory at a Later Age than now Required							
Agree	106	64		70	39	66	92
Undecided	27	41		46	36	38	39
Disagree	64	92		69	49	40	24
Retirement made Compulsory at an Earlier Age than now Required							
Agree	25	88		21	7	17	5
Undecided	18	67		34	12	27	13
Disagree	150	42		126	103	100	129
Earlier Retirement with Full Medical Disability Benefits							
Agree	155	172		119	118	114	140
Undecided	22	15		47	6	16	9
Disagree	18	10		26	5	24	9

a. As in Tables 1A–36A, where totals do not equal N, the discrepancy is due to questions left unanswered.
b. Omitted from the questionnaire.

220

TABLE 31B[a]

Proper Measures for Professional Organizations

	London England N = 200	Helsinki Finland N = 200	West Munich Germany N = 112	Detroit U.S.A. N = 199	Windsor Canada N = 179
Organizing and Leading Strikes to get needed Salary Raises or other Benefits					
Agree	15	23	32	24	13
Undecided	19	33	9	26	16
Disagree	165	140	69	136	141
Putting Pressures other than Strikes on the Government for Better Salaries and other Benefits					
Agree	174	136	71	140	108
Undecided	13	25	14	23	23
Disagree	12	38	23	22	38
Publishing Newspapers and Professional Journals					
Agree	169	168	101	164	146
Undecided	23	25	7	16	15
Disagree	7	5	1	7	7
Setting up Workshops and Discussion Groups, and furthering other means of Professional Growth					
Agree	148	178	104	175	155
Undecided	38	17	4	9	9
Disagree	13	3	2	4	8
Providing Local Meeting Places and Organizing Social Groups					
Agree	135	74	83	101	65
Undecided	48	90	16	57	53
Disagree	16	34	11	30	51

221

TABLE 31B—continued

| | | | | EAST | | | |
	Seoul Korea N = 200	Manila, the Philippines N = 200	Yokohama Japan N = 200	Bangkok Thailand[b] N = 200	Lahore Pakistan N = 132	Madras India N = 159	Saigon Vietnam N = 161
Organizing and Leading Strikes to get needed Salary Raises or other Benefits							
Agree	21	10	64		35	30	20
Undecided	31	22	76		39	16	40
Disagree	142	166	59		55	99	90
Putting Pressures other than Strikes on the Government for Better Salaries and other Benefits							
Agree	50	81	86		85	80	41
Undecided	26	37	63		22	21	37
Disagree	118	80	51		21	50	72
Publishing Newspapers and Professional Journals							
Agree	154	161	149		92	93	101
Undecided	28	28	37		25	31	27
Disagree	13	10	13		11	26	22
Setting up Workshops and Discussion Groups, and furthering other means of Professional Growth							
Agree	163	187	173		48	73	131
Undecided	25	7	20		47	29	16
Disagree	6	5	6		31	44	9
Providing Local Meeting Places and Organizing Social Groups[c]							
Agree	67	171	145			71	57
Undecided	65	21	44			40	65
Disagree	62	7	10			34	22

a. As in Tables 1A–36A, where totals do not equal N, the discrepancy is due to questions left unanswered.
b. Thailand was omitted from the questionnaire.
c. Omitted in the Pakistan questionnaire.

TABLE 32B[a]

Type of Teacher Training Institution

	London England N = 200	Helsinki Finland N = 200	WEST		
			Munich Germany N = 112	Detroit U.S.A. N = 199	Windsor Canada N = 179
Training institutions set up specifically to prepare primary teachers	22	97	35	22	101
Common training institutions which prepare both primary and secondary teachers, but with separate curriculums	47	46	29	47	28
Common training institutions for both primary and secondary teachers, with some general curriculums in common	94	34	5	86	35
Almost identical training programs for primary and secondary teachers with a small amount of specialization for each group	37	23	41	36	12

TABLE 32B—*continued*

	Seoul Korea N = 200	Manila, the Philippines N = 200	Yokohama Japan N = 200	Bangkok Thailand N = 200	Lahore Pakistan N = 132	Madras India N = 159	Saigon Vietnam N = 161
				EAST			
Training institutions set up specifically to prepare primary teachers	51	135	35	80	52	53	120
Common training institutions which prepare both primary and secondary teachers, but with separate curriculums	5	50	22	85	39	33	21
Common training institutions for both primary and secondary teachers, with some general curriculums in common	28	8	49	16	12	33	11
Almost identical training programs for primary and secondary teachers with a small amount of specialization for each group	115	5	89	16	27	35	7

a. As in Tables 1A–36A, where totals do not equal N, the discrepancy is due to questions left unanswered.

224

TABLE 33B[a]

Methods of In-service Training

			WEST		
	London England N = 200	Helsinki Finland N = 200	Munich Germany N = 112	Detroit U.S.A. N = 199	Windsor Canada N = 179
Reading Professional Books and Magazines					
Agree	186	196	109	181	164
Undecided	11	3	2	8	10
Disagree	1	—	1	7	3
Attending Professional Meetings and Discussion Groups					
Agree	165	172	99	162	152
Undecided	26	17	11	26	19
Disagree	8	10	2	9	4
Returning to Teacher Training Schools for Additional Courses					
Agree	160	153	47	153	122
Undecided	28	34	26	27	24
Disagree	11	9	37	16	28
Studying to be Qualified for the next Higher Level of Teaching					
Agree	48	130	43	56	119
Undecided	69	47	22	73	22
Disagree	81	22	45	62	31
Carrying on Independent Research					
Agree	122	94	84	110	94
Undecided	50	68	22	54	60
Disagree	27	33	6	31	19

225

TABLE 33B—*continued*

	Seoul Korea N = 200	Manila, the Philippines N = 200	Yokohama Japan N = 200	EAST Bangkok Thailand N = 200	Lahore Pakistan N = 132	Madras India N = 159	Saigon Vietnam N = 161
Reading Professional Books and Magazines							
Agree	177	189	190	184	122	143	150
Undecided	15	5	2	2	7	6	2
Disagree	4	2	7	9	2	5	6
Attending Professional Meetings and Discussion Groups							
Agree	163	186	189	142	107	125	147
Undecided	31	9	3	35	18	19	2
Disagree	3	1	8	17	4	10	7
Returning to Teacher Training Schools for Additional Courses							
Agree	21	172	92	121	103	68	85
Undecided	38	18	70	38	19	32	35
Disagree	135	6	38	30	8	49	31
Studying to be Qualified for the next Higher Level of Teaching							
Agree	79	152	103	159	113	99	117
Undecided	62	33	69	18	13	25	27
Disagree	52	11	25	14	5	29	13
Carrying on Independent Research							
Agree	157	113	169	173	118	60	130
Undecided	28	49	23	9	9	30	15
Disagree	10	33	8	11	3	59	12

a. As in Tables 1A–36A, where totals do not equal N, the discrepancy is due to questions left unanswered.

meetings. As for returning to school for additional training, Korean teachers were opposed and Japanese teachers were uncertain. In the West there was general agreement that teachers read professional material and attended professional meetings. Only Germans were uncertain about continued study at training institutions. English, German and American teachers showed little disposition to qualify for the next higher level of teaching. In all countries, a large number wished to carry on independent research.

On methods of licensing (Table 34B), in the East, all countries but Korea favored a subject matter examination, while all chose a test in pedagogical subjects. Demonstration teaching likewise was accepted, except by Korean teachers. A satisfactory record of work in teacher training studies, but not letters of recommendation, was also considered important.

Countries in the West showed unanimity in agreeing that all methods listed in the table were legitimate means of licensing, except letters of recommendation, which was rejected by Finland and Germany. England and Canada were uncertain concerning this method.

Table 35B gives the position which the teachers took toward their own culture and that of other nations. In the East, the teachers generally took a very conservative view. Only in Korea and Japan did they tend to question their own culture as the superior way of life. Only the Japanese rejected the idea that their past culture was superior to that of the present day. All except the Japanese showed some uncertainty about the equal value of all cultures, but were agreed that the potential for equality is certain.

Teachers in the West strongly rejected the idea that their own culture is the superior way of life and, except for Germany, that the past is superior to the present. Only Finnish teachers felt that all cultures are equally good, but teachers in all countries were in agreement about the potential that all nations have for attaining equality. All admitted there are strengths and weaknesses in all cultures.

The countries of the East were in close agreement in accepting all the methods listed in Table 36B for studying the modern world, except that of making study of a foreign language compulsory. This was strongly rejected by the Philippines and strongly accepted by Vietnam. In other countries, opinion on this point was divided.

The same was true of the countries of the West, with Finnish teachers somewhat less concerned about contacts with foreigners, with inviting

TABLE 34B[a]

Methods of Licensing Teachers

	London England N = 200	Helsinki Finland N = 200	WEST Munich Germany N = 112	Detroit U.S.A. N = 199	Windsor Canada N = 179
Passing an Examination in General Subjects such as History, Mathematics, etc.					
Agree	169	132	72	115	135
Undecided	13	31	16	38	18
Disagree	17	35	24	44	19
Passing an Examination in Pedagogy, Psychology, Teaching Methods					
Agree	173	156	108	86	149
Undecided	14	26	3	37	16
Disagree	13	18	1	73	7
Passing an Examination by Demonstration Teaching					
Agree	169	187	105	117	154
Undecided	17	8	4	29	9
Disagree	14	5	2	50	9
A Satisfactory Record of Work in Teacher Training Studies					
Agree	188	179	98	184	162
Undecided	7	14	6	6	4
Disagree	5	6	8	6	6
Presenting Letters of Recommendation from Instructors in Teacher Training Schools					
Agree	88	44	4	123	57
Undecided	60	50	12	37	48

TABLE 34B—*continued*

	Seoul Korea N = 200	Manila, the Philippines N = 200	Yokohama Japan N = 200	EAST Bangkok Thailand N = 200	Lahore Pakistan N = 132	Madras India N = 159	Saigon Vietnam N = 161
Passing an Examination in General Subjects such as History, Mathematics, etc.							
Agree	69	145	149	110	104	100	107
Undecided	47	26	23	36	14	10	16
Disagree	82	27	25	44	10	45	27
Passing an Examination in Pedagogy, Psychology, Teaching Methods							
Agree	163	159	165	178	111	128	149
Undecided	21	24	15	7	13	10	4
Disagree	14	15	20	9	4	16	6
Passing an Examination by Demonstration Teaching							
Agree	76	115	137	98	101	85	138
Undecided	56	57	39	47	19	38	12
Disagree	65	23	24	44	4	27	9
A Satisfactory Record of Work in Teacher Training Studies							
Agree	120	165	136	71	100	101	107
Undecided	36	22	46	53	18	24	30
Disagree	42	11	18	66	14	29	15
Presenting Letters of Recommendation from Instructors in Teacher Training Schools							
Agree	44	53	43	64	18	30	45
Undecided	39	33	65	43	24	16	47
Disagree	115	110	91	84	80	103	60

a. As in Tables 1A–36A, where totals do not equal N, the discrepancy is due to questions left unanswered.

229

Attitudes toward Cultures

	London England N = 200	Helsinki Finland N = 200	WEST Munich Germany N = 112	Detroit U.S.A. N = 199	Windsor Canada N = 179
The Culture of One's Own Country is the Superior Way of Life					
Agree	23	27	5	32	18
Undecided	26	30	16	28	30
Disagree	147	140	87	128	122
The Past Culture of One's Own Country was in most Respects Superior to its Present Day Culture					
Agree	12	5	38	7	5
Undecided	29	21	27	23	15
Disagree	155	170	43	157	149
The Cultures of all Nations are Equally Good					
Agree	45	109	9	65	56
Undecided	35	29	20	32	20
Disagree	116	59	75	87	94
The Cultures of all Nations Including One's Own, have Strengths and Weaknesses which have Historical Origins					
Agree	192	194	108	179	166
Undecided	3	4	2	6	4
Disagree	2	2	—	3	2
Every Nation has the Potential for Developing a High Degree of Culture which fits its People to Live in Equality with all other Peoples in the Modern World					
Agree	173	163	97	167	146
Undecided	12	27	6	15	12

		EAST					
	Seoul Korea N = 200	Manila, the Philippines N = 200	Yokohama Japan N = 200	Bangkok Thailand N = 200	Lahore Pakistan N = 132	Madras India N = 159	Saigon Vietnam N = 161
The Culture of One's Own Country is the Superior Way of Life							
Agree	87	139	63	165	113	118	114
Undecided	66	33	82	17	10	7	16
Disagree	43	27	55	9	6	20	5
The Past Culture of One's Own Country was in most Respects Superior to its Present Day Culture							
Agree	66	95	16	79	83	83	80
Undecided	56	56	83	62	20	36	47
Disagree	73	48	101	41	26	26	21
The Cultures of all Nations are Equally Good							
Agree	68	121	50	65	31	92	83
Undecided	50	46	55	53	50	32	47
Disagree	76	30	94	67	46	25	20
The Cultures of all Nations including One's Own, have Strengths and Weaknesses which have Historical Origins							
Agree	176	176	141	129	95	83	128
Undecided	15	17	13	33	26	32	18
Disagree	7	5	10	22	9	28	5
Every Nation has the Potential for Developing a High Degree of Culture which fits its People to Live in Equality with all other Peoples in the Modern World							
Agree	181	186	176	168	100	105	119
Undecided	10	12	13	18	16	21	18
Disagree	6	1	10	8	13	23	8

a. As in Tables 1A–36A, where totals do not equal N, the discrepancy is due to questions left unanswered.

TABLE 36B[a]

Methods and Means for Understanding the Modern World

	London England N = 200	Helsinki Finland N = 200	WEST Munich Germany N = 112	Detroit U.S.A. N = 199	Windsor Canada N = 179
Careful Study of the Work of the United Nations and its Agencies					
Agree	128	151	69	153	124
Undecided	51	31	31	29	33
Disagree	15	7	10	11	16
Contact with Foreigners Living in One's Country					
Agree	172	86	92	141	108
Undecided	19	72	17	35	48
Disagree	4	32	2	16	16
Inviting Teachers from Foreign Countries to Teach in the Schools					
Agree	174	98	84	165	144
Undecided	15	60	16	21	23
Disagree	6	30	11	7	7
Study, Travel, and Teaching in Foreign Countries					
Agree	181	168	107	175	163
Undecided	9	19	4	12	6
Disagree	5	5	—	6	5
Membership in Teachers' International Organizations					
Agree	131	98	51	128	119
Undecided	48	71	33	48	36
Disagree	16	21	25	15	18
Compulsory Foreign Language Training					
Agree	52	103	58	65	35
Undecided	38	31	27	41	55
Disagree	104	56	26	72	82

232

	Seoul Korea N = 200	Manila, the Philippines N = 200	Yokohama Japan N = 200	Bangkok Thailand N = 200	Lahore Pakistan N = 132	Madras India N = 159	Saigon Vietnam N = 161
				EAST			
Careful Study of the Work of the United Nations and its Agencies							
Agree	103	181	162	160	117	124	108
Undecided	69	10	27	27	6	8	30
Disagree	20	7	10	5	2	14	12
Contact with Foreigners Living in One's Country							
Agree	95	145	115	120	111	103	118
Undecided	69	41	70	49	11	27	23
Disagree	31	10	14	15	7	16	11
Inviting Teachers from Foreign Countries to Teach in the Schools							
Agree	117	134	75	81	79	101	114
Undecided	41	38	87	70	28	24	32
Disagree	32	24	37	34	22	20	9
Study, Travel, and Teaching in Foreign Countries							
Agree	168	166	140	82	111	115	125
Undecided	18	25	49	58	10	14	23
Disagree	9	7	11	42	6	19	6
Membership in Teachers' International Organizations							
Agree	159	154	142	123	103	110	102
Undecided	25	26	46	45	15	14	35
Disagree	10	17	12	22	6	24	10
Compulsory Foreign Language Training							
Agree	78	52	96	86	21	60	126
Undecided	60	46	71	51	32	25	18
Disagree	56	99	30	45	73	57	12

a. As in Tables 1A–36A, where totals do not equal N, the discrepancy is due to questions left unanswered.

233

foreign teachers into their schools. German teachers did not favor membership in international organizations. Finland was, however, the only country which believed strongly that training in a foreign language should be compulsory.

V

THE POSITION OF STUDENTS
IN TEACHER TRAINING

Through improved and inspired teaching everywhere,
all peoples of the world
can achieve a better and happier life.
Waldo Emerson Lessenger

AS A KIND OF CHECK ON THE POSITIONS TAKEN BY TEACHERS (BOTH
younger and older members of the profession) a small sample was taken
of students in training in three widely separated cities: Detroit, U.S.A.;
Hong Kong (under British control); and London, England. These
students were in the latter part of their training period. Since the
length of their schooling and the pattern of courses they had completed
varied greatly, they were asked only general questions concerning their
position on a number of matters relating to the profession.

As closely as possible, the questionnaire devised for them paralleled
the questionnaire given to the teachers. The tables containing their
responses closely parallel those presented in Chapters III and IV.
Tables 37C–49C cover responses given by the students to a number
of additional questions.

The present discussion notes any marked deviation of responses
between teachers and students within the three groups sampled. Where
no pronounced difference of position appears, the comments made on

teachers in Chapter III indicate how students felt concerning matters pertaining to the role and status they expected to assume as future teachers.

As Table 1C indicates, the proportion of women was high in Detroit and London. This may be due in part to the fact that a school enrolling only women was sampled in London.

TABLE 1C[a]

Sex, Age, and Family Status

	Detroit N = 100	Hong Kong N = 100	London N = 85	Total N = 285	Percent of total
Sex					
Male	13	55	—	68	24
Female	87	45	85	217	76
Age					
20–29	59	97	79	235	82
30–39	24	—	—	24	28
40–49	11	—	3	14	5
50–59	1	—	—	1	—
60–69	—	—	—	—	—
Marital Status					
Unmarried	52	99	82	233	82
Married	42	1	3	46	16
Divorced or widowed	6	—	—	6	2
Number of children					
None	57	100	81	238	84
1–3	27	—	3	30	11
4–6	6	—	—	6	2
Over 6	—	—	—	—	—

a. N = number of samples. The percents ignore decimals and are the closest in round numbers. Where totals do not equal N, the discrepancy is due to questions left unanswered.

Marriage was far more common among the students in Detroit than elsewhere; it was practically non-existent in Hong Kong. Furthermore, one-third of those married in Detroit had children and considerably above a third of the total number were older than one would expect for students in training.

Table 3C shows the longer period of training for students in the U.S.A. Students in London and Hong Kong spent far more time in observing or teaching children than had students in Detroit. Three-

TABLE 3Cᵃ

Qualifications for Teaching

	Detroit N = 100	Hong Kong N = 100	London N = 85	Total N = 285	Percent of total
Total Number of Years spent in School as a Student (including Primary School, Secondary School and all others)					
11	—	—	1	1	
12	—	2	—	2	1
13	2	11	6	19	7
14	5	15	6	26	9
14.5	1	—	—	1	
15	26	24	18	68	24
15.5	2	—	—	2	1
16	30	26	40	96	34
16.5	1	—	—	1	
17	13	18	6	37	13
17.5	2	—	—	2	1
18	8	1	3	12	4
More than 19	10	2	—	12	4
Preparation for Full Qualification					
Yes	97	92	82	271	95
No	3	7	2	12	4
Method of Qualifying					
Regular government examination	7	20	32	59	21
Special examination	3	8	19	30	11
Completion of the training course	94	91	75	260	91
Special arrangement	6	—	—	6	2
Clock Hours spent in Observing or Teaching Children					
None at all	6	—	—	6	2
10–50	42	4	1	47	16
51–100	10	18	1	29	10
101–200	14	28	8	50	18
More than 200	28	45	73	146	51

a. N = number of samples. The percents ignore decimals and are the closest in round numbers. Where totals do not equal N, the discrepancy is due to questions left unanswered.

237

fourths of the group in Hong Kong and almost all of the group in London reported one hundred and more hours spent in this activity. This difference may reflect only a difference in the sequence program of the training.

The three cities reported similar influences in choosing education as a profession and, in general, satisfaction with the choice made (Table 4C). There were definite variations, however, in the length of time these students believed they would remain in the profession. Large numbers of those in Detroit and London were certain they would drop out to care for children of their own. Half of those in Detroit, slightly over half in Hong Kong, but only one-fourth in London said they expected to remain in teaching until retirement age. One-fourth of those in Hong Kong hoped to enter some other profession.

Table 5C shows that a majority of students in Detroit and Hong Kong were recruited from a large city; over 70 percent of those in London came from smaller locales. Both in Detroit and London students came from homes where religious teaching was considered important. Three-fourths of those from Hong Kong said little or no attention was paid to religion in their homes. Students in Detroit and London were more insistent on higher moral standards for teachers than were those in Hong Kong. The majority of students in the three cities wished to be placed in teaching positions in their home communities or not too far from home, although a third of the students in London said they had no preference as to where they might be assigned.

More students in Hong Kong preferred a salary which gave them fringe benefits beyond pension than did students in the other two areas (Table 7C).

Table 8C shows there were no marked differences concerning their ideas as to the proper proportion of female teachers in a primary school, except that Hong Kong students were more liberal in accepting women both as staff and as head of the school.

In the rankings assigned various professions and vocations (Table 9C) students in Detroit gave higher rank to the clergyman, to the lawyer, to the businessman, than did students in the other two areas. Students in Hong Kong rated the secondary school teacher and the university professor much higher than did students in the other cities. Students in all three cities agreed on the extremely low status of primary school teachers. This was in spite of the fact that slightly over one-third (except in London, where it was one-fourth) believed that his

TABLE 4Cª

Factors in the Choice of Teaching as a Profession

	Detroit N = 100	Hong Kong N = 100	London N = 85	Total N = 285	Percent of total
Satisfaction with Choice					
Definitely would go into teaching	53	42	44	139	49
Probably would go into teaching	27	13	32	72	25
Uncertain; depends on opportunities	12	38	8	58	20
Would possibly choose another occupation	3	3	1	7	2
Would surely choose another occupation	4	4	—	8	3
People who Approve of Choice					
Parents	81	70	78	229	80
Brothers, sisters	60	44	51	155	54
Fiance	17	11	24	52	18
Husband or wife	35	1	2	38	13
Close friends	72	46	55	173	61
Former teachers	56	45	69	170	60
Anticipated length of professional service					
Until married	8	5	13	26	9
Until have one's own children to care for	42	13	76	131	46
Until one's children are grown	9	12	1	22	8
Until have enough savings to retire on	7	24	1	32	11
Retirement age	50	60	26	—	48
Other profession	1	26	3	30	11
Disillusionment	20	23	17	60	22
Other's support	8	12	20	40	14
New location	3	16	5	24	8
Changes in attitude					
Changed very much	41	23	42	106	37
Changed a little	51	58	38	147	52
Changed not at all	3	12	4	19	7
Don't know	5	7	—	12	4

a. N = number of samples. The percents ignore decimals and are the closest in round numbers. Where totals do not equal N, the discrepancy is due to questions left unanswered.

TABLE 5C[a]

Environmental Background and Choice of Teaching Environment

	Detroit N = 100	Hong Kong N = 100	London N = 85	Total N = 285	Percent of total
Environment of Childhood					
Rural area or small village	13	9	28	50	18
Small city or town (25,000–100,000)	12	10	33	55	19
Large city (*over* 100,000)	60	80	9	149	52
Suburbs of a large city	14	1	15	30	11
Parents' regard for Religious Training					
Paid little if any attention to religion	12	70	10	92	32
Had child observe special rituals and ceremonies	9	2	6	17	6
Placed some emphasis on understanding the basic meaning of religion	38	13	50	101	35
Considered religious instruction very important	40	13	19	72	25
Attitude toward Morals for Teachers					
Higher than for other professions	13	39	5	57	20
Higher than for general public	54	52	48	154	54
Same as for general public	32	7	31	70	25
Choice of Teaching Location					
Rural area or small village	3	4	11	18	6
Small city or town	27	12	32	71	25
Large city	19	40	7	66	23
Suburbs of a large city	39	32	8	79	28
No preference	10	12	26	46	17
Teaching Location with Reference to Home					
Remain in home community	29	36	13	78	27
Go to a community not too far from present home	34	45	29	108	38
Go a considerable distance from present home	15	10	14	39	14
No preference	22	9	29	60	21

a. N = number of samples. The percents ignore decimals and are the closest in round numbers. Where totals do not equal N, the discrepancy is due to questions left unanswered.

TABLE 7C[a]

Choice of Remuneration

	Detroit N = 100	Hong Kong N = 100	London N = 85	Total N = 285	Percent of total
Highest possible salary without other benefits	21	26	17	64	22
Lower than maximum salary with a pension system after retirement	58	21	43	122	43
Still lower salary with provisions for housing, health insurance, and a pension system after retirement	10	39	22	71	25
Minimum salary with all the benefits mentioned above, plus others, such as life insurance, credit and loan arrangements, recreation facilities	10	10	2	22	8

a. N = number of samples. The percents ignore decimals and are the closest in round numbers. Where totals do not equal N, the discrepancy is due to questions left unanswered.

TABLE 8C[a]

Proportion of Male and Female Personnel

	Detroit N = 100	Hong Kong N = 100	London N = 85	Total N = 285	Percent of total
Proportion of Female Teachers					
0–19	1	—	—	1	—
20–39	3	3	—	6	3
40–59	55	14	43	112	39
60–79	34	72	37	143	50
80–100	3	9	3	15	5
Principal or Head					
Female	10	18	6	34	12
Male	56	38	43	137	48
No preference	34	41	34	109	38

a. N = number of samples. The percents ignore decimals and are the closest in round numbers. Where totals do not equal N, the discrepancy is due to questions left unanswered.

241

TABLE 9C[a]

Ranking of Fifteen Vocations as to Prestige

	Detroit N = 100	Hong Kong N = 100	London N = 85	Total N = 285	Percent of total
Governmental Official					
1– 3[b]	45	46	48	139	49
4– 6	27	31	20	78	27
7– 9	15	18	6	39	14
10–12	6	3	6	15	5
13–15[c]	3	2	4	9	3
Government Worker or Civil Servant					
1– 3	1	4	6	11	4
4– 6	6	16	8	30	11
7– 9	6	24	22	52	18
10–12	42	35	24	101	35
13–15	41	21	24	86	30
Doctor of Medicine					
1– 3	90	80	61	231	81
4– 6	5	11	20	36	13
7– 9	—	3	2	5	2
10–12	1	2	1	4	1
13–15	—	4	—	4	1
Lawyer					
1– 3	69	43	51	163	57
4– 6	19	37	24	80	28
7– 9	6	10	7	23	8
10–12	1	5	2	8	3
13–15	1	5	—	6	2
Shopkeeper					
1– 3	—	—	—	0	—
4– 6	—	—	1	1	—
7– 9	5	3	—	8	3
10–12	21	19	9	49	17
13–15	70	78	74	222	78
Artist, Musician or Actor					
1– 3	5	7	5	17	6
4– 6	22	15	7	44	15
7– 9	25	25	21	71	25
10–12	25	31	21	77	27
13–15	19	22	30	71	25

TABLE 9C[a]—*continued*

	Detroit N = 100	Hong Kong N = 100	London N = 85	Total N = 285	Percent of total
Priest or Clergyman					
1– 3	40	27	21	88	31
4– 6	38	28	46	112	39
7– 9	13	18	11	42	15
10–12	4	19	3	26	4
13–15	1	8	3	12	4
Farmer					
1– 3	1	—	—	1	—
4– 6	—	4	2	6	2
7– 9	3	3	25	31	11
10–12	14	12	17	43	15
13–15	78	80	40	198	69
Banker					
1– 3	12	12	8	32	11
4– 6	40	30	27	97	34
7– 9	23	28	30	81	28
10–12	18	22	15	55	19
13–15	3	7	4	14	5
Secondary School Teacher					
1– 3	1	9	2	12	4
4– 6	10	22	9	41	14
7– 9	43	48	29	120	42
10–12	35	19	39	93	33
13–15	7	—	5	12	4
Businessman					
1– 3	7	4	5	16	6
4– 6	39	22	22	83	29
7– 9	26	20	27	73	26
10–12	19	36	24	79	28
13–15	5	17	6	28	10
Primary School Principal or Head					
1– 3	1	6	3	10	4
4– 6	25	31	27	83	29
7– 9	56	42	31	129	45
10–12	13	20	22	55	19
13–15	1	—	1	2	1

243

TABLE 9C[a]—*continued*

	Detroit N = 100	Hong Kong N = 100	London N = 85	Total N = 285	Percent of total
University Professor					
1– 3	14	59	41	114	40
4– 6	51	35	31	117	41
7– 9	30	5	8	43	15
10–12	1	1	2	4	1
13–15	—	—	2	2	1
Primary School Teacher					
1– 3	2	3	—	5	2
4– 6	3	10	6	19	7
7– 9	28	34	15	77	27
10–12	53	44	42	139	49
13–15	10	9	21	40	14
Skilled Craftsman					
1– 3	—	—	1	1	—
4– 6	3	8	2	13	5
7– 9	9	19	18	46	16
10–12	35	32	25	92	32
13–15	49	41	38	128	45

a. N = number of samples. The percents ignore decimals and are the closest in round numbers. Where totals do not equal N, the discrepancy is due to questions left unanswered.
b. Denotes highest rank.
c. Denotes lowest rank.

status had improved in recent times, as Table 10C shows. Table 10C also shows why young people are deterred from going into teaching. Hong Kong students gave highest priority to too little opportunity for advancement as the reason, while students in the other cities gave first place to too low salary.

The students in Detroit showed themselves highly in favor of using only qualified teachers when shortages occur, even though rather drastic adjustment would have to be made in schools (Table 11C). Students in the other cities believed more strongly that unqualified teachers should be used and that length of training periods should be shortened to meet emergencies.

Detroit students spent more time in transportation and in doing school work at home than did the other students (Table 12C). No great differences were reported in time spent daily in some form of

TABLE 10C[a]

Present Status of Primary School Teachers

	Detroit N = 100	Hong Kong N = 100	London N = 85	Total N = 285	Percent of total
Direction of Change of Status					
No change	34	38	27	99	35
Improved a great deal	40	35	19	94	33
Deteriorated	25	27	39	91	32
Reasons why Young People Hesitate to choose this Profession					
Shortage of positions	5	36	4	45	16
Working conditions in schools too unattractive and difficult	53	30	51	134	47
Too little intellectual stimulation in working with children	14	37	12	63	22
Too few teachers who have intellectual interests and tastes	8	19	8	35	12
Too little respect shown to teachers	50	17	31	98	34
Weak teachers' organizations	8	7	2	17	6
Too little opportunity for advancement	57	83	64	204	72
Too much interference from government and superiors	10	22	3	35	12
Too low salary	90	38	75	203	71
Living conditions in rural areas and villages too difficult	2	7	—	9	3

a. N = number of samples. The percents ignore decimals and are the closest in round numbers. Where totals do not equal N, the discrepancy is due to questions left unanswered.

recreational activity (median time was something over an hour). In doing clerical work connected with school, such as correcting children's papers more than half spent less than an hour. More students in Detroit worked longer hours in gainful employment.

Hong Kong students had been absent for illness during the past year considerably more than the others (Table 13C).

Table 14C shows that students in Hong Kong read professional journals less frequently, took fewer trips (dictated, no doubt, by the peculiar political and geographical situation of the city) and attended

TABLE 11C[a]

Ways of Meeting Teacher Shortages

	Detroit N = 100	Hong Kong N = 100	London N = 85	Total N = 285	Percent of total
Using only qualified teachers, however large classes have to be	69	39	28	136	48
Using only qualified teachers, but dividing large classes into double or triple shifts each day	84	79	51	214	75
Using only qualified teachers, but limiting the number of days per week that each child may attend school	58	44	32	134	47
Using unqualified teachers as required	30	47	48	125	44
Relaxing compulsory attendance laws to cut down on the number of children in school	2	10	1	13	5
Closing as many schools as necessary until a sufficient number of qualified teachers are trained	5	7	—	12	4
Shortening the period of teacher training so that more teachers become quickly available	42	64	64	170	60

a. N = number of samples. The percents ignore decimals and are the closest in round numbers. Where totals do not equal N, the discrepancy is due to questions left unanswered.

TABLE 12C[a]

Minutes Spent Daily in Various Activities

	Detroit N = 100	Hong Kong N = 100	London N = 85	Total N = 285	Percent of total
Traveling to and from School					
Less than 20	4	20	22	46	16
20– 39	8	19	3	30	11
40– 59	16	8	2	26	9
60– 79	29	14	5	48	17
80– 99	12	12	2	26	9
100–119	3	4	—	7	2
120–139	15	19	13	47	16
140–159	7	1	4	12	4
160–179	—	—	—	—	—
More than 180	3	1	8	12	4
Correcting Papers or Preparing Lessons at Home					
Less than 20	4	4	1	9	3
20– 39	4	4	—	8	3
40– 59	1	3	—	4	1
60– 79	4	22	1	27	9
80– 99	6	10	2	18	6
100–119	1	3	1	5	2
120–139	25	22	6	53	19
140–159	3	4	5	12	4
160–179	—	4	—	4	1
More than 180	46	15	37	98	34
Engaging in some form of Recreational Activity					
Less than 20	11	7	5	23	8
20– 39	13	20	5	38	13
40– 59	1	6	2	9	3
60– 79	28	19	21	68	24
80– 99	5	3	2	10	4
100–119	1	3	—	4	1
120–139	15	19	5	39	14
140–159	5	2	—	7	2
160–179	—	—	—	—	—
More than 180	6	13	7	26	9

247

TABLE 12C[a]—*continued*

	Detroit N = 100	Hong Kong N = 100	London N = 85	Total N = 285	Percent of total
Doing Clerical Work Connected with School					
Less than 20	29	42	25	96	34
20– 39	15	13	4	32	11
40– 59	3	1	—	4	1
60– 79	9	18	3	30	11
80– 99	3	1	—	4	1
100–119	2	—	—	2	1
120–139	2	—	—	2	1
140–159	—	—	—	—	—
160–179	—	—	—	—	—
More than 180	2	—	1	3	1
Working for Money					
Less than 20	32	43	34	109	38
20– 39	2	1	—	3	1
40– 59	—	2	—	2	1
60– 79	3	14	2	19	7
80– 99	2	4	—	6	2
100–119	—	1	—	1	—
120–139	5	6	—	11	4
140–159	—	1	—	1	—
160–179	—	—	—	—	—
More than 180	23	4	—	27	9

a. N = number of samples. The percents ignore decimals and are the closest in round numbers. Where totals do not equal N, the discrepancy is due to questions left unanswered.

TABLE 13C[a]

Number of Days Absent for Illness During Past Year

	Detroit N = 100	Hong Kong N = 100	London N = 85	Total N = 285	Percent of total
None	65	37	45	147	52
1– 5	28	49	22	99	35
6–10	5	7	2	14	5
11–15	—	1	2	3	1
16–20	—	3	—	3	1
Over 20	—	1	—	1	—

a. N = number of samples. The percents ignore decimals and are the closest in round numbers. Where totals do not equal N, the discrepancy is due to questions left unanswered.

TABLE 14C[a]
Regular Cultural Activities

	Detroit N = 100	Hong Kong N = 100	London N = 85	Total N = 285	Percent of total
Daily general newspaper	99	97	78	274	96
Professional newspaper or journals	47	27	49	123	43
Daily radio listening	91	82	79	252	88
Popular magazines and journals	83	81	64	228	80
Daily television viewing	77	20	15	112	39
Taking one yearly trip of at least 300 kilometers (200 miles) away from home	81	4	75	160	56
Attending at least one professional or cultural meeting each month	34	17	41	92	32
Seeing at least one motion picture a month	61	78	64	203	71
Attending at least one concert or theatre performance during the year	75	67	83	225	79
Visiting a library at least once each month	91	80	76	247	87
Reading at least one book each month	73	68	79	220	77
None of the above	—	—	—	—	—

a. N = number of samples. The percents ignore decimals and are the closest in round numbers. Where totals do not equal N, the discrepancy is due to questions left unanswered.

fewer cultural meetings than did students in the other cities. Detroit students saw much more TV than did the others. In other matters, London and Detroit students followed much the same pattern in their cultural activities.

Nor did they vary much in their ideas about the proper kinds of community work in which teachers might like to engage (Table 15C). A higher proportion in Hong Kong suggested that teaching adults to read and write and directing children and youth in community improvement projects as community activities were legitimate activities for teachers.

TABLE 15C[a]

Participation in Community Activities related to Education

	Detroit N = 100	Hong Kong N = 100	London N = 85	Total N = 285	Percent of total
Teaching adults to read and write	37	58	36	131	46
Teaching adults such skills as sewing, cooking, animal care, crop raising, sanitary measures	20	47	35	102	36
Directing children and youth in projects to improve the community	63	88	71	222	78
Working in projects to improve the community	62	71	55	188	66
No community work except that closely connected to the regular work of the school	25	8	4	37	13

a. N = number of samples. The percents ignore decimals and are the closest in round numbers. Where totals do not equal N, the discrepancy is due to questions left unanswered.

Students in the three cities were remarkably well agreed on the chief goals of primary education (Table 17C). Those in Hong Kong placed more stress on teaching moral values than did the others. Those in Detroit placed less stress on teaching facts and habits of good health and on teaching religious values and ideals. London students played down teaching civic skills and facts about history and other content subjects and skill in group thinking.

Chief Goals of Primary Education

	Detroit N = 100	Hong Kong N = 100	London N = 85	Total N = 285	Percent of total
Moral values	44	78	49	171	60
Basic skills such as reading, writing and simple arithmetic	96	86	79	261	92
Social skills such as learning how to get along with other people inside and outside the family	82	82	79	243	85
Facts of history, geography, mathematics	26	23	7	56	20
Civic skills necessary to democratic government	50	23	—	73	26
Vocational skills to be used later in earning a living	24	22	15	61	21
Facts and habits of good health	28	54	60	142	50
To reason and think	86	66	82	234	82
Religious values and ideals	3	13	36	52	18
Obedience in obeying orders	13	19	12	44	15
Skill in group thinking	27	17	4	48	17

a. N = number of samples. The percents ignore decimals and are the closest in round numbers. Where totals do not equal N, the discrepancy is due to questions left unanswered.

Table 18C covers students' opinions on teachers' responsibility in the conduct of school matters. They felt that outside authority should be strongly relied upon: in handling a child who does not work well (Detroit); in deciding time teachers should arrive and leave school (Detroit and Hong Kong); and in deciding matters of reporting to parents (Hong Kong). Matters in which the initiative of the teacher is demanded were: handling a child who does not work well (Hong Kong and London); deciding on methods of classroom teaching (Hong Kong and London); deciding on class schedule (Detroit); contacting parents (Detroit and Hong Kong). Thus there was considerable disagreement among the students of the three cities as to

TABLE 18C[a]

Teacher's Responsibility in the Conduct of School Matters

	Detroit N = 100	Hong Kong N = 100	London N = 85	Total N = 285	Percent of total
Handling a Child who does Not Work Well					
A	41	9	—	50	18
B	59	27	12	98	34
C	—	64	71	135	47
Disciplining a Child who is Disobedient					
A	8	9	—	17	6
B	66	58	36	160	56
C	25	33	47	105	37
Deciding Methods of Classroom Teaching					
A	3	8	1	12	4
B	57	41	35	133	47
C	39	51	47	137	48
Deciding the Time Teachers Arrive and Leave School					
A	58	66	32	156	55
B	35	29	37	101	35
C	7	5	14	26	9
Handling a Child who is Late					
A	6	13	1	20	7
B	48	55	45	148	52
C	46	32	37	115	40
Deciding the Schedule of Classes					
A	6	26	3	35	12
B	52	58	53	163	57
C	42	16	27	85	30
Contacting Parents					
A	6	1	9	16	6
B	42	38	51	131	46
C	52	61	23	136	48

TABLE 18C[a]—*continued*

	Detroit N = 100	Hong Kong N = 100	London N = 85	Total N = 285	Percent of total
Deciding on Methods of Reporting to Parents					
A	24	41	21	86	30
B	60	46	50	156	55
C	16	13	12	41	14
Deciding on Content of Subject Matter					
A	13	4	3	20	7
B	73	76	57	206	72
C	14	20	23	57	20

KEY:
  A. Teachers to follow strict rules laid down by higher authority.
  B. Teachers to follow general rules but to allow for the situations.
  C. No set rules; teachers to use their own judgment.

a. N = number of samples. The percents ignore decimals and are the closest in round numbers. Where totals do not equal N, the discrepancy is due to questions left unanswered.

what are the proper spheres for relying on authority and for the teacher using his own initiative.

There was considerable unanimity among the students of the three cities concerning the proper guides for determining the content of the curriculum, with the Hong Kong students showing slightly more definite leanings toward authorities and the guide sent by the school (Table 19C).

In general, the Hong Kong students were more liberal than students in Detroit and London in providing supplementary aids to children and their parents (Table 20C). The Detroit and London students rejected free meals. Detroit students were generally opposed to any sort of health service or of grants to parents. More than one-half of the London students favored free birth control clinics, while only one-fourth of the students in each of the other cities took this position.

All the students were definitely certain that large classes are a reason for poor school achievement (Table 21C). London students were not so aware of too many duties for teachers outside the classroom. Students in Hong Kong were more certain that inadequate help from supervisors or school heads contributed to poor achievement. Hong Kong students also felt heterogeneous grouping, poor buildings and

Guides for Determining Content of Curriculum

	Detroit N = 100	Hong Kong N = 100	London N = 85	Total N = 285	Percent of total
Textbook					
Agree	17	11	—	28	10
Undecided	26	15	6	47	16
Disagree	54	69	76	199	70
The Curriculum Guide sent by School Authorities such as Ministry of Education					
Agree	37	65	33	135	47
Undecided	30	15	27	72	25
Disagree	29	17	24	70	25
The Time Schedule sent by School Authorities					
Agree	23	52	22	97	34
Undecided	27	30	21	78	27
Disagree	47	15	40	102	36
The Curriculum Guide worked out by Teachers and Principal of the School					
Agree	82	82	78	242	85
Undecided	11	9	3	23	8
Disagree	4	6	3	13	5
The Curriculum Plan worked out by the Individual Teacher					
Agree	79	61	75	215	75
Undecided	9	19	3	31	11
Disagree	11	16	6	33	12
The Content of the Examinations which have been given in Recent Years by School Authorities for Entrance to the Next Higher School					
Agree	21	43	21	85	30
Undecided	26	27	19	72	25
Disagree	51	27	44	122	43

a. N = number of samples. The percents ignore decimals and are the closest in round numbers. Where totals do not equal N, the discrepancy is due to questions left unanswered.

TABLE 20C[a]

Supplementary Aids to Regular Instruction

	Detroit N = 100	Hong Kong N = 100	London N = 85	Total N = 285	Percent of total
Free Meals in School for all Children					
Agree	14	43	14	71	25
Undecided	18	18	15	51	18
Disagree	65	31	53	149	52
Free Medical and Dental Check-ups in School					
Agree	31	84	78	193	68
Undecided	23	3	2	28	10
Disagree	43	5	3	51	18
Free Medical and Dental Service in School					
Agree	17	84	68	169	59
Undecided	22	3	6	31	11
Disagree	58	5	10	73	26
Grants to Parents with Many Children					
Agree	15	50	26	91	32
Undecided	21	23	21	65	23
Disagree	61	17	37	115	46
Free Textbooks and School Supplies					
Agree	62	51	73	186	65
Undecided	22	23	6	51	18
Disagree	13	19	4	36	13
Grants to Widows for Support of Children					
Agree	27	65	68	160	56
Undecided	26	12	11	49	17
Disagree	43	16	5	64	22
Free Psychological Clinics and Counselling for Children					
Agree	82	65	64	211	74
Undecided	9	18	8	35	12
Disagree	4	10	10	24	8

TABLE 20C[a]—*continued*

	Detroit N = 100	Hong Kong N = 100	London N = 85	Total N = 285	Percent of total
Free Birth Control Clinics					
Agree	27	26	50	103	36
Undecided	19	24	19	62	22
Disagree	51	39	14	104	36
Special Schools for Children Not fitted to Attend Regular Schools					
Agree	87	78	83	248	87
Undecided	7	11	—	18	6
Disagree	3	1	—	4	1
Grants to Very Poor Parents					
Agree	34	72	61	167	59
Undecided	24	8	15	47	16
Disagree	39	11	6	56	20

a. N = number of samples. The percents ignore decimals and are the closest in round numbers. Where totals do not equal N, the discrepancy is due to questions left unanswered.

TABLE 21C[a]

Reasons for Poor Achievement by Children

	Detroit N = 100	Hong Kong N = 100	London N = 85	Total N = 285	Percent of total
Too many Children in the Classes					
Agree	61	74	75	210	74
Undecided	19	10	4	33	12
Disagree	18	13	5	36	13
Too many Duties for the Teacher Outside the Classroom					
Agree	52	41	29	122	43
Undecided	24	20	23	67	24
Disagree	21	36	32	89	31
Too Little Help for the Teacher from Inspectors and Heads or Principals					
Agree	26	47	18	91	32
Undecided	33	25	28	86	30
Disagree	37	23	36	96	34

TABLE 21C[a]—*continued*

	Detroit N = 100	Hong Kong N = 100	London N = 85	Total N = 285	Percent of total
Too many Dull Children in the Same Classes with Bright Children					
Agree	15	57	34	106	37
Undecided	21	21	14	56	20
Disagree	61	18	36	115	40
Poor Buildings and Equipment					
Agree	36	57	42	135	47
Undecided	32	13	16	61	21
Disagree	29	27	26	82	29
Not Enough Books and Teaching Materials					
Agree	63	49	48	160	56
Undecided	16	22	14	52	18
Disagree	18	25	21	64	22
Poor Home Training of the Children					
Agree	59	81	55	195	68
Undecided	24	9	13	46	16
Disagree	14	7	14	35	12
Too much Time Required for Preparing for Examinations to the Next Higher School					
Agree	15	72	65	152	53
Undecided	30	7	11	48	17
Disagree	51	18	7	76	27

a. N = number of samples. The percents ignore decimals and are the closest in round numbers. Where totals do not equal N, the discrepancy is due to questions left unanswered.

equipment, and poor home training of children were serious handicaps. Detroit students were keenly aware of a lack of books and supplies but did not feel pressed by the demands of preparing the children for an examination.

Nor were students at all persuaded of the need for nursery school education (Table 22C). Only the Hong Kong students were strongly in favor of it.

Hong Kong and London students were more disposed to use intelligence tests in deciding on promotion for children than were Detroit

TABLE 22C[a]

Importance of Nursery School Education

	Detroit N = 100	Hong Kong N = 100	London N = 85	Total N = 285	Percent of total
Required by all Children before they enter Regular Schools					
Agree	23	64	14	101	35
Undecided	27	13	10	50	18
Disagree	49	15	58	122	43
Provided by the Government for Parents who wish their Children to have these Experiences					
Agree	25	63	73	158	55
Undecided	11	12	4	27	9
Disagree	61	17	4	82	29
Provided for Parents by Private Agencies					
Agree	50	41	15	106	37
Undecided	19	25	22	66	23
Disagree	29	25	44	98	34
Strongly Discouraged and Parents urged to keep their Children at Home Until they Reach School Age					
Agree	6	7	3	16	6
Undecided	12	7	3	22	8
Disagree	79	77	75	231	81

a. N = number of samples. The percents ignore decimals and are the closest in round numbers. Where totals do not equal N, the discrepancy is due to questions left unanswered.

students (Table 23C). Only the Hong Kong students favored examinations made and administered by the government.

Students in the three cities were in favor of modified centralization of school systems (Table 24C).

All but the Hong Kong students favored a multilevel professional organization for teachers (Table 25C). These leaned toward an exclusive organization for primary teachers only.

258

TABLE 23C[a]

Admission Procedures to Higher Schools

	Detroit N = 100	Hong Kong N = 100	London N = 85	Total N = 285	Percent of total
Intelligence Tests					
Agree	16	59	48	123	43
Undecided	29	18	11	58	20
Disagree	53	15	23	91	32
Examinations made and Administered by the Government					
Agree	4	59	13	76	27
Undecided	26	14	17	57	20
Disagree	66	19	52	137	48
Satisfactory Record of Work in the Primary School					
Agree	94	74	73	241	85
Undecided	3	11	5	19	7
Disagree	2	5	4	11	4
Recommendation of Teachers and Head of the Primary School					
Agree	75	48	60	183	64
Undecided	16	21	5	42	15
Disagree	6	22	17	45	16
Examinations made by Professional Organizations Based on Research					
Agree	15	38	28	81	28
Undecided	32	25	23	80	28
Disagree	49	27	31	107	38

a. N = number of samples. The percents ignore decimals and are the closest in round numbers. Where totals do not equal N, the discrepancy is due to questions left unanswered.

For the control and discipline of teachers (Table 26C), Hong Kong students were more in favor of regulations from a ministry of education and less in favor of regulations by a principal than were the students in the other cities. Detroit students were more willing to rely on regulations made by the staff of a school. Perhaps the most interesting fact to be deduced from the table is the willingness of future teachers

TABLE 24C[a]

Degree of Centralization for Schools

	Detroit N = 100	Hong Kong N = 100	London N = 85	Total N = 285	Percent of total
Highly centralized system of licensing and placing teachers, with a uniform salary scale, uniform curriculum, textbooks and common standards of achievement for pupils	10	14	7	31	11
A centralized system of licensing and placing teachers, uniform salary scale, but local variations in curriculum, text-books, and standards of achievement for pupils	65	76	64	205	72
Completely decentralized system with local regulations and variations for teachers and for pupils	24	8	13	45	16

a. N = number of samples. The percents ignore decimals and are the closest in round numbers. Where totals do not equal N, the discrepancy is due to questions left unanswered.

TABLE 25C[a]

Preferred Type of Teacher Organization

	Detroit N = 100	Hong Kong N = 100	London N = 85	Total N = 285	Percent of total
For primary teachers only	30	45	10	85	30
For secondary and primary teachers	18	16	16	50	18
For all levels of teachers: primary, secondary, university, technical	50	35	57	142	50

a. N = number of samples. The percents ignore decimals and are the closest in round numbers. Where totals do not equal N, the discrepancy is due to questions left unanswered.

TABLE 26C[a]

Control and Discipline of Teachers

	Detroit N = 100	Hong Kong N = 100	London N = 85	Total N = 285	Percent of total
The Best Means of Control					
Laws passed by the government	25	17	12	54	19
Rules made by the ministry of education	10	70	40	120	42
Regulations by supervisors or inspectors	29	19	14	62	22
Regulations by the principal or head of the school	61	39	57	157	55
Regulations made by teachers' organizations	41	47	22	110	39
Regulations made by organizations of parents	5	5	9	19	7
Regulations made by the teachers of the school	50	30	31	111	39
Individual teacher's own self-discipline	71	63	69	203	71
Type of Discipline (Depending on Seriousness of Offense)					
Permanent dismissal	48	23	44	115	40
Temporary dismissal with loss of pay	23	26	8	57	20
Permanent reduction of salary	1	4	2	7	2
Temporary reduction of salary	9	—	8	17	6
Removal to an undesirable position or area	4	23	—	27	9
Letter of apology to the principal, head or other administrative officer	35	72	49	156	55
Public reprimand from principal, head or other officer	—	7	—	7	2
Private reprimand from principal, head or other official	68	58	77	203	71

a. N = number of samples. The percents ignore decimals and are the closest in round numbers. Where totals do not equal N, the discrepancy is due to questions left unanswered.

to rely on many means of authoritarian control. However, they also wish to rely on self-discipline for teachers.

Probably because there was a considerable number of men among the Hong Kong students, more of them said men teachers should receive a higher salary than women (Table 27C). They also favored

TABLE 27C[a]

Special Regulations for Teachers

	Detroit N = 100	Hong Kong N = 100	London N = 85	Total N = 285	Percent of total
When a Woman Marries she should be Required to Stop Teaching					
Agree	2	8	1	11	4
Undecided	1	12	1	14	5
Disagree	95	70	79	244	86
Men Teachers should have a Higher Salary than Women					
Agree	15	37	24	76	27
Undecided	10	10	7	27	9
Disagree	73	43	51	167	59
Teachers should not be Paid Salaries according to the Years they Teach, but According to their Merit					
Agree	39	43	15	97	34
Undecided	26	26	18	70	25
Disagree	34	22	49	105	37
If Teachers Discontinue Teaching to take other Positions, they should Not be Permitted to Return to Teaching					
Agree	4	21	5	30	11
Undecided	6	14	3	23	8
Disagree	88	56	74	218	76
Women Should be Allowed Liberal Maternity Leaves with Full Pay					
Agree	17	71	32	120	42
Undecided	18	7	6	31	11
Disagree	63	12	34	109	38
Teachers should Receive Liberal Allowances for Sick Leave and Disability					
Agree	63	79	76	218	76
Undecided	21	8	4	33	12
Disagree	14	3	2	19	7

a. N = number of samples. The percents ignore decimals and are the closest in round numbers. Where totals do not equal N, the discrepancy is due to questions left unanswered.

262

merit pay and were strongly in favor of a liberal policy concerning maternity leaves for women with full pay.

Hong Kong students were more in favor of rewarding good teachers through promotion and by serving in a teachers' organization than were the other students (Table 28C). Both Detroit and Hong Kong students favored increased pay; all wanted a choice of teaching positions. London students strongly rejected all ideas of using medals, honors or citations as a means of reward.

In checking possible grounds for the dismissal of teachers, students in Hong Kong felt mostly strongly that immoral conduct was a legitimate cause (Table 29C). Students in Detroit and London gave high rating to irresponsibility. Detroit students felt, more strongly than the other two groups, that teaching ideas contrary to government policy was a serious offense, though as many were against the notion as were for it. The London students were the most liberal on this point. In all cities, however, there was division among the student group from each city.

The positions taken regarding retirement showed considerable variation (Table 30C). Detroit students did not choose the same regulations for men and women and did not feel that a widow should be provided for. Also, that they had given little thought to retirement was clear in that a large proportion voted both for earlier and for later retirement than is now usual. Hong Kong students wanted earlier retirement; London students seemed agreed that the present retirement age is satisfactory to them.

That student teachers tend to be conservative, particularly in Detroit, is shown in Table 31C. Students generally did not favor strikes, two-thirds of their combined groups indicating their opposition mildly. Even putting other pressures on the government was not strongly advocated, although over half the students in Detroit and London felt such measures were legitimate. The students seemed content to let professional organizations occupy themselves with purely professional matters.

Only the Hong Kong students showed much liking for a teacher training unit exclusively for educating primary teachers (Table 32C). London students favored a common training institution for both primary and secondary teachers with some general curriculums in common.

In thinking about future in-service training, only the students in Detroit showed much inclination for returning to teacher training

TABLE 28C[a]

Methods of Recognizing and Rewarding Good Teachers

	Detroit N = 100	Hong Kong N = 100	London N = 85	Total N = 285	Percent of total
Simple Promotion					
Agree	28	75	37	140	49
Undecided	29	9	24	62	22
Disagree	39	13	24	66	23
Increased Pay or Allowance					
Agree	64	62	47	173	61
Undecided	18	16	12	46	16
Disagree	14	19	25	58	20
Promotion to a Higher School					
Agree	10	68	8	86	30
Undecided	29	16	20	65	23
Disagree	52	13	55	120	42
Citations, Medals, Honors					
Agree	26	35	—	61	21
Undecided	19	23	3	45	16
Disagree	49	38	80	167	56
Choice of Teaching Position					
Agree	56	49	51	156	55
Undecided	18	21	18	57	20
Disagree	21	26	15	62	22
Selection to Office in Teachers' Organization					
Agree	17	42	6	65	23
Undecided	29	25	38	92	32
Disagree	48	28	39	115	40
Self-satisfaction of work Well Done; No other Reward Needed					
Agree	60	55	63	178	62
Undecided	17	13	7	37	13
Disagree	21	28	15	64	22

a. N = number of samples. The percents ignore decimals and are the closest in round numbers. Where totals do not equal N, the discrepancy is due to questions left unanswered.

Grounds for Dismissal of Teachers

	Detroit N = 100	Hong Kong N = 100	London N = 85	Total N = 285	Percent of total
Immoral Conduct					
Agree	69	90	46	205	72
Undecided	10	4	14	28	10
Disagree	19	5	25	49	17
Harsh Discipline of Children					
Agree	30	43	36	109	38
Undecided	41	26	20	87	31
Disagree	25	28	29	82	29
Laziness or Failure to Meet their Responsibilities in Teaching and Maintaining Discipline					
Agree	60	54	62	176	62
Undecided	20	17	7	44	15
Disagree	15	26	15	56	20
Teaching Ideas Contrary to Government Policy					
Agree	33	21	17	71	25
Undecided	32	28	22	82	29
Disagree	32	47	46	125	44
Frequent or Prolonged Illness					
Agree	13	17	7	37	13
Undecided	33	28	26	87	31
Disagree	51	52	51	154	54
Disagreement with Principal or other School or Government Official					
Agree	8	7	3	18	6
Undecided	13	13	13	39	14
Disagree	76	76	68	220	77
Lack of Sufficient Knowledge of their Subject Matter					
Agree	57	37	27	121	42
Undecided	18	23	33	74	26
Disagree	24	37	24	85	30

a. N = number of samples. The percents ignore decimals and are the closest in round numbers. Where totals do not equal N, the discrepancy is due to questions left unanswered.

TABLE 30C[a]

Retirement Regulations

	Detroit N = 100	Hong Kong N = 100	London N = 85	Total N = 285	Percent of total
Same Regulations for Men and Women					
Agree	16	55	60	131	46
Undecided	29	14	5	48	17
Disagree	53	18	17	88	31
Provision for the Widow and Minor Children when a Teacher Dies before retirement					
Agree	4	71	78	153	54
Undecided	26	8	2	36	13
Disagree	66	6	2	74	26
Retirement made Compulsory at a Later Age than now Required					
Agree	94	42	10	146	51
Undecided	3	25	24	52	18
Disagree	2	20	48	70	25
Retirement made Compulsory at an Earlier Age than now Required					
Agree	75	9	4	88	31
Undecided	16	21	24	61	21
Disagree	6	57	53	116	41
Earlier Retirement with Full Medical Disability Benefits					
Agree	15	65	69	149	52
Undecided	32	13	3	48	17
Disagree	49	8	9	66	23

a. N = number of samples. The percents ignore decimals and are the closest in round numbers. Where totals do not equal N, the discrepancy is due to questions left unanswered.

TABLE 31C[a]

Proper Measures for Professional Organizations

	Detroit N = 100	Hong Kong N = 100	London N = 85	Total N = 285	Percent of total
Organizing and Leading Strikes to get Needed Salary Raises or Other Benefits					
Agree	15	21	9	45	16
Undecided	13	10	3	26	9
Disagree	68	55	69	192	67
Putting Pressures other than Strikes on the Government for Better Salaries and other Benefits					
Agree	58	29	56	143	50
Undecided	15	14	12	41	14
Disagree	24	42	13	79	28
Publishing Newspapers and Professional Journals					
Agree	84	52	67	203	71
Undecided	11	24	9	44	15
Disagree	2	10	3	15	5
Setting up Workshops and Discussion Groups, and Furthering Other Means of Professional Growth					
Agree	92	55	58	205	72
Undecided	4	18	20	42	15
Disagree	1	12	1	14	5
Providing Local Meeting Places and Organizing Groups					
Agree	61	66	52	179	63
Undecided	22	13	22	57	20
Disagree	4	14	5	23	8

a. N = number of samples. The percents ignore decimals and are the closest in round numbers. Where totals do not equal N, the discrepancy is due to questions left unanswered.

TABLE 32C[a]

Type of Teacher Training Institution

	Detroit N = 100	Hong Kong N = 100	London N = 85	Total N = 285	Percent of total
Training institutions set up specifically to prepare primary teachers	10	44	9	63	22
Common training institutions which prepare both primary and secondary teachers, but with separate curriculums	34	23	14	71	25
Common training institutions for both primary and secondary teachers, with some general curriculums in common	44	18	55	117	41
Almost identical training programs for primary and secondary teachers with a small amount of specialization for each group	11	12	7	30	11

a. N = number of samples. The percents ignore decimals and are the closest in round numbers. Where totals do not equal N, the discrepancy is due to questions left unanswered.

schools for further work (Table 33C). Only the Hong Kong students wanted to study for the next higher level of teaching. Fifty-four percent of all the students felt they would like to do some form of independent research.

The Detroit students were not as keen on using examinations, either in subject matter or professional subjects, as a method for certification as were the others (Table 34C). There were no other strong differences of position on methods of licensing teachers.

The students in Hong Kong were definitely more chauvinistic than were the other students (Table 35C). Detroit students were particularly certain that the past culture of one's country is not superior to present cultural conditions, and London students tended to agree.

Students in the three cities showed themselves eager to study the modern world and to cooperate with teachers from other cultures (Table 36C). Detroit and Hong Kong students were somewhat uncertain about compulsory language training, but London students strongly opposed it.

TABLE 33C[a]

Methods of In-Service Training

	Detroit N = 100	Hong Kong N = 100	London N = 85	Total N = 285	Percent of total
Reading Professional Books and Magazines					
Agree	93	84	75	252	88
Undecided	3	3	4	10	4
Disagree	3	3	2	8	3
Attending Professional Meetings and Discussion Groups					
Agree	87	75	66	228	80
Undecided	9	8	15	32	11
Disagree	2	5	1	8	3
Returning to Teacher Training Schools for Additional Courses					
Agree	84	38	53	175	61
Undecided	9	25	18	52	18
Disagree	5	25	11	41	14
Studying to be Qualified for the Next Higher Level of Teaching					
Agree	26	64	17	107	38
Undecided	32	15	30	77	27
Disagree	38	9	34	81	28
Carrying on Independent Research					
Agree	50	65	40	155	54
Undecided	31	18	31	80	28
Disagree	16	6	9	31	11

a. N = number of samples. The percents ignore decimals and are the closest in round numbers. Where totals do not equal N, the discrepancy is due to questions left unanswered.

Tables 37C to 49C are special items which were included in the questionnaire for students only and are not, therefore, parallel with the tables presented in Chapters III and IV. These additional tables have largely to do with the students' anticipations concerning their future careers as teachers.

269

TABLE 34Cª

Methods of Licensing Teachers

	Detroit N = 100	Hong Kong N = 100	London N = 85	Total N = 285	Percent of total
Passing an Examination in General Subjects such as History, Mathematics					
Agree	38	67	57	162	57
Undecided	22	10	13	45	16
Disagree	39	20	15	74	26
Passing an Examination in Pedagogy, Psychology, Teaching Methods					
Agree	29	73	67	169	59
Undecided	20	12	8	40	14
Disagree	49	12	10	71	25
Passing an Examination by Demonstration Teaching					
Agree	63	68	81	212	74
Undecided	13	15	1	29	10
Disagree	23	14	3	30	14
A Satisfactory Record of Work in Teacher Training Studies					
Agree	92	74	78	244	86
Undecided	4	8	6	18	6
Disagree	4	14	1	19	7
Presenting Letters of Recom- mendation from Instructors in Teacher Training Schools					
Agree	47	39	36	122	43
Undecided	21	22	25	68	24
Disagree	31	35	24	90	32

a. N = number of samples. The percents ignore decimals and are the closest in round numbers. Where totals do not equal N, the discrepancy is due to questions left unanswered.

In Table 37C, the largest number of Detroit and London students indicated that they expect to have their greatest rewards from teaching in intellectual stimulation, professional growth and service to children. The Hong Kong students agree, but more of them mentioned

TABLE 35C[a]

Attitudes Toward Cultures

	Detroit N = 100	Hong Kong N = 100	London N = 85	Total N = 285	Percent of total
The Culture of One's Own Country is the Superior Way of Life					
Agree	18	42	6	66	23
Undecided	21	26	11	58	20
Disagree	58	17	63	138	48
The Past Culture of One's Own Country was in most Respects Superior to its Present Day Culture					
Agree	3	29	3	35	12
Undecided	11	31	14	56	20
Disagree	83	25	63	171	60
The Cultures of all Nations are Equally Good					
Agree	49	62	24	135	47
Undecided	18	16	27	61	21
Disagree	30	6	30	66	23
The Cultures of all Nations, including One's Own, have Strengths and Weaknesses which have Historical Origins					
Agree	95	66	77	238	84
Undecided	—	13	3	16	6
Disagree	3	5	1	9	3
Every Nation has the Potential for Developing a High Degree of Culture which fits its People to Live in Equality with all Other Peoples in the Modern World					
Agree	84	64	72	220	77
Undecided	7	12	7	26	9
Disagree	6	8	2	16	6

a. N = number of samples. The percents ignore decimals and are the closest in round numbers. Where totals do not equal N, the discrepancy is due to questions left unanswered.

TABLE 36C[a]

Methods and Means for Understanding the Modern World

	Detroit N = 100	Hong Kong N = 100	London N = 85	Total N = 285	Percent of total
Careful Study of the Work of the United Nations and its Agencies					
Agree	61	61	49	171	60
Undecided	28	7	24	59	21
Disagree	10	16	6	32	11
Contact with Foreigners Living in One's Country					
Agree	67	69	67	203	71
Undecided	26	10	9	45	16
Disagree	6	5	3	14	5
Inviting Teachers from Foreign Countries to Teach in the Schools					
Agree	68	62	73	203	71
Undecided	23	14	4	41	14
Disagree	8	8	3	19	7
Study, Travel and Teaching in Foreign Countries					
Agree	81	75	78	234	82
Undecided	12	5	2	19	7
Disagree	7	3	—	10	4
Membership in Teachers' International Organizations					
Agree	74	67	66	207	73
Undecided	18	8	12	13	13
Disagree	7	8	1	16	6
Compulsory Foreign Language Training					
Agree	25	30	16	71	25
Undecided	35	24	18	77	27
Disagree	39	30	45	114	40

a. N = number of samples. The percents ignore decimals and are the closest in round numbers. Where totals do not equal N, the discrepancy is due to questions left unanswered.

TABLE 37C[a]

Expected Grounds for Satisfaction in Teaching

	Detroit N = 100	Hong Kong N = 100	London N = 85	Total N = 285	Percent of total
Prestige	6	21	2	29	10
Salary	16	25	9	50	18
Security	19	28	9	56	20
Intellectual stimulation	46	44	37	127	45
Good working conditions	18	24	20	62	22
Service	40	45	30	115	40
Little competition	3	11	11	25	9
Professional growth	63	48	55	166	58
Service to children	83	48	72	203	71

a. N = number of samples. The percents ignore decimals and are the closest in round numbers. Where totals do not equal N, the discrepancy is due to questions left unanswered.

service, prestige, salary, security, and good working conditions than did the others.

In anticipating impediments to teaching, the students agreed quite well on conservative administrators as a chief hindrance, although considerable numbers of Detroit and Hong Kong students feared radical pressures (Table 38C). The London students were sure that keeping abreast in the profession, uncooperative colleagues, and low salary would be definite hindrances.

In their observations of teaching conditions, the students were asked to indicate what problems in primary schools they felt were most obvious (Table 39C). All were aware of too large classes. The Hong Kong students said there was too much confusion and disorder in the schools; the Hong Kong and London students complained of old buildings, the Detroit and Hong Kong students charged that teachers were using the same old methods in their teaching.

Table 40C shows that all the students preferred heterogeneous, average children, though Hong Kong students had a somewhat greater preference for bright children. Detroit and London students showed marked preference for the 6–8 year old children; Hong Kong students for older children.

273

TABLE 38Cᵃ

Anticipated Impediments to a Teaching Career

	Detroit N = 100	Hong Kong N = 100	London N = 85	Total N = 285	Percent of total
Conservative administrators, parents, officials and lay groups	44	53	33	130	46
Radical administrators, parents, officials and other lay people	31	48	12	91	32
Boredom	14	20	7	41	14
Unreasonable moral standards	2	14	3	19	7
Uncooperative colleagues	18	—ᵇ	25	43	15
Community work	21	7	5	33	12
Non-teaching duties	24	15	17	56	20
Inadequate salary	5	3	23	31	11
Lack of supervisory help	4	19	10	33	12
Keeping abreast in the profession	26	17	26	69	24

a. N = number of samples. The percents ignore decimals and are the closest in round numbers. Where totals do not equal N, the discrepancy is due to questions left unanswered.
b. Omitted in the questionnaire.

The two problems which the students in the three cities agreed would give them greatest difficulty were meeting the individual needs of children and discipline (Table 41C).

London students would like to think of themselves as inspectors or supervisors sometime in their future career (Table 42C). Detroit students had no such aspirations but hoped to remain primary school teachers; a few hoped for an administrative post or positions as special teachers. Hong Kong students looked toward an administrative post or a position in a teacher training college.

Many of the future teachers hoped to travel and to work in a foreign land as a means of improving themselves (Table 43C). Only the Hong Kong students showed much interest in writing, speaking, organizing professional groups or holding office in teachers' organizations. Only the Detroit and Hong Kong students were interested to any degree in assisting in teacher training as part of their future careers.

274

TABLE 39C[a]

Problems in Primary Schools

	Detroit N = 100	Hong Kong N = 100	London N = 85	Total N = 285	Percent of total
Too many children in each classroom	86	77	59	222	78
Too much confusion and disorder in the school	20	48	8	76	27
Teachers lack the proper books and other teaching materials	36	46	30	112	39
Buildings are often old and generally unattractive	27	40	40	107	38
Children are wasting a great deal of time	22	28	6	56	20
Too much regimentation of the children	32	29	14	75	26
Teachers are using the same old methods	50	69	27	146	51
No particular problems	7	3	2	12	4

a. N = number of samples. The percents ignore decimals and are the closest in round numbers. Where totals do not equal N, the discrepancy is due to questions left unanswered.

TABLE 40C[a]

Preference for Kinds of Children in Class

	Detroit N = 100	Hong Kong N = 100	London N = 85	Total N = 285	Percent of total
General Type					
Physically handicapped children	17	17	18	52	18
Mentally handicapped children	18	5	13	36	13
Bright children	35	72	30	137	48
Average, heterogeneous children	72	66	62	200	70
Low economic groups	41	42	33	116	41
Upper economic groups	26	35	16	77	27
No preference	10	11	15	36	13
Age Group					
3– 5	17	—	12	29	10
6– 8	81	7	41	129	45
9–11	71	33	30	134	47
12–14	23	38	2	63	22
15–17	5	20	—	25	9
18–20	—	2	—	2	1

a. N = number of samples. The percents ignore decimals and are the closest in round numbers. Where totals do not equal N, the discrepancy is due to questions left unanswered.

TABLE 41C[a]

Anticipated Problems in Working with Children

	Detroit N = 100	Hong Kong N = 100	London N = 85	Total N = 285	Percent of total
Suffering boredom	1	13	1	15	5
Challenging bright children	11	4	3	18	6
Motivating dull children	12	18	4	34	12
Raising the cultural level of deprived children	4	10	7	21	7
Meeting the needs of individual children	40	18	29	87	31
Guiding unruly and unresponsive children	14	22	22	58	20
Establishing warm, positive, teacher-pupil relationships	5	9	1	15	5
Assigning grades or marks and deciding on promotion for individual children	8	4	15	27	9

a. N = number of samples. The percents ignore decimals and are the closest in round numbers. Where totals do not equal N, the discrepancy is due to questions left unanswered.

TABLE 42C[a]

Future Vocational Plans as a Teacher

	Detroit N = 100	Hong Kong N = 100	London N = 85	Total N = 285	Percent of total
Administrator	18	31	10	59	21
Inspector or supervisor	2	18	76	96	34
Special school officer (psychological tester, counsellor, etc.)	10	12	4	26	9
Special teacher (of the blind, deaf, etc.)	17	1	24	42	15
Primary teacher	41	4	36	81	28
Secondary teacher	4	7	4	15	5
Teacher training college	6	25	5	36	13

a. N = number of samples. The percents ignore decimals and are the closest in round numbers. Where totals do not equal N, the discrepancy is due to questions left unanswered.

TABLE 43C[a]

Interest in Professional Activities

	Detroit N = 100	Hong Kong N = 100	London N = 85	Total N = 285	Percent of total
Writing textbooks for children	12	33	7	52	18
Writing articles for professional journals and magazines	8	42	9	59	21
Giving speeches at meetings for teachers	11	20	—	31	11
Organizing study groups for teachers	8	21	2	31	11
Holding office in teachers' organizations	18	29	4	51	18
Holding membership in teachers' organizations	50	34	28	112	39
Carrying on research	28	60	10	98	34
Teaching in a foreign country	44	31	63	138	48
Assisting in training student teachers	46	35	13	94	33
Traveling	75	83	70	228	80
Simply teaching the children in class	44	11	39	94	33

a. N = number of samples. The percents ignore decimals and are the closest in round numbers. Where totals do not equal N, the discrepancy is due to questions left unanswered.

Tables 44C and 45C cover plans for advanced study and for future vacation time. Only the students in Detroit and Hong Kong planned on formal advanced study, and these not in large numbers. Two-thirds of the students in each city said they counted on doing occasional study. Only a few indicated that they planned to use vacations for studying teaching methods or some other field than teaching.

Since it is said that teachers usually teach as they have been taught, the students were asked to indicate at what levels in their own schooling they had experienced good teaching among their own teachers.

TABLE 44C[a]

Plans for Advanced Study

	Detroit N = 100	Hong Kong N = 100	London N = 85	Total N = 285	Percent of total
None at all	—	1	1	2	1
Some, but less than one full school year	9	5	10	24	8
At least one full year	38	14	14	66	23
At least two full years	14	10	—	24	8
More than two full years	13	43	4	60	21
Occasional study throughout the teaching career	69	68	67	204	72

a. N = number of samples. The percents ignore decimals and are the closest in round numbers. Where totals do not equal N, the discrepancy is due to questions left unanswered.

TABLE 45C[a]

Plans for Future Vacation Time

	Detroit N = 100	Hong Kong N = 100	London N = 85	Total N = 285	Percent of total
Relaxing and resting	42	50	48	140	49
Studying methods of teaching independently	19	22	3	44	15
Studying methods of teaching at some institution	31	10	—	41	14
Studying some other field than teaching	14	42	18	74	26
Traveling	80	69	78	227	80
Working to earn money	20	13	17	50	18
Pursuing hobbies, home improvement, creative activities of various types	70	57	68	195	68
Doing community service without pay, such as directing recreational activities for children	21	27	17	65	23

a. N = number of samples. The percents ignore decimals and are the closest in round numbers. Where totals do not equal N, the discrepancy is due to questions left unanswered.

Example of Good Teaching shown by Students' Own Teachers

	Detroit N = 100	Hong Kong N = 100	London N = 85	Total N = 285	Percent of total
Teachers in the primary school	59	29	69	157	55
Teachers in the secondary school	37	67	36	140	49
Professors in the teacher training college or university	40	38	34	112	39
Special tutors or teachers in special schools	5	20	11	36	13
None at all	6	4	2	12	4

a. N = number of samples. The percents ignore decimals and are the closest in round numbers. Where totals do not equal N, the discrepancy is due to questions left unanswered.

Table 46C gives their responses. Students in Detroit were agreed that they had most often experienced good teaching in the primary school. The Hong Kong students said for them it was at the secondary level. Over one-third in each group indicated that good teachers had been encountered in teacher training institutions.

Table 47C presents the image of the contemporary primary school teacher the students hold. In general it is a complimentary image, particularly for the Detroit students who rated the teacher high on all positive characteristics, low on the negative ones. Hong Kong students were less complimentary, while the London students about equalled the Detroit on the negative characteristics but were less generally favorable on the positive evaluation.

That the students knew little about their current instructors in the teacher training programs they were taking is shown in Table 48C. The only item known to any considerable number was their marital status. Many Hong Kong students also knew their home addresses. More Detroit students knew of the philosophy of education held by their instructors and more Hong Kong students knew of their previous experience and their feelings of satisfaction concerning their work.

On their attitude toward their training program, more Detroit students seemed to feel that their work load was too heavy than did the students of the other cities, both as to academic and educational

TABLE 47C[a]

Image of the Contemporary Primary Teacher

	Detroit N = 100	Hong Kong N = 100	London N = 85	Total N = 285	Percent of total
They tend to complain a good deal about their work	6	46	9	61	21
They are genuinely fond of children and like to be with them	87	56	78	221	78
They accomplish what is expected of them	64	49	55	168	59
They are respectful of the uniqueness and dignity of children	67	28	44	139	49
They do work beyond the call of duty	64	26	61	151	53
They are working primarily for the salary involved	6	42	8	56	20
They know their subject matter well	71	59	44	174	61
They are often absorbed in their own personal problems	6	26	7	39	14
They are worthy models for children and youth to follow	70	37	42	149	52
They are proud of being teachers	76	37	49	162	57

a. N = number of samples. The percents ignore decimals and are the closest in round numbers. Where totals do not equal N, the discrepancy is due to questions left unanswered.

courses (Table 49C). They felt, too, that their professional courses tended to be repetitious, vague, and dull, but that they did offer practical help for teaching. The students in Hong Kong and London were slightly less critical of their professional courses.

From so limited a sample of a questionnaire study in three large cities representing different types of cultures, one can certainly draw no valid conclusions concerning the positions taken by teachers in training at the present time. One can say, however, that no areas of extreme divergence of opinion exist, that there seems to be, as there

Knowledge of Present Teacher Training Instructors

	Detroit N = 100	Hong Kong N = 100	London N = 85	Total N = 285	Percent of total
Marital status	69	85	75	229	80
Work of spouse	11	29	15	55	19
Number of children	10	27	28	65	23
Home address	15	68	35	118	41
Future length of teaching	13	27	10	50	18
Philosophy of education	36	24	22	82	29
Satisfaction with present position	35	42	22	99	35
Previous experience	29	36	17	72	25

a. N = number of samples. The percents ignore decimals and are the closest in round numbers. Where totals do not equal N, the discrepancy is due to questions left unanswered.

was among the teacher groups sampled, fairly common agreement among both teachers and students as to the role taken by the teacher of today and fairly common agreement concerning his status in various cultures.

These students, preparing for teaching as a life career, live in a large city and indicate a preference for continuing to work there. They accord the primary school teacher low status in their respective cultures, and feel that young people are deterred from entering the profession because of this low status. Little opportunity for advancement and low salaries contribute greatly to discouraging the best young people from entering the profession.

These students lead a rather restricted cultural life and participate to a very limited degree in community activities. They generally feel that teachers need strong direction in carrying out their classroom activities and in deciding educational policy.

In supplying supplementary aids to children such as health care and free meals, the students took a conservative position. They were also conservative concerning special benefits for teachers.

TABLE 49C[a]

Attitude toward Present Training Program

	Detroit N = 100	Hong Kong N = 100	London N = 85	Total N = 285	Percent of total
General Academic Load					
Too heavy	33	12	10	55	19
Too light	1	14	2	17	6
About right	30	21	10	61	21
Sometimes one, sometimes the other	33	51	63	147	52
Education Courses					
Seem about the right number	27	47	42	116	41
Too many	32	23	5	60	21
Too few	1	11	12	24	8
Incompetent to judge	39	14	26	79	28
Content of Education Courses					
Stimulating and challenging	20	25	30	75	26
Repetitious	58	36	35	129	45
Dull, too much obvious material included	42	30	22	94	33
Practical, with good suggestions for teaching	51	48	37	136	48
Too theoretical and vague	37	42	40	119	42
Too difficult to understand	2	9	4	15	5
Too easy and lacking in challenge	20	15	5	40	14
Incompetent to judge	6	8	6	20	7

a. N = number of samples. The percents ignore decimals and are the closest in round numbers. Where totals do not equal N, the discrepancy is due to questions left unanswered.

They were fully aware of the problems arising from large classes and insufficient teaching aids and materials. However, their future plans did not include a great deal of in-service training.

Perhaps it is fair to say that these future teachers, although not impressed by the place accorded their profession in their society, did not demonstrate any great desire to change the status and role of the primary teacher nor did they advance any evidence that they were prepared to take whatever appropriate action they could to improve that role and status.

VI

HIGHLIGHTS OF THE STUDY

I find the great thing in this world is not so much
where we stand as in what direction we are moving.
Oliver Wendell Holmes

THE PRESENT STUDY REPRESENTS A VERY LIMITED SAMPLE OF THE TOTAL
teaching staff of the twelve countries included. Only teachers in large
urban centers responded. In not all cases could it be determined that
the sample obtained was a true sample in the sense of being entirely
random. There were problems of translations from English to the
language of the country sampled, so that the meanings of the questions
asked were not exactly the same for all teachers responding. Finally, as
has long been demonstrated, the questionnaire method in educational
research has very serious drawbacks in arriving at exact conclusions.
Data obtained by this method cannot lend themselves to sophisticated
statistical analysis. For this study only simple percentages have been
figured from raw data. For all of these reasons, the conclusions to be
drawn must remain tenuous. Since it is a pioneering study, perhaps its
chief value lies more in pointing to the need for getting answers to
important questions through more precise research techniques than in
giving exact information about the current role and status of teachers
in various cultures of the world.

Three major conclusions, however, seem warranted. First, the primary school teachers of the twelve cities sampled present few marked differences of opinion concerning their role and status. They are a singularly unified group, although the societies they serve vary greatly. Second, where there are differences, these seem to reflect rather accurately the current political, economic and social philosophies of each country as these impinge upon policies and practices in education. Third, older teachers, even in countries where recent change has been extremely rapid and profound, vary but little in their point of view from their younger colleagues.

Sex and Family Status. The teaching profession is composed largely of women, with more males in the East than in the West. A considerable number are married and have children to support.

Placement and Qualification. There is slightly more stability of placement for teachers in the West than in the East. Most of the teachers are fully qualified, although there is wide variation in the amount of preparation they had received for teaching.

Choice of Profession. Two-thirds of the teachers said they had chosen teaching as a profession because they felt it was a rewarding way of life. However, only one-half were definite in feeling they would go into teaching again, could they make a second choice. Teachers in the East showed slightly less satisfaction with their profession than did teachers in the West. Parents and former teachers influenced a considerable number in making their professional choice.

Teachers in the East acknowledged greater change in their ideas concerning education since they entered the profession than did teachers in the West.

Early Environment. Although the teachers were all currently employed in large cities, nearly two-thirds in the East and slightly over half in the West were reared in small towns or rural areas. About 10 percent in each region indicated a willingness to teach in a rural area. Teachers in the West and the older ones in both East and West indicated that a significant proportion came from homes where religious training was considered important. However, teachers in the East were more insistent on a high standard of morals for teachers. In general, the younger teachers were laxer than the older ones in the standards they considered important.

Adequacy of Income. About half of all the teachers reported they did not supplement their regular salary. Among those reporting that they did supplement their salary the largest proportion was the older teachers in the East. In general, teachers in the East are much more concerned about generous fringe benefits and pension systems than are teachers in the West. Young teachers were less concerned than older ones about pensions and retirement benefits in general.

Proportion of Sexes Considered Desirable. Neither East nor West was opposed to large numbers of women as teachers in elementary schools, but in both regions a male was definitely preferred as the head of the school. Students had no real preference as to the sex of staff or head of a school.

Prestige Value Assigned to Various Occupational Groups. The occupations given high ranking by teachers in both East and West were the government official, the doctor of medicine and the university professor. Of the teaching occupations, the primary school head, the secondary school teacher, and the primary school teacher were rated in the order listed, but very much lower than the three highest ranks. There was little difference in the rating assigned the primary school teacher by the East and the West. In the West 67 percent and in the East 57 percent of teachers placed the rank of this profession in the two lowest categories. There were no marked differences between young and old teachers and students.

About one-half of the teachers in the West and slightly more than half in the East believed that the status of the teaching profession has deteriorated in recent times. Older teachers were more certain of this trend than were the younger ones.

Deterrents to Recruiting Excellent Young People for Teaching. The main grounds given by all the teachers for thinking that many excellent young people are discouraged from seeking teaching as a life career were unattractive working conditions in schools, too little respect shown teachers, too little opportunity for advancement and too low salaries. Teachers in the West were more concerned about low salaries and limited opportunities for advancement than were teachers in the East.

Ways of Meeting Teacher Shortages. The teachers were generally certain that only qualified teachers should be employed when shortages exist, even though compromises would have to be made in teaching conditions. Shortening training periods to make teachers available more rapidly was looked upon more favorably in the East than in the West.

Time Spent in Extra Teaching Duties. Approximately 50 percent of the teachers both in the East and the West, indicated that they spent no more than forty minutes a day in travelling to and from school and about the same proportion said they spent no more than an hour and a half daily in checking papers and doing other related tasks at home. In some countries of the East, a considerable number of teachers spent more than two hours daily in work of this sort. There were no marked differences reported by the older and younger teachers.

Absence Due to Illness. Oddly enough, the record of absence due to illness for the East and the West was exactly identical: 40 percent in each region reported no days lost during the past year (1963) for illness; 32 percent said they had lost from one to five days for this reason. The record of older teachers compared favorably with that of younger ones.

Regular Cultural Activities. Teachers are limited in their cultural activities by the opportunities they find to engage in them. Since the teachers of the study lived in large, metropolitan communities, it can be assumed that numerous cultural advantages were available to them. However, only three-fourths or more of them reported daily newspaper reading and radio listening. A larger proportion of teachers in the West reported reading both professional and popular periodicals, viewing TV programs, taking yearly trips, and attending concerts and theatres. Teachers in the East went to movies slightly more than those in the West. One-half in both regions reported reading a book a month. More older teachers reported reading books and journals than younger ones, while younger teachers went more often to movies and other events in the community.

Participation in Community Activities. On the type of community activity the teachers believed proper for the primary school teacher, the activity most commonly favored was directing children and youth in community improvement. Second in popularity was active participation by teachers in such projects. Slightly over half the teachers in the East said they felt primary teachers should assist in the literacy programs for adults. One-third of the teachers in the West and one-fourth of those in the East thought that the primary teacher should not be asked to participate in work outside the school. Students in training were more favorably disposed toward community work than were teachers.

Professional and Political Activities. Teachers in the East and in the West, old and young, were interested in membership in teachers' organizations both at the local and the national level, although this interest is stronger in the West and among the older teachers. Only in the West did any considerable number indicate membership in professional associations other than those strictly concerned with teachers.

The primary school teacher in all countries sampled was definitely not politically oriented. Voting regularly was the only activity reported by any large number in both East and West. One-fifth of the teachers in the East said they took no part in political affairs. There were no marked differences between the younger and the older ones.

The Chief Goals of Primary Education. The three goals of the primary school which were designated by the largest numbers of teachers in the West were teaching children to read and write, to reason and think, and to get along with others, in this order of importance. Teachers in the East named teaching children to read and write, moral values, and to get along with others as of greatest importance. Teachers in the West gave higher value to teaching religion than did those in the East, while the latter emphasized civic skills, vocational skills, and facts and habits of health. The younger teachers were more inclined to choose social skills than the basic skills of reading and writing, but the difference from the older teachers was slight.

The Responsibility of the Teacher in Dealing with School Matters. In the conduct of school affairs, there are few areas where teachers want implicit direction from high authority and likewise few areas where they wish to take full responsibility for dealing with such matters on their own. In general, teachers in the East indicated a stronger need for direction from above than did teachers in the West. There were no marked differences between older and younger.

Determining the Content of the Curriculum. Teachers in both East and West indicated they desired some guidance in determining the content of the curriculum (three-fourths of those in the West and one-half of those in the East). Those in the East said they relied more on the textbook and on guides sent by school authorities and on the requirements of examinations than did teachers in the West. The widest differences were in the greater reliance placed by teachers in the East on the textbook and on the time schedules sent out by school authorities. Teachers in both regions showed a strong disposition to share in curriculum development by making the adjustments the children needed in particular situations. In general younger teachers showed a stronger disposition to rely less on authority and more on their own judgment in determining what should be taught at the primary school level.

Supplementary Aids to Regular Instruction. The practice of supplementing instruction in school with health care and other social welfare aids varies widely in different areas of the world. In general, the opinion of the teachers concerning the importance and propriety of such aids reflected rather closely the current policies of individual countries, particularly in the West. In the countries where supplementary social benefits for children are few, the teachers opposed them. In countries where they are commonly supplied to children, the teachers favored them. In general, however, the teachers in the East were definitely inclined toward social welfare programs of all sorts. Older teachers in the East and younger teachers in the West took somewhat more liberal positions than the younger in the East and older in the West.

Teachers in the West voted more strongly than did those in the East for special services and special schools for atypical children, particularly those needing psychological counselling. These attitudes may be partially due to the enrollment of all children in school in the West. Atypical children may often be the early dropouts in the East.

Justifiable Reasons for Low Achievement in Primary Schools. On questions concerning the reasons for low achievement of children, the one item on which there was general agreement in both East and West was that of too large classes. (Since the questionnaire did not define "large class," presumably the exact number of children would vary from locale to locale.) In addition to this factor, teachers in the East were troubled most by too many duties outside the classroom, too many dull children, poor buildings and equipment, the lack of textbooks and other teaching materials, and the poor home training of children. Teachers in the West felt most hampered by duties outside the classroom, too many dull children, not enough teaching materials, and poor home training of the pupils. There were no marked differences between the younger and the older teachers.

Importance of Pre-School Education. Despite the fact that teachers generally complained of the poor home training of children, they were not strongly in favor of pre-school education, either compulsory or voluntary. They were somewhat in agreement that such schools should be provided for those parents who choose to send their children. Both younger and older teachers subscribed to this opinion.

Admission Procedures to Higher Schools. Since there are wide differences in the countries of the study in the proportion of children completing primary school who continue on to a higher school, there are likewise wide differences in the procedures followed in determining the basis on which such promotion should be made. The methods strongly approved by teachers in the West were a satisfactory record of work in the elementary school and the recommendation of the teacher. External testing was considered much more important in the East than in the West.

Degree of Centralization for Schools. In both East and West there was a consensus that the optimal degree of centralization should concern uniform practices in licensing and placing teachers and a uniform salary scale throughout the country, but that there should be local option in such matters as curriculum development, choice of text and teaching materials, and standards of achievement for pupils. Older and younger teachers were in close agreement on this point.

Type of Teacher Organization. Teachers in the West leaned more toward an exclusive organization for primary school teachers than did those in the East, who were more in favor of an organization embracing teachers at all levels. Older teachers were slightly more in favor of the exclusive type than were younger teachers.

Means of Teacher Control. Teachers, both in the East and in the West, rated control of their conduct by teachers' organizations rather low. One-half in both East and West gave supervision by the principal or head of the school first place in regulating their conduct. Teachers in the West wanted more authority given to supervisors and inspectors than teachers in the East. Both regions felt that self-discipline was extremely important. Younger teachers were less willing to accept regulations from outside the school than were older ones.

As a disciplinary measure, the possibility of permanent dismissal was accepted by about half of the teachers in the West, but only by one-quarter in the East. Reduction of salary either temporary or permanent and removal to a less desirable locale were more palatable to teachers in the East than in the West. Both regions favored handling disciplinary cases in a quiet manner.

Special Regulations for Teachers. All teachers were fairly well agreed that men and women should receive equal treatment and that they should receive liberal allowances for sick leave and disability. Teachers in the West were generally not in favor of merit pay nor of paid maternity leaves, whereas teachers in the East were more disposed to accept such measures. Younger teachers were generally more liberal in their point of view concerning the equal treatment of men and women and various special allowances.

289

Methods of Recognizing and Rewarding Excellent Teachers. Promotion within the primary school and promotion to teach in a higher school were the favored ways of rewarding excellent service in the West. In the East, promotion within the primary school and increased salary, above the regular scale, were the favored ways. Only teachers in the East, to any considerable extent, wanted citations, medals or honors for their work. Differences between the older and the younger teachers were slight.

Grounds for Dismissal of Teachers. The possible grounds for dismissal on which teachers in both East and West showed much agreement were immoral conduct (sufficient cause), disagreement with a principal or other official (insufficient cause). On lack of knowledge of subject matter as a ground there was no uniformity of opinion. More teachers in the West allowed failure to meet teaching responsibilities as a just cause, while more teachers in the East felt that teaching ideas contrary to government policy should be a just ground. Older teachers were more certain than younger ones that immoral conduct should be cause for dismissal of teachers.

Retirement Regulations. Teachers were generally agreed that retirement regulations should apply equally to men and to women and that illness or disability should be provided for in retirement policies. There was some disagreement about the age at which retirement should be compulsory: teachers in the West were more in favor of earlier retirement and teachers in the East were in favor of later retirement. Generally, older teachers were in favor of the more liberal retirement policies.

Proper Measures for Professional Organizations. Teachers were generally opposed to the calling of strikes by their organizations, but they did favor putting pressure on governments to gain benefits. They strongly favored such activities as the publication of professional journals and setting up in-service courses. They were undecided about social activities organized by their associations, although younger teachers tended to favor them.

Type of Teacher Training Institution. The type of institution most generally favored for the training of primary school teachers was the single purpose institution, although there was considerable difference of opinion, particularly in the West.

Method of In-Service Training. Primary school teachers generally preferred to rely on informal methods of in-service education such as professional reading and attendance at professional meetings. Three-fourths of teachers in the West and one-half of those in the East favored additional course work at teacher training schools. Carrying on independent research interested the majority in each region. Older teachers showed slightly more interest in professional meetings than did younger ones.

Methods of Licensing Teachers. Only in the West would a considerable number of teachers rely on a satisfactory record of work in a teacher training college as the basis for licensing, although various types of examinations were generally thought necessary and acceptable.

Attitudes Toward Cultures. Teachers in the East were more inclined toward chauvinism than were those in the West and more agreed that the past surpassed the present in cultural achievement. They were all well disposed toward active participation in programs involving contacts with teachers of cultures other than their own and welcomed membership in international teachers' organizations.

In final summary of this study, it can be said that the primary school teachers sampled in twelve countries have very low regard for their own position in the society in which they work. They likewise feel no strong responsibility to work actively within their organizations or within the body politic to improve their status. They show little inclination to push for changes which might enhance their position. Even in matters having to do with their activities within their own classrooms they are reluctant to assume responsibility. The wish of Sir Ronald Gould, general secretary of the National Union of Teachers in the United Kingdom and president of the World Confederation of the Organizations of the Teaching Profession, does not seem possible of immediate fulfillment if the findings of this study are valid: "I would like to think that teachers could take the lead in deciding what changes are necessary." If teachers in the primary school are to help themselves to achieve more favorable status in their own eyes and in the eyes of the general public, they will need more adequate training in their preparation for teaching, more stimulating leadership from their professional organizations, and more understanding of the importance of their role from society in general.

APPENDIX A
QUESTIONNAIRE TO TEACHERS

Many inquiries have previously been made into the place teachers hold in various countries of the world. Usually opinions have been given by others than the teachers themselves. This present study is an attempt to ask teachers in primary schools in a number of nations what they themselves think are their role and status in their own country. Their answers will be of great help in evaluating school practices and development, not only in the countries studied, but throughout the world.

There are two parts to this inquiry. Part I asks you for certain information about you as a teacher. Part II asks you for value judgments which you as a teacher are qualified to make. You are not asked to sign your name. Please do your best to give honest answers to all questions.

PART I

Teachers' Data

1. Sex: Male___ Female___
2. Marital Status: Unmarried___ Married___ Divorced___ Widowed___
3. Children: None___ 1–3___ 4–6___ over 6___

4. Your Age Range: 20's___ 30's___ 40's___ 50's___ 60's___
5. Years of *Total* Teaching Experience: Less than 1 full year___ 1–5 yrs.___ 10–20 yrs.___ over 20 yrs.___
6. Years of Teaching Experience in Your *Present* School: Less than 1 full year___ 1–2 yrs.___ 3–6 yrs.___ 7–10 yrs.___ 11–20 yrs.___ over 20 yrs.___
7. In which type of school do you teach at the present time? Public (Chiefly tax supported by the government)___ Private (Supported chiefly by non-government agency)___
8. What is the total number of years you have spent in school as a student? (Include elementary school, secondary school, and all other) ___years
9. Are you a fully qualified teacher for the primary school? Yes___ No___
10. How did you receive your first license, permit, or certificate for teaching? (Check *as many* as apply.)
    ___Regular government examination
    ___Special examination
    ___Satisfactory completion of the course for training teachers
    ___Special arrangement
11. During the time you were studying teacher training, approximately how many clock hours did you spend in a classroom, either observing or teaching children? (Check *one*.)
    ___None at all
    ___10–50 hours
    ___51–100 hours
    ___101–200 hours
    ___more than 200 hours
12. Where did you spend most of your childhood? (Check *one*.)
    ___Rural area or small village
    ___Small city or town (25,000–100,000)
    ___Large city (over 100,000)
13. If you could have your choice, in which community described above would you prefer to teach for the rest of your life? (Check *one*.)
    ___Rural area or small village
    ___Small city or town
    ___Large city
14. If you had it to do over again would you go into teaching or some other occupation? (Check *one*.)
    ___I'm sure I would go into teaching
    ___Probably would go into teaching
    ___Uncertain; depends on opportunities
    ___Think I would choose another occupation
    ___Quite sure I would choose another occupation
15. Think of the 5 teachers you know best in the school where you are now teaching. For how many of these could you give the following information? (Place a number from 0 to 5 for *each* of the questions below.)
    ___Marital status, i.e., married, single, etc.
    ___If married, what their husbands or wives do?

___Where they live?
___How long they intend to go on teaching?
___What philosophy of education they hold?
___How well they like their present position?
___How they discipline their students?
___What position in the school system they would like some day to have?

16. How do you think the following situations should be taken care of?
    a. Teachers made to follow strict rules (Mark these items *a*.)
    b. Teachers asked to follow rules, but allowed to make some changes to suit the situation (Mark these items *b*.)
    c. No set rules, teachers allowed to use their own judgment (Mark these items *c*.)
    (Place a, b, or c before *each* of these statements.)
    ___Handling a child who does not work well
    ___Disciplining a child who is disobedient
    ___Deciding methods of classroom teaching
    ___Deciding what time teachers must arrive at and leave school building
    ___Handling a child who is late
    ___Deciding the amount of time to be spent on different subjects each week
    ___Contacting parents
    ___Deciding the form of report on child's school work to parents
    ___Deciding what is to be taught in each subject

17. How much would you say that your ideas about the general purposes or aims of education have changed since you began your training as a teacher? (Check *one*.)
    Changed very much___   Changed a little___
    Hardly changed at all___   Don't know___

18. When you were growing up, what importance did your parents place on seeing that you were taught religion? (Check *one*.)
    ___Paid little if any attention to religion
    ___Had you observe special rituals and ceremonies
    ___Placed some emphasis on your understanding the basic meaning of religion
    ___Considered religious instruction very important

19. In addition to the regular salary and other benefits you receive as a teacher, do you supplement your income? (Check *as many* as apply.)
    ___Not at all
    ___By teaching in other schools
    ___By tutoring pupils privately
    ___By writing educational books or articles
    ___By working at jobs other than educational ones
    ___By the paid work of your husband or wife
    ___Other ways

20. If you do supplement your regular salary, how much do you generally earn in one year? (Check the *one* that applies.)
    ___Less than one month of your regular teaching salary
    ___One to three months of your regular teaching salary

___Four to nine months of your regular salary
___More than your regular yearly salary

21. Check the professional organizations of which you are *now* a regular member. (Check *as many* as apply.)
___Local teachers' organization
___Regional or provincial teachers' organization
___National teachers' organization
___Other professional association or organization
___None

22. To what extent do you take part in the political life of your country? (Check *as many* as apply.)
___By holding public office at the local level
___By holding public office at higher than the local level
___By voting regularly
___By holding membership in a political party
___By participating in public rallies, protest demonstrations, etc.
___Not at all

23. What sources of information do you regularly have? (Check *as many* as apply.)
___Daily general newspaper
___Professional newspaper or journals
___Daily radio listening
___Popular magazines and journals
___Daily television viewing
___Taking one yearly trip of at least 300 kilometers (200 miles) away from your home
___Attending at least one professional or cultural meeting each month
___Seeing at least one motion picture a month
___Attending at least one concert or theatre performance during the year
___Visiting a library at least once each month
___Reading at least one book each month
___None of the above

24. Who or what influenced you most in deciding to become a teacher? (Check *all that strongly apply*.)
___One or both of your parents or a close relative was a teacher
___You had at least one teacher you strongly admired and wished to follow as an example
___You felt that teaching offered a rewarding way of life
___You were disappointed in getting into the vocation you really wanted and took teaching as second choice
___Your school marks were high
___Don't know; no special reason

25. Ordinarily, how many minutes do you spend each school day
___Traveling to and from school?
___Checking papers or preparing lessons at home?
___Engaging in some form of recreational activity?
___Doing clerical work connected with school?

26. For the year past, how many days were you absent from school because of illness?

___days

PART II

Teachers' Opinion Sections

In these sections you are asked to give your opinion about certain matters pertaining to primary school teachers and primary school practices.

There are no right or wrong answers to any of the items.

Please give your honest opinion concerning each statement.

Section A

1. Below are listed a number of vocations and professions. Please rank these in the order in which they are respected and honored in your country by placing the number 1 before the one which ranks highest; number 2 before the second and so on, until you have ranked them all.

___Government official

___Government worker or civil servant

___Doctor of medicine

___Lawyer

___Shopkeeper

___Artist, musician or actor

___Priest or clergyman

___Farmer

___Banker

___Secondary school teacher

___Businessman

___Primary school principal or head

___University professor

___Primary school teacher

___Skilled craftsman

2. What do you think has happened to the respect shown to the primary teachers in your country?

___It has remained about the same

___It has improved a great deal

___It has become lower than it was in former times

3. In countries where many of the most intelligent young people do not become teachers, these reasons are sometimes given. (Check the *three* you consider the strongest reasons for your country.)

___Shortage of positions

___Working conditions in schools too unattractive and difficult (Poor facilities, large classes, etc.)

___Too little intellectual stimulation in working with children

___Too few persons who have intellectual interests and tastes to be found among teachers

___Too little respect shown to teachers
___Weak teachers' organizations
___Too little opportunity for advancement
___Too much interference from government and superiors
___Too low salary
___Living conditions in rural areas and villages too difficult

4. When there is a shortage of teachers in a country, there are several ways of meeting the crisis. (Check the *three* you consider most desirable for your country.)

___Using only qualified teachers, however large classes have to be to keep children in school

___Using only qualified teachers, but dividing large classes into double or triple shifts each day

___Using only qualified teachers but limiting the number of days per week that each child may attend school

___Using unqualified teachers, as required

___Relaxing compulsory attendance laws to cut down on the number of children in school

___Closing as many schools as necessary until a sufficient number of qualified teachers are trained

___Shortening the period of teacher training so that more teachers become quickly available

5. In countries where industrial development is low and a very limited amount of support is available for education, a government must make choices in allocating funds. (Check the *three* you consider the best choices.)

___Use most of the education budget for technological and industrial development with very little for schools of any sort

___Use most of the education budget for literacy campaigns for adults

___Use most of the education budget for primary schools

___Use most of the education budget for training highly skilled professional people and technicians at university levels

___Divide the education budget among all levels of education (primary, secondary, higher, technical) as equally as possible

6. There are several administrative patterns possible for the primary schools in a national educational system. (Check the *one* which you consider best.)

___A highly centralized system of licensing and placing teachers, with a uniform salary scale; uniform curriculum, textbooks, and common standards of achievement for pupils

___A centralized system of licensing and placing teachers, uniform salary scale, but local variations in curriculum, textbooks and standards of achievement for pupils

___A completely decentralized system with local regulations and variations for teachers and for pupils

7. A nation can expect to have the most qualified and best prepared primary teachers which makes certain requirements for training them. (Check the *one* requirement which seems to you best.)

___Training institutions set up specifically to prepare primary teachers

___Common training institutions which prepare both primary and secondary teachers, but with separate curriculums and programs

___Common training institutions for both primary and secondary teachers, with some general curriculums in common

___Almost identical training programs for primary and secondary teachers with a small amount of specialization for each group

8. Moral standards for teachers are often under discussion. (Check the *one* which you feel should be required.)

___The standards should be higher for teachers than for other respected professional workers

___The standards should be higher than for the general public

___The standards should be the same as for the general public

9. Teachers often have a choice between maximum salary and certain other benefits. (Check the *one* which you favor most.)

___Highest possible salary, without other benfits

___Lower than maximum salary, with a pension system after retirement

___Still lower salary with provisions for housing, health insurance, and a pension system after retirement

___Minimum salary with all the benefits mentioned above, plus others, such as life insurance, credit and loan arrangements, recreation facilities.

10. Teachers are controlled and regulated in various ways. (Check the *three* which you believe are most important to insure good results in primary schools.)

___Laws passed by the government

___Rules made by Ministry of Education

___Regulation by supervisors or inspectors

___Supervision by the principal or head of the school

___Regulations made by teachers' organizations

___Regulations made by organizations of parents

___Regulations made by the teachers of the school

___Individual teacher's own self-discipline

11. Primary teachers can hope for the greatest benefits from one or another form of teacher organization. (Check the *one* you prefer.)

___An organization for primary teachers only

___An organization for secondary and primary teachers

___An organization including all levels of teachers: primary, secondary, university, technical

12. Teachers are often asked to do various types of community work. (Check *as many* as you think should be the proper concern of teachers.)

___Teaching adults to read and write

___Teaching adults various skills, such as sewing, cooking, animal care, crop raising, sanitary measures

___Directing children and youth in projects to improve the community

___Working as participants in projects to improve the community

___No community work except that closely connected to the regular work of the school

13. In primary school children are required to learn a number of things (Check the *five* below which you consider of greatest importance.)
    ___Moral values
    ___Skills such as reading, writing and numbers
    ___Social skills such as learning how to get along with other people in the family and other groups
    ___Facts about history, geography, mathematics
    ___Civic skills necessary to democratic government
    ___Vocational skills to be used later in earning a living
    ___Facts and habits of good health
    ___To reason and think
    ___Religious values and ideals
    ___Obedience in obeying orders
    ___Skill in group thinking
14. Which kinds of discipline (depending on the seriousness of the offense) do you feel should be given to teachers? (Check *as many* as apply.)
    ___Permanent dismissal
    ___Temporary dismissal with loss of pay
    ___Permanent reduction of salary
    ___Temporary reduction of salary
    ___Removal to an undesirable position or undesirable area
    ___Letter of apology to the principal, head, or other administrative officer
    ___Public reprimand from principal, head, or other officer
    ___Private reprimand from principal, head, or other official
15. For the best results, the proportion of male and female teachers in the primary school should be: (Be sure the two figures equal 100%)
    ___% female teachers
    ___% male teachers
16. For the principal or head of a primary school which do you prefer? (Check *one*.)
    ___Male
    ___Female
    ___No preference

Section B

In Section B, you are asked to check the relative importance you attach to each of a number of statements pertaining to propositions that have to do with teachers and teaching in the primary school. Mark each statement this way:

① 2   3   4   5   means that you agree with the statement fully
1   ② 3   4   5   means that you tend to agree with the statement
1   2   ③ 4   5   means that you are uncertain about the statement. You are neither strongly for nor strongly against what it says
1   2   3   ④ 5   means that you tend to disagree with the statement
1   2   3   4   ⑤ means that you strongly disagree

Be sure to circle the number that shows how you feel about each statement.

299

1. Before being licensed or certified to teach, a young teacher should be required to demonstrate his ability by:
   1 2 3 4 5 Passing an examination in a number of general subjects, such as literature, history, mathematics
   1 2 3 4 5 Passing an examination in pedagogy, psychology, teaching methods
   1 2 3 4 5 Passing an examination by demonstration teaching
   1 2 3 4 5 A satisfactory record of work in his teacher training studies
   1 2 3 4 5 Presenting letters of recommendation from instructors in teacher training schools

2. The ways of encouraging and rewarding good teachers should be by:
   1 2 3 4 5 Promotion to be a principal, head, inspector, or other administrative positions
   1 2 3 4 5 Increased pay or allowances, above regular scale
   1 2 3 4 5 Promotion to teach in a higher school
   1 2 3 4 5 Citations, medals, honors
   1 2 3 4 5 Choice of teaching position
   1 2 3 4 5 Selection to office in teachers' organization
   1 2 3 4 5 Self-satisfaction of work well done; no other reward needed

3. Teachers should be permanently dismissed from service for:
   1 2 3 4 5 Immoral conduct
   1 2 3 4 5 Harsh disciplining of children
   1 2 3 4 5 Laziness or failure to meet their responsibilities in teaching and maintaining discipline
   1 2 3 4 5 Teaching ideas contrary to government policy
   1 2 3 4 5 Frequent or prolonged illness
   1 2 3 4 5 Disagreement with principal or other school or government official
   1 2 3 4 5 Lack of sufficient knowledge of their subject matter

4. The content of what is to be taught in the primary school should be determined by:
   1 2 3 4 5 The textbook
   1 2 3 4 5 The curriculum guide sent by school authorities, such as ministry of education
   1 2 3 4 5 The time schedule sent by school authorities
   1 2 3 4 5 The curriculum guide worked out by the teachers and principal of the school
   1 2 3 4 5 The curriculum plan worked out by the individual teacher
   1 2 3 4 5 The content of the examinations which have been given in recent years by school authorities for entrance to the next class or the next higher school

300

5. Poor achievement of children in the primary school may be justified because of:

1 2 3 4 5 Too many children in the classes

1 2 3 4 5 Too many duties for the teacher outside the classroom

1 2 3 4 5 Too little help for the teacher from inspectors and heads or principals

1 2 3 4 5 Too many dull children in the same classes with bright children

1 2 3 4 5 Poor buildings and equipment

1 2 3 4 5 Not enough books and teaching materials

1 2 3 4 5 Poor home training of the children

1 2 3 4 5 Too much time required for preparing for examinations to the next higher school

6. Even though the government may have to take funds from the general budget for education, it should spend money for:

1 2 3 4 5 Free meals in school for all children

1 2 3 4 5 Free medical and dental checkups in school

1 2 3 4 5 Free medical and dental services in school

1 2 3 4 5 Grants to parents with many children

1 2 3 4 5 Free textbooks and school supplies

1 2 3 4 5 Grants to widows for support of children

1 2 3 4 5 Free psychological clinics and counselling for children

1 2 3 4 5 Free birth control clinics

1 2 3 4 5 Special schools for children not fitted to attend regular schools

1 2 3 4 5 Grants to very poor parents

7. Pre-school or nursery education should be:

1 2 3 4 5 Required of all children before they enter regular schools

1 2 3 4 5 Provided by the government for parents who wish their children to have these experiences

1 2 3 4 5 Provided for parents by private agencies

1 2 3 4 5 Strongly discouraged and parents urged to keep their children at home until they reach school age

8. The proper basis for admitting children from the primary school to the next higher school should be:

1 2 3 4 5 Intelligence tests

1 2 3 4 5 Examinations made and administered by the government

1 2 3 4 5 Satisfactory record of work in the primary school

1 2 3 4 5 Recommendation of teachers and principal or head of the primary school

1 2 3 4 5 Examinations made by professional organizations based on research

9. Teachers should be subjected to special laws and regulations:
   1 2 3 4 5   When a woman marries she should be required to stop teaching
   1 2 3 4 5   Men teachers should have a higher salary than women
   1 2 3 4 5   Teachers should not be paid salaries according to the years they teach, but according to the quality of their work
   1 2 3 4 5   If teachers discontinue teaching to take other positions, they should not be permitted to return to teaching
   1 2 3 4 5   Women should be allowed liberal time for maternity leaves and should receive full pay for such leaves
   1 2 3 4 5   Teachers should receive liberal allowances for sick leave and disability

10. The ways by which teachers should keep up to date in their profession are:
   1 2 3 4 5   Reading professional books and magazines
   1 2 3 4 5   Attending professional meetings and discussion groups
   1 2 3 4 5   Returning to teacher training schools for additional courses
   1 2 3 4 5   Studying to be qualified for the next higher level of teaching
   1 2 3 4 5   Carrying on independent research

11. Arrangements for the retirement of teachers should be:
   1 2 3 4 5   The same regulations for men and women
   1 2 3 4 5   Provision for the widow and minor children when a teacher dies before retirement
   1 2 3 4 5   Retirement from service made compulsory at a later age than now required
   1 2 3 4 5   Retirement from service made compulsory at an earlier age than now required
   1 2 3 4 5   Early retirement with full benefits for serious health reasons

12. Teachers should take part in the social and political life of their country and community by:
   1 2 3 4 5   Voting in political elections
   1 2 3 4 5   Holding political office
   1 2 3 4 5   Attending public meetings where political and social matters are discussed
   1 2 3 4 5   Holding meetings for the parents of the children
   1 2 3 4 5   Visiting the homes of parents
   1 2 3 4 5   Belonging to professional organizations
   1 2 3 4 5   Holding membership in a political party
   1 2 3 4 5   Refraining from any sort of active participation in political life

13. Teachers' organizations should engage in various types of activities to further the welfare of teachers:

1 2 3 4 5 Organizing and leading strikes to get needed salary raises or other benefits

1 2 3 4 5 Putting pressures other than strikes on the government for better salaries and other benefits

1 2 3 4 5 Publishing newspapers and professional journals

1 2 3 4 5 Setting up workshops and discussion groups, and furthering other means of professional growth

1 2 3 4 5 Providing local meeting places and organizing social groups

14. The teacher should hold certain beliefs about cultures:

1 2 3 4 5 That the culture of one's own country is the superior way of life

1 2 3 4 5 That the past culture of one's own country was in most respects superior to its present day culture

1 2 3 4 5 That the cultures of all nations are equally good

1 2 3 4 5 That the cultures of all nations, including one's own, have strengths and weaknesses which have historical backgrounds

1 2 3 4 5 That every nation has the potential for developing a high degree of culture which fits its people to live in equality with all other peoples in the modern world

15. Teachers should develop an understanding of the modern world by:

1 2 3 4 5 Careful study of the work of the United Nations and its agencies

1 2 3 4 5 Contact with foreigners living in one's country

1 2 3 4 5 Inviting teachers from foreign countries to teach in the schools

1 2 3 4 5 Study, travel, and teaching in foreign countries

1 2 3 4 5 Membership in teachers' organizations which are international

1 2 3 4 5 Compulsory foreign language training

APPENDIX B
DIRECTIONS TO ADMINISTRATORS

Translating and Typing

1. Translation should follow the meaning expressed in English as closely as possible.
2. If possible, check the translation with a small group of teachers to see that the wording is clear.
3. In typing, follow the numbering system exactly.
4. Do not crowd items; do not separate the items of a question by placing part of it on one page and part of it on the next page.
5. Make sure that the hectographed or mimeographed copy is easily read.

Sampling

1. A sample of 100 teachers with 1–5 years' experience (Sample I) is wanted; and a sample of 100 teachers with more than ten years' experience (Sample II) is wanted.
2. Choose 300 names of teachers at random (every fifth name or every tenth name, etc., depending on how long the list of names is for the city from which you draw the sample).
3. Check the length of teaching experience of these 300 teachers, making sure that about 150 names will fall in *each* of Sample I and Sample II. If there are not enough names in one sample or the other, continue picking names from the list until you have about 150 names in each of Sample I and Sample II.
4. Keep the names of the teachers to be sampled, in case a follow-up letter is needed.

Sending Out the Questionnaire

1. Please write a covering letter (signed by a school official or by you) to be sent with the questionnaire, stating: the purpose of cooperating in this study; the need for prompt and careful response to the questionnaire; the request that the questionnaire be returned within *one week*. Please emphasize the anonymity of the replies.
2. Mail your letter with the questionnaire, enclosing an addressed envelope (addressed to you or to the official to whose office it is to be sent) with sufficient postage on it for returning the questionnaire. If possible, mail to the teacher's home address (school address only if the home address is not known.) *Please do not mail questionnaires to principals or heads of schools.*

Follow-up

1. No later than ten days after the date of mailing of the questionnaires, check to see how many replies have been received. If either Sample I or Sample II has fewer than ninety replies, send a simple letter of request to all included in that Sample, saying that more replies are needed to make a fair picture for your country.
2. Wait ten days for additional replies. If more do not come, we will have to be satisfied with the sample received.
3. Return all questionnaires in Samples I and II as soon as possible to C.E.R.I. —#8 Yejang Dong, Choong-Ku—Seoul, Korea. Please investigate the costs of sending the package of questionnaires by air freight and notify Miss Edman. She will decide if this is too expensive or not. The data for all countries will be processed by the research staff of the Central Education Research Institute.

   It is hoped that some type of interim report on the results of the research can be sent to you.

   Thank you for your cooperation.

APPENDIX C
INTERVIEW SCHEDULE

Country_____   Date_____

Status and Role of Primary School Teachers

Name of Person Interviewed_____
Position_____

   I. Teacher education

     Level of institution?_____

     Entrance level?_____

     Finishing level?_____

     Proportion of professional education?_____

     Student teaching?_____

     Proposed charges?_____

  II. Teacher certification

     How achieved?_____

     How long valid?_____

     How renewed?_____

 III. Teacher supply

     Adequacy?_____

     Turnover?_____

APPENDIX C

Men or women?_____
How provide for shortages?_____
IV. Policies concerning placement, transfer, and dismissal
 V. In service education
Compulsory?_____
How given?_____
Supervisory helps?_____
Ability of principal or supervisor?_____
VI. Teacher responsibility
Pupil load?_____
Working week?_____
Textbook?_____
Curriculum and time schedule?_____
Community development and extra-curricular?_____
VII. Special regulations
Concerning women?_____
Political activities?_____
Supplementing income?_____
VIII. Salary and reimbursement
Fringe benefits, such as housing, cost of living, etc.?____
Urban vs. rural?_____
IX. Retirement and insurance benefits
Maternity leaves?_____
Sick leaves_____
Retirement age and benefits?_____
Other benefits?_____
X. Professional organizations
Number of organizations?_____
Character of organizations_____
Size of largest ones?_____
Activities:
Publications?_____
Legislative lobbying?_____
In-service workshops and seminars?_____
Strikes?_____

APPENDIX D
QUESTIONNAIRE TO STUDENTS

SELF-CONCEPT OF THE ROLE AND STATUS OF THE URBAN TEACHER
IN THE PRIMARY SCHOOLS OF SELECTED COUNTRIES

This questionnaire is addressed to students who are preparing to be primary school teachers in various countries and parallels the one submitted to teachers who are presently at work in the primary schools. Your answers to the following questions will be an important supplement to the opinions the teachers express concerning their role and status in their country.

There are two parts to this inquiry. Part I asks for certain information about you as a student who plans to be a teacher. Part II asks you for value judgments about your future position as a teacher. You are not asked to sign your name. Please do your best to give honest answers to all questions.

PART I
Student's Data

1. [1.ª] Sex: Male___ Female___
2. [2.ª] Marital Status: Unmarried___ Married___ Divorced or widowed___
3. [3.ª] Children: None___ 1–3___ 4–6___ over 6___
4. [4.ª] Your Age Range: 20's___ 30's___ 40's___ 50's___ 60's___

5. [8.ª] What is the total number of years you have spent in school as a student? (Include elementary school, secondary school, and all other.)
___years

a. Numbers in brackets indicate identical questions in the questionnaire to teachers, Appendix A.

6. [9.ᵇ] Do you expect to become fully qualified for teaching? Yes___ No___

7. [10.ᵇ] How do you expect to be qualified for teaching? (Check as many as apply.)
___Regular government examination
___Special examination
___Satisfactory completion
___Special arrangement

8. [11.] During the time you have been studying teacher training, approximately how many clock hours did you spend in a classroom, either observing or teaching children? (Check one.)
___None at all
___10–50 hours
___51–100 hours
___101–200 hours
___More than 200 hours

9. [12.] Where did you spend most of your childhood? (Check one.)
___Rural area or small village
___Small city or town (25,000–100,000)
___Large city (over 100,000)

10. [13.] If you could have your choice, in which community described above would you prefer to teach for the rest of your life? (Check one.)
___Rural area or small village
___Small city or town
___Large city

11. [14.ᵇ] If you had it to do over again would you choose teaching or some other occupation? (Check one.)
___I'm sure I would go into teaching
___Probably would go into teaching
___Uncertain; depends on opportunities
___Think I would choose another occupation
___Quite sure I would choose another occupation

12. In your own experience as a student, where have you found the best teachers? (Check as many as apply.)
___Teachers in the primary school
___Teachers in the secondary school
___Professors in the teacher training college or university
___Special tutors or teachers in special schools
___None at all

13. [15.ᵇ] Of the teachers you now have in your teacher training school, indicate which facts you know about the five known best.

____Marital status
____Work of spouse
____Number of children
____Home address
____Future length of teaching
____Philosophy of education
____Satisfaction with present position
____Previous experience

b. Not identical but very similar in the two questionnaires.

14.   Of the primary teachers you now know, check the statements which
       you think pertain to them generally. (Check as many as apply.)
       ____They tend to complain a good deal about their work
       ____They are genuinely fond of children and like to be with them
       ____They accomplish what is expected of them
       ____They are respectful of the uniqueness and dignity of children
       ____They do work beyond the call of duty
       ____They are working primarily for the salary involved
       ____They know their subject matter well
       ____They are often absorbed in their own personal problems
       ____They are worthy models for children and youth to follow
       ____They are proud of being teachers
15. [16.] How do you think the following situations should be taken care of?
       a. Teachers made to follow strict rules (Mark these items a.)
       b. Teachers asked to follow rules, but allowed to make some changes
          to suit the situation (Mark these items b.)
       c. No set rules, teachers allowed to use their own judgment (Mark
          these items c.)
       (Place a, b or c before each of these statements.)
       ____ Handling a child who does not work well
       ____ Disciplining a child who is disobedient
       ____ Deciding methods of classroom teaching
       ____ Deciding what time teachers must arrive at and leave school
          building
       ____ Handling a child who is late
       ____ Deciding the amount of time to be spent on different subjects each
          week
       ____Contacting parents
       ____ Deciding the form of report on child's school work to parents
       ____Deciding what is to be taught in each subject
16. [17.ᵇ] How much would you say that your ideas about the general purposes
       or aims of education have changed since you began your work as a
       student? (Check one.)
       Changed very much____   Changed a little____
       Hardly changed at all____   Don't know____

b. Not identical but very similar in the two questionnaires.

17. [18.] When you were growing up, what importance did your parents place on seeing that you were taught religion? (Check one.)
___Paid little if any attention to religion
___Had you observe special rituals and ceremonies
___Placed some emphasis on your understanding the basic meaning of religion
___Considered religious instruction very important

18. [23.] What sources of information do you regularly have? (Check as many as apply.)
___ Daily general newspaper
___ Professional newspaper or journals
___ Daily radio listening
___ Popular magazines and journals
___ Daily television viewing
___ Taking one yearly trip of at least 300 kilometers (200 miles) away from your home
___ Attending at least one professional or cultural meeting each month
___ Seeing at least one motion picture a month
___ Attending at least one concert or theatre performance during the year
___ Visiting a library at least once each month
___ Reading at least one book each month
___ None of the above

19. [24.] Who or what influenced you most in deciding to become a teacher? (Check all that strongly apply.)
___One or both of your parents or a close relative was a teacher
___ You had at least one teacher you strongly admired and wished to follow as an example
___ You felt that teaching offered a rewarding way of life
___ You were disappointed in getting into the vocation you really wanted and took teaching as second choice
___ Your school marks were high
___ Don't know; no special reason

20. [25.] Ordinarily, how many minutes do you spend each school day?
___ Traveling to and from school?
___ Checking papers or preparing lessons at home?
___ Engaging in some form of recreational activity?
___ Doing clerical work connected with school?

21. [26.] For the year past, how many days were you absent from school because of illness?
___days

22. Please indicate your reactions to your present study program.
GENERAL ACADEMIC LOAD (Check one.)
___Too heavy
___Too light
___About right
___Sometimes one, sometimes the other

311

EDUCATION COURSES (Check one.)
___Seem about the right number
___Too many
___Too few
___Incompetent to judge
CONTENT OF EDUCATION COURSES (Check as many as apply.)
___Stimulating and challenging
___Repetitious
___Dull, too much obvious material included
___Practical, with good suggestions for teaching
___Too theoretical and vague
___Too difficult to understand
___Too easy and lacking in challenge
___Incompetent to judge

23. What do you expect to find the greatest satisfactions in being a teacher? (Check as many as apply.)
___Prestige
___Salary
___Security
___Intellectual stimulation
___Good working conditions
___Service
___Little competition
___Professional growth
___Service to children.

24. What impediments do you expect to doing your best work as a teacher? (Check as many as seem of major importance.)
___Conservative administrators, parents, officials and lay groups
___Radical administrators, parents, officials and other lay groups
___Boredom
___Unreasonable moral standards
___Uncooperative colleagues
___Community work
___Non-teaching duties
___Inadequate salary
___Lack of supervisory help
___Keeping abreast in the profession

25. What do you consider the hindrances to good work in the primary school? (Check only the ones you consider of major importance.)
___Too many children in each classroom
___Too much confusion and disorder in the school
___Lack of proper books and other teaching materials
___Buildings too old and generally unattractive
___Children wasting a great deal of time
___Too much regimentation of the children
___The same old methods of teaching in most schools
___No particular problems

26. What preferences do you have for teaching? (Check as many as apply.)
GENERAL TYPE
___Physically handicapped children
___Mentally handicapped children
___Bright children
___Average, heterogeneous groups
___Low economic groups
___Upper economic groups
___No preference
AGE GROUP
___3–5
___6–8
___9–11
___12–14
___15–17
___18–20

27. What problems do you anticipate in working with children? (Check as many as apply.)
___Suffering boredom
___Challenging bright children
___Motivating dull children
___Raising the cultural level of deprived children
___Meeting the needs of individual children
___Guiding unruly and unresponsive children
___Establishing warm, positive, teacher–pupil relationships
___Assigning grades or marks and deciding on promotion for individual children

28. What would you eventually like to become? (Check one.)
___Administrator
___Inspector or supervisor
___Special school officer (psychological tester, counselor, etc.)
___Special teacher (of the blind, deaf, etc.)
___Primary teacher
___Secondary teacher
___Teacher training college

29. In what professional activities, in addition to teaching, would you like to engage? (Check all that apply.)
___Writing textbooks for children
___Writing articles for professional journals and magazines
___Giving speeches at meetings for teachers
___Organizing study groups for teachers
___Holding office in teachers' organizations
___Holding membership in teachers' organizations
___Carrying on research
___Teaching in a foreign country
___Assisting in training student teachers
___Traveling

30.   What are your plans for advanced study after completion of your present course? (Check one.)

__None at all

__Some, but less than one full school year

__At least one full year

__At least two full years

__More than two full years

__Occasional study throughout the teaching career

31.   How do you plan to use future vacations? (Check as many as apply.)

__Relaxing and resting

__Studying methods of teaching independently

__Studying methods of teaching at some institution

__Studying some other field than teaching

__Traveling

__Working to earn money

__Pursuing hobbies, home improvement, creative activities of various types

__Doing community service without pay, such as directing recreational activities for children

PART II

Students' Opinion Sections

This part is exactly the same as Part II of the questionnaire used to discover teachers' opinions.

BIBLIOGRAPHY

Publications dealing primarily with
cross-cultural studies of teacher role and status

Bereday, George Z. F. and Joseph Lauwerys, eds. *The Education and Training of Teachers*. "The Yearbook of Education," 1963. New York: Harcourt, Brace and World, 1963.

Biddle, Bruce J. and others. *Contemporary Research in Teacher Effectiveness*. New York: Holt, Rinehart and Winston, 1964.

———. *Role Theory: Concepts and Research*. New York: John W. Wiley & Sons, 1966.

———. *Studies in the Role of the Public School Teacher*. 6 vols., Columbia, Mo., University of Missouri Press, 1961–64.

Fédération Internationale Syndicate de l'Enseignement. *Enquête et Rapport de Synthèse sur la Condition des Enseignants en U.R.S.S., Hongrie, Pologne, Bulgarie et en Romanie*. Paris: UNESCO, 1965.

Hall, Robert King, Nicholas, Hans and J. A. Lauwerys, eds. *Status and Position of Teachers*. "The Yearbook of Education," 1953. New York: World Book Company, 1953.

International Bureau of Education. *Training of Primary Teacher Training Staffs*. A Comparative Study. Twentieth International Conference on Public Education. Paris: UNESCO, 1957. Pub. No. 182.

UNESCO. *World Survey of Education*. Paris: UNESCO, 1958. Vol. 2.

UNESCO Institute for Education. *Preparing Teachers for Education for International Understanding*. Edited by J. B. Willcock. Hamburg: the Institute, 1962.

315

World Union of Catholic Teachers. *Inquiry and Comparative Report on the Condition of Private School Teachers in Seven European Countries.* Rome: the World Union, 1964.

World Confederation of the Organizations of the Teaching Profession. *Conditions of Work for Quality Teaching.* 1963 WCOTP Theme Study. Washington: the Confederation, 1963.

_____. *Introductory Report to the Draft Recommendations Concerning the Status of Teachers.* Washington: the Confederation, 1966. Mimeographed.

_____. *Status of the Teaching Profession.* Washington: the Confederation, 1955.

_____. *Survey of the Teaching Profession in the Americas.* Washington: the Confederation, 1964.

_____. *Survey of the Status of the Teaching Profession in Asia.* Washington: the Confederation, 1963.

_____. "The UNESCO/ILO Expert Meeting on The Status of Teachers," *Education Panorama*, VIII, No. 2, 1966.

NOTES

Chapter I

1. George Z. F. Bereday and Joseph A. Lauwerys, eds., *The Education and Training of Teachers.* "The Yearbook of Education," 1963 (New York, 1963), p. xii.
2. See Chapter II for various studies dealing with these matters.
3. See Appendices A and B for a complete copy of the questionnaire and the written directions given to educational authorities for administering them.
4. See Appendix C.
5. Marion Edman, *Primary Teachers of Korea Look at Themselves* (Seoul, 1962). Distributed by Cellars Book Shop, Box 6, College Park Station, Detroit, Michigan, U.S.A., 48221.
6. *Ibid.,* pp. 103–104.

Chapter II

1. A study involving several of these forms and several thousand teachers in the United States has been reported by David G. Ryans, *Characteristics of Teachers; Their Description, Comparison and Appraisal; A Research Study* (Washington, 1960), p. 416.
2. Bruce J. Biddle and others, "Bibliographies on Role Terms, Role Conflict, and the Role of the Teacher," Vol. B of *Studies in The Role of The Public School Teacher.* (Columbia, Mo., 1961), 127–136.
3. Bruce J. Biddle and others, *Contemporary Research on Teacher Effectiveness* (New York, 1964), p. 27.

317

4. Jean F. Floud, "Teaching in the Affluent Society," *British Journal of Sociology*, 13 (December, 1962), 299.
5. *Ibid.*, p. 308.
6. Claude Russell, "Tradition and Change in the Concept of the Ideal Teacher" in Bereday and Lauwerys, p. 24.
7. See Bibliography for individual studies.
8. WCOTP, *Resolutions of the 1955 General Assembly of the World Confederation of the Organizations of the Teaching Profession* (Washington, 1955), pp. 6–7.
9. *Introductory Report to the Draft Recommendation Concerning the Status of Teachers* (Washington, 1966), p. 4. Mimeographed.
10. Bryan Wilson, "The Teacher's Role—A Sociological Analysis," *British Journal of Sociology*, 13, No. 1 (March, 1962), 24–25.
11. Margaret Mead, *The School in American Culture*; Inglis Lecture, 1950 (Cambridge, Mass., 1951), pp. 2–3.
12. Albert C. Pryor, "An Analysis of Teacher Perception of Professional Role and Predicted Professional Action." Doctoral dissertation, University of Connecticut, 1963, and F. T. Jacobs, "Perceptions of the Professional Role Held on Educators in a Large City System." Doctorial dissertation, University of California, 1962.
13. K. M. Bolte, *Sozialer Aufsteig und Absteig*. Doctoral dissertation, University of Hamburg, 1958.
14. Helena W. F. Stellwag, "The Attitudes of Teachers Towards Their Profession in the Netherlands," in Bereday and Lauwerys, p. 430.
15. Bryan Wilson, pp. 15–32.
16. WCOTP, *Conditions of Work for Quality Teaching*, 1963 WCOTP Theme Study (Washington, 1963), pp. 1–9.
17. "Revalue the Teacher," *Panorama*, 5, No. 1 (April–June, 1963), 26.
18. "Difficulties Facing Primary School Teachers in Seven New Nations," *Panorama*, 5, No. 1 (April–June, 1963), 2–4.
19. *Introductory Report to the Draft Recommendation Concerning the Status of Teachers*, p. 9.
20. Ethics Committee, National Education Association, *Code of Ethics of the Education Profession* (Washington, 1963).
21. *Introductory Report to the Draft Recommendation Concerning the Status of Teachers*, p. 3.
22. International Bureau of Education, *The Training of Primary Teacher Training Staffs* (Paris, 1957), Pub. No. 182, p. 11.
23. *Ibid.*, p. 11.
24. Brian Holmes, "Organization of Teacher Training," in Bereday and Lauwerys, p. 124.
25. For complete programs of sixty-six countries, see International Bureau of Education. *op. cit.*, pp. 13–36.
26. WCOTP, *Conditions of Work for Quality Teaching*, pp. xvii, xviii.
27. International Bureau of Education, *Bulletin*, Fourth Quarter 1963. No. 149, pp. 215–216.
28. Margaret Mead, pp. 33–34.
29. See Carl Hendrick Wittrock, "In-Service Training to Attain Quality Teaching," *Panorama*, 5, No. 1 (April–June, 1963), 5.

30. International Bureau of Education, *Bulletin*, First Quarter 1962, No. 142, pp. 187–191.

Chapter III

1. International Bureau of Education, *Bulletin*, Third Quarter 1962, No. 144, pp. 201–204; UNESCO, *World Survey of Education* (Paris, 1958), Vol. 2.
2. Robert Ulich, *The Education of Nations* (Cambridge, Mass., 1961).

Chapter IV

1. See page 000 for a description of the role of the ILO in the Geneva Conference of 1966.
2. Philippine Bureau of Civil Service, Ministry of Education, *Bureau of Public Schools Survey*, Chap. VI, "Teacher Personnel and Teacher Training" (Manila, 1960), p. 5. Mimeographed.
3. WCOTP, *Survey of the Status of the Teaching Profession in Asia* (Washington, 1963), p. 31.
4. *Ibid.*, p. 34.
5. *Ibid.*, p. 89.
6. Department of Research and Planning, Ministry of Education, *Education in Vietnam, 1965* (Saigon, 1965).

INDEX

321

Marion Edman earned her Ph.D. degree at the University of Minnesota. A one-time public-school teacher, she has served as educational adviser in half-a-dozen countries around the world and has published various professional articles. She is Professor of Education at Wayne State University.

The manuscript was edited by Alexander Brede. The book was designed by Peter Nothstein. The type face used is Monotype Times Roman, designed by Stanley Morison in 1931.

The book is printed on S. D. Warren's Olde Style Antique paper and bound in Columbia Mills' Bayside Vellum cloth. Manufactured in the United States of America.